Oh,
To Be 50
Again!

Books by Eda LeShan

FOR ADULTS:

When Your Child Drives You Crazy
Living Your Life
Winning the Losing Battle
In Search of Myself and Other Children
The Wonderful Crisis of Middle Age
Natural Parenthood
How Do Your Children Grow?
Sex and Your Teenager
The Conspiracy Against Childhood
How to Survive Parenthood

FOR CHILDREN:

When a Parent Is Very Sick
Grandparents: A Special Kind of Love
The Roots of Crime
What's Going to Happen to Me:
   When Parents Separate and Divorce
Learning to Say Goodbye:
   When a Parent Dies
You and Your Feelings
What Makes Me Feel This Way?

EDA LeSHAN

Oh, To Be 50 Again!

On Being Too Old for

a Mid-Life Crisis

BOOKS

All rights reserved under International and
Pan-American Copyright Conventions.
Published in the United States by Times Books,
a division of Random House, Inc.,
New York, and simultaneously in Canada by
Random House of Canada Limited, Toronto.

Library of Congress Cataloging-in-Publication Data
LeShan, Eda J.
Oh, to be 50 again.
Bibliography: p.
1. Aged—United States—Attitudes.
2. Old Age. I. Title.
II. Title: Oh, to be fifty again.
HQ1064.U5L469   1986   305.2'6'0973   86-5829
ISBN 0-8129-1238-1

Designed by Ann Gold
Manufactured in the United States of America

9   8   7   6   5   4   3   2

First Edition

PERMISSIONS ACKNOWLEDGMENTS

Grateful acknowledgment is made to the following for permission to reprint
previously published material:
American Medical Association: Excerpt from "Death Is Not the Enemy" by
Richard Landow, M.D., and James Gustafson, Ph.D., from the *Journal of
the American Medical Association,* November 2, 1984, Volume 252, No.

For May Sarton, who wrote, "Old age
is not an illness, it is a timeless ascent.
As power diminishes, we grow towards more light."

and

In loving memory of Burr Tillstrom,
for telling me of Oliver J. Dragon's belief,
"If you go on growing you learn
to enjoy living more completely."

CONTENTS

ACKNOWLEDGMENTS

~~~~~~

LITERALLY HUNDREDS OF PEOPLE SHARED their experiences and ideas with me, and I am deeply grateful to all of them. The following are people to whom I owe a special thank-you.

Helene Arnstein, Pat Carroll, Phyllis Contini, Virginia Edwards, Edith Engel, Sylvia Halpern, Lillian Handel, Alice B. Hinchcliff, Sadie and Lawrence Hofstein, Marjorie Ilgenfritz, Edgar Jackson, Mary Kinsella, Paul Krooks, D.D.S., Ann Landers, Mrs. Leroy Lewis, Bertha Maslow, Marvin Meitus, M.D., Mitch Miller, Leoni Nowitz, M.S.W., Harry Olin, Jean Payne, Hilda Pearlman, Lee Polk, Joanne Rogers, Sandor Rogers, Ruth Rosen, May Sarton, Sara and Harry Schacter, Burr Tillstrom, Myra Woodruff, Richard Worthington, Ph.D., and Hattie Yanks.

I also want to thank Jo-ann Straat for her infinite patience in typing the most complicated cut-and-paste puzzle of a manuscript I have ever written, and to Elizabeth Scharlatt and Phyllis Wender for moral support, above and beyond the call of duty. Thanks also to Milagros Ortega for keeping my household afloat. And special love to my husband, Larry, and my father, Max Grossman, who share this crisis of getting old with me.

INTRODUCTION

~~~~~~

IF YOU WALK INTO ANY REASONABLY
large library or bookstore chances are that you will be able
to find quite an assortment of books dealing with the later
years of life. I've done just that, and mostly what I've found
has fallen into two categories: First, there are some excellent books with valuable and expert advice about what one
needs to know about health and hospitalization, retirement
benefits, Social Security, housing, and other specific factual
information, and second, there are some upbeat books ex-
tolling the joys of old age—the "prime of your life."

This book falls into neither category. It is primarily
about feelings—mine and those of the hundreds of people
I talked to, in and out of nursing homes, rich and poor,
educated and uneducated, from sixty to ninety, living alone
and married, healthy and ill, happy and miserable.

What I feel I have come to understand is really simply
this: none of us has any choice when it comes to getting old.
It's above all else a fact of life. There are surely some pleasures left, but also plenty of tough challenges, often coming
at a time when we feel least equipped to face them. Old age
is about courage; it is about making the choice as to

whether or not to be defeated by aging or to live out one's remaining years with style. Looking back, I guess my whole life and certainly my work have been devoted to the idea that human beings have incredible and thrilling potential and that the goal of our lives ought to be to come as close as possible to fulfilling what is so unique and remarkable about each of us. Never have I been more inspired, more touched, by the human spirit than I am now, as I face my own twilight years and share it with my peers.

There was a beautiful play (and then a movie) by Arthur Laurents called *Home of the Brave* about soldiers returning from war, wounded in body and mind. Two soldiers, terribly afraid of the future but ready to help each other as they move back toward civilian life, pick up their bags as one says to the other, "Coward, take my coward's hand." That's what I feel now. Coward, take my coward's hand as we face the ultimate test of our courage and our humanity.

Oh,
To Be 50
Again!

~~~~~~

It's
Not Over
Yet

I AM SIXTY-THREE YEARS OLD. I hate getting old. I can't bear the fact that so much more of my life is behind me than in front of me. Some days I feel ninety, other days, thirty. My friend Ginny and I compare notes on just how stiff we are when we get out of bed in the morning and the arthritis in our feet is acting up. She says she beats me by a mile because once she got up suddenly, took a step, and fell flat on her face.

I feel three and a half years old when I'm playing make-believe with my granddaughter, younger than springtime when my husband and I are feeling most in love, and seventy-five when someone gives me a seat on a bus.

A friend tells me, "The difference between young and old is that old hurts." Malcolm Cowley, literary critic and historian, wrote about his eighty-sixth year. He wrote:

"How does a man *feel* when he enters the second half of his ninth decade? Sometimes he feels terrible . . . 'After 70,' a friend told me, 'if you wake up without any pains at all, you're dead.' Little daily routines are harder to carry out and take more time. The old man can no longer depend on his instinctive reflexes.

He has to learn new methods of doing everything as if he were starting over in early childhood . . ."*

There is nothing wonderful about getting old. No matter how well preserved we may be, no matter how healthy and active, no matter if we are fulfilling our dreams and are happier than we've ever been before, the simple fact is that we are in the last third or quarter of our lives and for the first time we are faced with a reality that we can't work our way 'out of, or buy our way out of—no matter how noble or creative or beautiful or kind we may be, old age is the time when we begin to understand that we each have a terminal disease. We caught it the moment we were conceived. Aging forces us to face mortality as we have never faced it before.

As I tried to solicit reactions about aging from other people, something very mysterious and upsetting began to happen. A man who has counseled hundreds of people on aging, illness, and dying closed up completely when confronted with personal questions. At a dinner party I asked a friend why she hadn't mailed back the questionnaire I'd sent her. She looked me straight in the eye and said, "Because I have very strong, personal feelings, which I don't wish to share." I was shocked. Dorothy is an educator whom I've known most of my adult life. She appears very outgoing, very responsive, more insightful about human problems than most people, and I know she respects me and knows I would never misuse any information she gave me. What were the great secrets of this very energetic, at-

*Malcolm Cowley, "Being Old Old," *The New York Times Magazine* (May 26, 1985).

tractive, young-looking professional woman, married for over forty years, with two apparently happy adult children and lots and lots of money?

The day after this episode I got back a blank questionnaire from a couple that had always seemed remarkably open about feelings, both personally and professionally. He refused altogether and his wife wrote, "This whole subject is just too much for me to handle right now. My attitudes are decidedly negative. I hope some day to become more rational and realistic, but at this time I don't want to share what I am feeling."

I can understand these feelings. I worry about being sick and dependent; I agonize most of all over the possibility of becoming widowed. It frustrates the hell out of me that things I did easily ten years ago—bicycling, gardening, walking ten miles—are now painful, exhausting. The idea of writing a book about aging upsets me; the subject depresses me; it makes me feel agitated. I want to live all the pleasures of my life over again; I want to do it all again and solve the problems—eliminate the mistakes, the disasters, the pain. I want to appreciate all the good times more than I did the first time around. I don't want to face getting old any more than anyone else does. Everything about it shocks me.

On a television newscast it was announced that "an elderly woman" was killed instantly while walking along a street; she was hit by a wooden plank that fell off a scaffolding. The newscaster added, "She was sixty years old." Is it *really possible* that sixty-year-olds are perceived as elderly? Of course it is! It's all relative to where one is. I thought my parents were old when they were in their forties! One moment of especially rude awakening occurred in 1980, the year of my fortieth high-school reunion, where I met a classmate I hadn't seen in all that time. When the party ended, and we'd enjoyed each other's company, I said, "I hope it won't be another forty years before we meet again." "Eda," she reminded me, *"it can't be."* I'm still in a state of shock five years later!

If I'm so upset, who am I to write a book about getting old? Who better! The truth is that most of us who are approaching old age or are already there know full well that talk of this being the "prime of our lives" is a romantic oversimplification of a complex and challenging time of our lives. The truth is there never was and never will be a single "prime time." Each stage of life brings with it both joy and pain, confusion and wisdom, trauma and triumph, and this is only more clear when we get old.

I have always struggled to try to master the challenges of each stage of my life, to use my experiences for growth. As a frightened young mother, I wrote *How to Survive Parenthood;* by the time it was published, I felt much more confident. When another phase of life seemed to overwhelm me, I wrote *The Wonderful Crisis of Middle Age;* I mastered the appropriate tasks of that stage more confidently when it was completed. Writing has been, for me, a way to become more introspective, a way to search for new insights, increased self-awareness, and inner strengths. After I explore my own thoughts and feelings, I then check with others to help broaden my perspective, confirm or deny the validity of my reflections, in order to see if there are universalities in what I've experienced.

It seems now, looking back over my life, that my central goal has been to increase my self-understanding so that I could then understand and, I hope, be helpful to others. I think this has worked. By struggling through a great deal of introspection, through many years of psychotherapy, I think I found out things about myself that were also true of the parents and children with whom I've worked most of my adult life. It seemes quite natural to me, now that I am facing a new time of my life—the last stage—to explore what is happening to me, and then to try to see if the same things are happening to other people—the purpose, the goal, being to master the skills, the attitudes, the actions, that will be most helpful to me and possibly to others as well.

Each period of our lives, up to now, has usually been anticipated with pleasure, with conscious awareness of change. When I was a little girl, I looked forward to the birthday when there would be "two numbers instead of one"—ten. I eagerly awaited the signs of maturation that would mean I was "in my teens," an adolescent. And while that turned out to be anything but a tranquil time of life, I viewed it as a necessary interval that would lead to the fulfillment of my dreams—falling in love, marrying, working, becoming a parent.

The only stage of life that seems to creep up on us— unasked for, unexpected, somehow a great betrayal—is getting old. My husband, Larry, a psychologist, went to visit William and Mary College, where he first studied this subject. In the hall of the psychology department he saw a glass case marked "Antiques of Psychology. Use Unknown"! The case contained instruments used when he was a student!

Old age came in small shock waves for me, and to just about everyone with whom I spoke or corresponded. One man asked me, "Isn't old age ten years older than you are right now?"

The first awareness of aging seemed most often to be related to some sudden physical change. One such moment was when the dentist told me he would have to make a "removable bridge." And then it was arthritic heel spurs, which curtailed the lovely long walks I had cherished, and the arthritic knees that ended my bicycling days. And then it was discovering I could no longer pull up the tougher weeds in my garden because of arthritis in my wrists.

A woman I've known for more than thirty years, who had been an extraordinary person of tremendous energy— a woman who was head of an important government agency and had done a superb job—seemed for some time to be moving into her later years with great dignity and spirit. She had remained active in volunteer community work, and was as enthusiastic and as full of fun as ever. I didn't see her for quite awhile, and when we met again she was far more somber, had drawn in upon herself. She was much less outgoing; obviously it was now an effort to maintain the social relationships she'd always loved and handled so well. When I began writing this book, I asked her what had happened. She wrote to tell me the origins of the change in her.

When I first moved to a retirement community I felt very sorry for all the older people, some of whom seemed confused and dependent on others for their care. It never dawned on me that I might get that way; I felt just fine, physically and mentally.

Then, one day in the swimming pool, I was helping an old man get into the water, and I turned and fell against a post behind me. I couldn't see! I tried to walk and I fell; I had a severe headache—not a bit like me. It turned out I'd had a "minor stroke" that had blinded me. All I kept thinking was, this can't be happening to *me!* I have recovered most of my sight, but I have felt old ever since.

Often our first awareness of aging occurs as a reflection of how we are treated by others. A friend wrote: "I began to think I was getting old when I realized that men had quit pinching my ass!"

During the winter when I was fifty-nine years old, I was shoveling the snow in my driveway. A neighbor rushed out of her house and ran over to me. "You're too old for that, it's dangerous!" she said. It was a loving and protective impulse on her part, but I went into the house to look at myself in the mirror, trying to see what she saw. It was a shock—for the first time I was really aware of new wrinkles and graying hair.

A retired English professor told me, "I was always a great beauty as a young woman, and I enjoyed the attention and appreciation of both men and women. Ironically, at the age of seventy, I'm exceptionally wrinkled and ravaged. Inside my head, I see someone beautiful; in other people's eyes, I see an ugly old woman." A similar response came from a woman who said, "I became invisible to men. They didn't look at me anymore. My good looks had always been money in the bank. Suddenly my account was closed. I felt ugly, misshapen, a stranger to myself."

A man of sixty-one told me, "The first time I realized I was getting old was last summer. A friend and I had climbed a mountain in Switzerland—ten thousand feet high, opposite the Matterhorn. It was a glorious experience and I was triumphant that I held up so well. We took a funicular back down. It was very crowded, and we had to stand. Suddenly I heard a mother say to her child, 'Get up and let that older man sit down.' And then I knew. And when I found myself gratefully accepting the seat—I *really* knew!"

A sense of aging may begin when a spouse dies. A sixty-seven-year-old widow said, "Ralph and I felt *young*. He was retired, we were planning a long vacation trip, we were both in good health. His sudden death made me feel like an old woman."

Sometimes a photograph will bring a shock wave. I showed my husband, Larry, a picture of himself with our granddaughter, when she was on a carousel. When he saw the photograph he was startled and said, "My god, I *really do* look old enough to be a grandfather!"

Because each of us carries an inner image of ourselves as much younger than we really are, we may notice the aging process far more sharply when we look at a spouse. I notice that Larry doesn't bend down to pick up something on the floor as easily as he did twenty years ago. His hair is gray and white and thinning on top. As his forehead gets broader, I remember with a sense of shock and momentary sadness the young man I married with the thick black hair. I remember how skinny he was in his World War II uniform, his face unlined. I am suddenly so frightened by the ravages of time—by the thought that neither of us will ever again look the way we did in our wedding picture.

We are more unprepared for aging than for any other stage in our growing and changing. British poet Stephen Spender at seventy-five was musing about getting older in an interview in *The New York Times Book Review.* He said, ". . . the funny thing about old age is the way it suddenly steals up on you even if you do think about it. You wake up and you're seventy-five and you wonder how you got there.

But that is probably because you still feel the same person inside."*

We are surely not alone as we try to face the special challenges and complexities of this time of our lives. The percentage of people over sixty-five has nearly tripled since 1900. In another fifty years, older people will represent 20 percent of the population. We are increasing in numbers at twice the rate of the general population. The number of states with more than a million older citizens has more than doubled since 1960.

We are each as unique as we have ever been; there are certainly individual differences in how we feel and what we do. But, as with all the other ages and stages in human development, there are some universal patterns, as well— common factors in the roles we play, common fears, common satisfactions and fulfillments. If there is no such thing as "the prime of one's life" at any stage of living, there are surely more and less successful ways of coping, and it is my fervent hope that while admitting to the difficulties, while trying never to cover up the problems, we can together search out how we can make the most of the rest of our lives.

Hilda writes:

I would like to add my voice in objection to the advertising world's message that "old is bad." I refuse to dye my hair, lie about my age, dress like a teenager, or pretend to be what I ain't! But, on the other hand, I am not about to join a "senior citizens" club, move to a "retirement community," or otherwise allow myself to be segregated with other "old" people. (Re-

*The New York Times Book Review (Feb. 26, 1984), p. 3.

duced-price tickets at movies and museums are the only "perc" I'll accept!) . . . We're too busy to think about getting old. I think energy level is the crux of the matter. If you continue to be active mentally, physically, sexually, and socially, then you really don't feel very different at sixty-five than you did at twenty-five, except smarter! We are newly retired, taking college courses and exercise classes, involved in community activities as volunteers, free to travel, catch up on reading, get some extra sleep, etc. etc. There is never enough time for all we want to do.

Paul writes, "A numbers game is not particularly productive for me. What is eighty years old, for example? Is it my eighty-two-year-old piano teacher who lives in a third-floor walk-up, who paints and reads and gives concerts, and gives fabulous parties? Or is it the eighty-year-old woman who has become senile, who sometimes forgets my name as well as her own?"

Beverly Sills, director of the New York State Opera, says she's too busy to think about getting older. Jean-Pierre Rampal, a world-famous flutist, was asked on the occasion of his sixtieth birthday when he planned to retire. His answer was, "I'm just starting—always starting—it will always be the beginning of my life."

May Sarton, the gifted poet, novelist, nonfiction writer, and a beloved friend, greeted her sixty-fifth year by writing:

My 65th year, just past, has been the happiest and most fruitful so far. I do not see diminution except in sustained energy, but the lack of energy is more than made up for by my knowing better how to handle myself. . . . I am less compulsive, less driven by time. . . . It is not, perhaps, that the old are a problem, but that the best things about old age are so outside our ethos that we cannot, some of us, even imagine a state of growth that might have to do with contemplation, pure joy, and above all the elimination of the nonessential . . .*

At seventy, she wrote:

I realize that seventy must seem extremely old to my young friends, but I actually feel younger than I did when I wrote *The House by the Sea* six years ago . . . previews of old age were not entirely accurate, I am discovering. And that, as far as I can see, is because I live more completely in the moment these days, am not anxious about the future, and am more detached from the areas of pain, the loss of love, the struggle to get work completed, the fear of death . . . The long hard work is bearing fruit . . . I am coming into a period of inner calm . . . One of the good elements in old age is that we no longer have to prove anything to ourselves or to anyone else. We are what are are. †

From the beginning of my professional life I've been interested in developmental sequences—ages and stages in human growth. As a young woman absorbed in studying the characteristic life tasks of young children, it never occurred to me that "ages and stages" went beyond childhood. The developmental tasks that concerned me were things like learning to crawl, learning to drink from a cup. learning to use the toilet, learning to separate from a parent. Of course, as I got older, I had to acknowledge the fact that developmental tasks change at every stage of living— preparing for work, adult love relationships, parenthood.

The New York Times (Jan. 30, 1978).
†May Sarton, *At Seventy* (New York: W. W. Norton & Co.,1984).

Now I face the last developmental stage in the human experience, and as with all the other sequences of life, there are new, specific tasks.

Whatever our individual differences, sooner or later we all face some aspects of this development—we face physical aging; we face widowhood; we face retirement; we face problems of illness and medical care; almost all of us face living on less income. Many of us must face the death of our parents and of close relatives and friends; we may also face responsibility for our aged parents.

Some developmental tasks are less somber, such as becoming grandparents, and if we are lucky and have worked hard for this, we may be experiencing a new friendship and companionship with grown children. Some of us have the time—perhaps for the very first time in our lives—to do some of the things we've always dreamed of doing. The tasks are different from any we have met with in the past, but they are similar in one important respect; as in all the other stages of our lives, we can make some choices. Whether our circumstances at any given moment are good or bad, painful or exciting, sad or happy, depressing or promising, to some degree each of us can still bring some creativity, some courage, some spirit of adventure to this last stage of our lives.

It became clear, as I talked with others, that those who were finding some ways in which to do things they wanted to do had the most positive, the most accepting attitudes toward aging. For others who were very reluctant and fearful of giving up earlier, now inappropriate tasks, aging was most painful and difficult. If the happiest years of a woman's life were nest-building and child-raising, old age might represent a time of loss, a feeling of isolation—an ending. For a man who may have had sexual problems in his early and middle years, there might be a sense of relief in feeling less pressured for sexual performance and a chance to feel more fulfilled in being an expert golfer or a very special grandpa. For those who didn't particularly enjoy the hurly-burly, the intensity, the constant crises of youth, the later years may well be a time of greater comfort and peace. For someone who is widowed, alone, frightened by financial insecurity, or for someone whose only feeling of personal identity came from an occupation demanding great physical strength, such as being a construction worker or a baseball coach, getting old can be hell.

Our attitudes toward aging also reflect our impressions of the old people we have known. I'm depressed by the memory of two wrinkled old aunts who I thought "smelled funny" when I was a child. I'm hopeful—even exhilarated—by a woman I knew, a social activist, Alice K. Pollitzer, who remained a full and beautiful and useful human being until the age of 102; in her nineties she was electioneering from a sound truck for Robert Kennedy for president.

Dena, sixty-seven wrote:

I remember what my grandmother was like when she was about my age and she seemed like a very old woman and now I wonder if young people think of me as old. I also think about the very crippled, seventy-eight-year-old mother of a dear friend of mine who told her daughter there was a slim young girl dancing inside her old worn-out body. I have a perky ninety-year-old aunt who learned to drive at *seventy-two* and hops in the car to go to her favorite restaurant if she gets lonely.

We observe such a variety of reactions to aging that we

ought to sense that the element of choice still exists for us. There are certainly differences over which we may *feel* we have no control, but the truth is that old people demonstrate individual coping options all the time.

Don said, "My father-in-law seemed senile to me when he was fifty. Other people, such as my friend's father, have a mind like a steel trap at eighty, and I play tennis sometimes with a man who's seventy-nine."

Hilda, a woman of sixty-two, wrote, "When my mother was eighty-five, she was still taking trips to Europe by herself. We know others in their seventies who won't walk around the block! It's all a matter of attitude. Anyway, eighty is much younger than it used to be."

Hattie, age ninety-two, never quite conquered the English language, but in simple eloquence she told me, "To live old and not to enjoy your life, not to have your health—I don't agree to that. You know the time has to come—so if you don't enjoy—then it should be over. When you are enjoying it, it's better to live than to die. Enjoying means you feel people still care about you. While I've living, let me have a good time."

Actress Pat Carroll, somewhat younger than most of the people I talked to, told me, "Looking at my mother, who is near eighty, I think of someone who is cheerful most of the time, helping others every day, full of wisdom, love . . . I think it would not be so bad to be eighty like her. I see others in their eighties and think I would turn it down were it offered!"

Dr. Richard Worthington, a California psychologist, reminded me that "you have undoubtedly seen sixteen-year-olds who are so solidified that their personalities resemble those of some retirees. . . . As a kid I felt so intensely about all events—well through adolescence, and into the thirties—that I used to look forward to the time when I would be as calm and peaceful as I thought older people were. . . . Now I sort of regret not having the keen edge of excitement that used to fill me when challenges come along."

Sonya, now seventy-three, told me, "I am delighted to identify with anyone who has spirit, their marbles, and doesn't complain about their ills, and is occupied. They are my role models!"

Old age, just exactly like every other stage of our lives, is full of ambiguities. What really bugs me about the "prime of your life" enthusiasts is not that they lie, but they settle for half-truths. There are those who *are* having "the time of their lives," but even for those there is the poignant ever-present background music of time running out. And for many—the chronically ill, the physically handicapped, the poor, the lonely—old age can be a disaster.

I live with ambiguities every day. I have a keener appreciation of nature than ever before in my life. I can sit and watch a bird at a feeder for twenty minutes and then go back to work thoroughly refreshed. But my father is eighty-nine and alone. I worry about him all the time and cannot have the feeling of freedom from responsibility for others' welfare that I expected to have. The reversal of roles moves on inexorably and with terrible pain, as I gradually become the caretaker instead of Daddy's little girl, as he changes from being my Rock of Gibraltar to someone who depends on me. My heart breaks for this old man who misses my mother terribly, and who, though one of the most private and dignified of men, must now endure my bearing witness to his increasing infirmities. Not only do I suffer for him, and with him, but he is a daily reminder of where *I* am heading.

My closest friends are more dear and special than ever before; we begin to be more selective, there is more quality than quantity in our social lives. No more dinner parties—just special, quiet times with those we care about the most. I know I've achieved a great deal in my lifetime—there are many rewards and gratifications—but as life closes in on me I am also more aware of the regrets, the experiences, the adventures, the risks I wish I'd taken when I was young.

In spite of a stiff back and a few other indications of the general deteriorations of the human body, Larry is at the top of his work life—more excited about the book he's writing now than any previous ones. But at the same time that he senses how much he has achieved, he also experiences a terrible sense of urgency: how can he ever accomplish all the things he still longs to do—how answer all the questions, realize fully the goals of his research.

In spite of every indication that he and I are moving into the beginning of the last stage of our lives, these things are also true: we are more happily married to each other now than during the previous forty years. We still love to travel together. We are thinking seriously about our future—where we want to live, how we can remain independent when we are very old and need to be taken care of. Our daughter, in her sweetness and goodness, says she'd *like* to take care of us, but we have been too autonomous to want to allow the reversal of roles we know can—would—occur. We want to take as much responsibility as we possibly can for our future, however long or short a time that may be. What I think we both feel most strongly is that whether we live ten more years, or twenty, or thirty, when death comes, we will have grown and changed and become different people than we are today.

What we face is that the "ages and stages" of life culminate in a time of life when the days become increasingly precious and must be used to the fullest possible advantage.

Since I have no choice about the outcome, I need to figure out what choices I still do have. One choice is very clear. I can have a miserable old age in which I spend all my time cursing my mortality, or maybe—just maybe—I can choose to spend my last years flying across the sky like a comet—a brilliant last light, toward a flaming end. Do I have the guts to wish for what Nikos Kazantzakis prayed for in *Report to Greco,* where he wrote, "For this was my greatest ambition; to leave nothing for death to take— nothing but a few bones."

What can we do with the knowledge that old age leads to dying? We can continue to exist in a kind of waiting game, in which we change nothing in our lives; we enjoy whatever pleasures may be part of our past and present and we give up in defeat and hopelessness about the inevitability of aging. Or we simply hope to die—and often, if the despair is profound enough, we may do exactly that, since the physical body responds only too skillfully to misery. Suicides take many forms, both conscious and unconscious. There is a saying in the Talmud: "If you don't want to get old, hang yourself when you are young."

In spite of the fact that I am aware of the terrifying fact that I seem to be forgetting at least one name and one word a day (a nightmare for a writer!); in spite of the fact that some young people patronize me and treat me as if I'm ready for the loony bin; in spite of the fact that I worry more than I ever did before about the possibilities of widowhood or chronic illnesses that might make me dependent on other people; in spite of new aches and pains, and not being able to garden with as much energy as I did ten years ago (oh, to be fifty again!), I have made my choice. I have decided to go on growing until my last breath.

I've been exceedingly fortunate in having observed a large portion of Larry's work in the last thirty years, which has had to do with psychotherapy with terminally ill cancer patients. This may seem a morbid field, but it is not. What I have learned from his work is that one *can* go on growing and changing until the moment of death.

One patient, who had hated his work and his life for twenty years, spent his last year doing what he'd always dreamed of doing—painting, visiting the great art museums of the world, living alone, developing the inner life he had so long neglected. Just before he died, he said, "*Now* I feel as if my life was worth having been lived!" Another patient told Larry, "It makes all the difference—knowing who *I really am* before I die."

Part of the challenge is to begin to make more conscious decisions about what matters most, what is really unimportant. Anne Morrow Lindbergh, speaking at her alumni reunion, class of 1928, at Smith College, said, "But certain losses are positive. At our age we can get rid of a lot of superficials. Vanity for one thing. We don't have to keep taking up or letting down the hems of our skirts to keep in style. We can relax in whatever is becoming and comfortable. We don't have to be 'house-proud' and struggle over our possessions . . . We don't see the dust on our furniture or mind the faded curtains. We need less in our lives—except for treasured books and pictures and music, and perhaps a small garden and a pair of bird glasses. We've lost some of our ego, too, our competitive ambition . . . some of our conflicts are over. Many of our duties to family, to town or country, have dropped. We are freer now to do what we want. We can choose our pleasures without guilt, be ourselves without pretense . . ."

Helen Hayes, in a television interview with Arlene Francis, said she now felt much freer to tell the truth as she saw it and was less concerned with other people's opinions of her.

There is a great difference between being fulfilled and being frenetic. Bill, sixty-eight, wrote: "I keep myself busy every minute—I work ten hours a day, I jog, I don't leave myself time to think about getting old." The person who feels most creative, most fulfilled, may be a person who likes to sit quietly and contemplate the petals of a lovely flower.

Fulfillment is never achieved; it can only be worked at. If we feel depressed, immobilized, or bored, we need to examine our lives, ask for help. When Sophia Loren was asked why she was happier—and even more beautiful—at fifty than she was at thirty, she replied that she had learned great inner discipline and was never afraid of new experiences.

A friend with whom I was discussing old age commented philosophically, "Life can't be cured." Indeed it can't, and there are bound to be moments of fear and rage against the coming dark. We have a tiny house in New Jersey, where I do most of my writing. That's where I am, right now, as I begin this book. Two years ago we planted a young Vermont sugar maple tree, because I wanted to have that brilliant fall coloring. Today the little tree is covered with autumn leaves—red and gold and orange. As I look at it, I glory in its beauty and I feel sad that I will not live to see it when it is as tall and as magnificent in its colors as I know it will become. But it is *there*. Let me see it as one small contribution to the future of my neighborhood. There are children riding their bicycles up and down the street. *They* will see it. It's a growing thing that I put there. Let me try to keep pace with its growing for as long as I can. I offer you that challenge—to go on growing, as a necessary endeavor. Psychologist Carl Rogers wrote there is a choice: "Growing older, or old and growing." May we all choose the latter.

I received a letter from a dear friend, Harry Schacter, eighty-eight, almost totally blind, and quite deaf, who has been dictating the interesting story of his life. He wrote: "I ended my autobiography with the following statement: . . . if I am still alive at eighty-nine, I will raise my arms to heaven and say as Michelangelo did when he was eighty-nine, 'Thank God I can still learn!'"

~~~~~~

TWO

Dealing with Change

LARRY AND I WERE WALKING toward our gate at the Los Angeles airport. As we approached, we noticed that the line of people waiting for seat assignments was unusually long and not moving. Ultimately there were several hundred people waiting, and the line was at a standstill. After about ten more minutes, Larry went to inquire what was happening. The young woman at the desk said, "The computer is down—we can't make seat assignments." Larry, rising to his full (and considerable) height, said, "Young woman, I know you won't believe this, but I must tell you that before you were even born, people were getting seat assignments on planes. It was done with pieces of paper, pencils or pens, which you may at some time have heard of, and by careful strokes of the human wrist and movements of the fingers." Needless to say, she assumed he was insane. (We waited another thirty minutes for the computer to "come up.")

Why am I always gleeful when the computer doesn't work at the supermarket or department store? Why do I revel in the fact that the dreams of the 1960s and '70s that teaching machines could replace many teachers turned out to be folly? Why do I cringe and cover my ears in midtown Manhattan when the horns and the sirens and the drilling are at their optimum cacophony? Why do I miss the sky so much, walking in the cavernous shadow of hundreds of skyscrapers, not one with a window capable of being opened? I'll tell you why: because I'm sixty-three years old. A record player is still a Victrola as far as I'm concerned; a refrigerator, an icebox; "grass" is something green on the ground; "gross" is a measurement of weight; "cool" is something neither hot nor cold.

Why, when I was in high school, was I taught that the atom was just the smallest thing there is? Because I'm sixty-three years old. More things have changed in my (and your) lifetime than in the preceding five hundred years. If we are conscious we are frequently ricocheting from wall to wall!

One of the most frightening and serious changes has occurred in connection with one particular word. For all the years when I was growing up, the word "future" meant everything getting better; peace and prosperity; justice and mercy. Better housing and enough food, clothing, and shelter for everyone; an integrated society where people were judged on their own merits, not on the color of their skin or their religious preferences. Where wonders of science would have made it possible to cure just about any disease—where rational, well-educated, well-raised men and women would be able to live in harmony with each other.

That was what I and millions of other children were being taught in the early 1920s and the 1930s. Before the Depression; before any of our schoolbooks told us what had really happened to black slaves and native American Indians. Long before we could have imagined that those unions struggling so hard, so bravely, for recognition in the 1930s would, in so many cases, turn out to be as corrupt and full of the same self-interest as some of the "capitalists" they were fighting. In the particular milieu in which I grew up—in a home where the new insights into human psychology were greatly emphasized—I grew up really believing this new field would be used for such noble and necessary causes as curing juvenile delinquency and adult crime, helping children to grow up able to live in peace with each other. I decided I would devote my adult life to this cause—using psychology in child-raising, so that for the first time in human history we could raise "good citizens."

During those years, there was an ideal, a belief in progress through idealistic movements, such as socialism in the case of my family. One needed to join with others in social movements to bring about important social changes. We also believed that if you worked hard you could accomplish anything you wanted.

A new "rational man" would emerge, and we would be able to solve all problems with reason. What we have found of course is what people have had to learn many times throughout history: social revolutions do bring about change, but rarely exactly what we hoped for. A significant change is evident in the now prevalent view that movements and institutions are not to be trusted as a source of change; that faith in them leads to disappointment and defeat.

Jerry Rubin, a well-remembered Yippie of the 1960s now approaching middle age, unlikely as that seems, who certainly believed at one time that movements could move mountains, expresses a different philosophy now—one that

I certainly never heard as a child. He says that he now believes change for the better can come about *only* through the actions of one person at a time. If someone is walking down a street and sees three things that are wrong and attempts to change one of them, that's the best we can hope for.

But during my most impressionable years, the "future" meant "perfectibility"; it now seems a naive dream. I approach old age feeling the same way most of the people I know now feel (from eight to eighty)—that the future is full of terror and danger and even the possible extinction of the human race, the destruction of our planet. Somewhere between Hiroshima and the Holocaust I along with millions of others around the world lost my innocence.

The world I grew up in seemed very quiet and safe. I was carefully protected from the painful, the violent, the suffering of other people. I played safely in the streets and parks of New York. As an adolescent, I often came home at midnight or later, often alone, or walked the streets of the city on Saturday night without fear. In those days there were so few private cars on the street that you could drive anywhere in the city and park! (If you think I'm exaggerating, the next time you watch an old movie of the '20s or '30s, notice how the heroes and heroines pull up and park in front of Macy's or the Plaza Hotel or the Empire State Building!)

Radio was an infant. I vaguely recall my grandmother listening to some quartet on a radio and marveling at it. It was really not part of my life until I was well into my school years, when the first soap operas, like *Mert and Marge,* entranced me, along with the Sunday-night comedians and singers—Al Jolson, Eddie Cantor, and Ed

Wynn. I played quietly with a neighbor's little girl until I was five—no nursery, no day care. My mother was a working woman, but we had a full-time sleep-in maid—I think it cost somewhere between thirty and fifty dollars a month in those days, every other Sunday off. There was also the extended family—grandparents, aunts, uncles, cousins— always nearby. The great excitement of the day was the coming of the iceman or the coal man. A big adventure was to go to the small, familiar grocery store or butcher shop. I never saw a movie until I was eight. When I was about ten, I went to a restaurant for the first time in my life; it was Chinese. I rode the Fifth Avenue double-decker bus, which you weren't allowed to board unless seats were available. The only outside entertainment I can recall was a rare and thrilling trip to the second balcony of Carnegie Hall for the Walter Damrosch children's concerts.

We are people who were born roughly in the first quarter of this century. We are the people of trolley cars; of children being quiet at the table. It is exceedingly unlikely that many of us learned about sex from our parents. We are the children of a time when there were more farms than big cities, a time of child labor, of smallpox, diphtheria, polio, tuberculosis. We are the children of family doctors who came to the house when we were sick, though often they were helpless to make us well. We are the children whose grandparents mostly died when we were very young. We come into our own later years totally unprepared for the problems of parents who live well into their nineties almost routinely. Many of us were children of poverty. The older we are now, the more likely it is that the most successful parents were those who could supply us with the bare necessities of life; who may well have worked ten hours a day, six days a week, for about twelve dollars a week. We are the children who grew up to believe that only hard work gave us our dignity, our sense of purpose in life. We are the children who grew up thinking women could be secretaries, nurses, and schoolteachers—or it was all right if they worked in a factory to feed their children. We are the children who grew up knowing that father was the head of the family, that fathers never changed diapers, that mothers let fathers discipline the children.

Is it any wonder we cannot understand the grandson who works only when he needs money to survive? Is it any wonder we are often horrified by the useless, unnecessary toys and gadgets and junk our grandchildren acquire? Is it any wonder we think we are about to go into cardiac arrest when we hear words that were forbidden to us as horrible and disgusting freely spoken at the dinner table by our grown-up children and our grandchildren?

There is almost nothing in our lives that hasn't changed. Patterns of family living, institutional controls and influences, moral values, social behavior. The equipment we use in daily living—from using the old rippled washboard and boiling clothes on the stove to the washing machine and dryer; from oatmeal that simmered all night to the little package to which you add boiling water. The way we travel—from the train or boat to the 747 flight. The changes in attitudes toward work are astounding, from honoring what often amounted to slave labor all the way to the concept of the three- or four-day work week.

Those changes that may interfere with our most deeply felt ethical ideals probably give us the most trouble. For example, one enormous change that really drives me mad is the relatively new and absolutely overwhelming preoccupation of young people with making money. Until a few years ago, I never heard about investments and money markets and CDs and all the other financial terms that I don't understand. I know that there have always been financiers and investors, but I never bothered them and they never bothered me! My father, perhaps too naively, was never interested in money, and while Larry and I have enjoyed the pleasures of travel and comfortable homes, there were surely easier ways of making a living than the ways we chose. It bores me, it angers me, to turn on the radio and find some expert discussing money matters any time of the day or night—it's a national obsession, which I think helps people avoid the real problems and challenges of life today. This is not much different from video games, Trivial Pursuit, and the preoccupation with sports events where, again, money is the chief factor.

For a two-year period, I did a short radio commentary five days a week on a major network. I talked about a wide range of human problems—child-raising, old age, dieting, grief, friendships, marriage problems—generally dealing with both large and small crises in human relationships. When I was fired, my boss said, "The truth is that people are interested in money and sports and not in the quality of life." What depresses me most is that I believe him.

There are, of course, changes I like a lot. Medicare, concern about child abuse, Planned Parenthood, and the legalization of abortion. (Whatever one's moral or legal views may be, abortion is a fact of life and when it was illegal, rich women went to Sweden or Puerto Rico, and poor women were butchered on tenement-house floors, or tried to do it themselves with coat hangers.) I love the greater concern about the environment and the growing awareness of the danger of nuclear war. I love the changes Martin Luther King, Jr., and other civil rights activists brought into being.

Perhaps nothing has changed so much as attitudes toward sex and how it influences life-styles. If my grandmother could have seen the pornography on TV and in the movies and in magazines, she would have dropped dead from the shock. During my parents' generation, most middle-class couples were chaste until after marriage, partly because the fear of pregnancy was so great. In my generation, there was some premarital experimentation, but not a lot; it began to be permissible to have sexual relations with one's fiancé—but not too long before the marriage.

In my daughter's generation, many parents found themselves shaking with fear when they discovered that twelve- or thirteen-year-old children were often more knowledgeable than their parents, and that they found the idea of "waiting for marriage" primitive, ludicrous.

We grew up in a more stable society; I can't recall anybody getting a divorce during my childhood. By early adolescence I was shocked at the idea that some of my friends' parents might be having affairs. As an adult I was amazed to learn that a few of the most proper ladies in my family had had illegal abortions. It was the Depression and there was terror of not being able to take care of more than one or two children. Among my adult peers, there were occasional divorces and many more affairs and abortions. In my daughter's generation each of these has become a normal part of life. My parents' generation struggled to find their own way toward sexual gratification, and kept it mighty quiet if they did. My generation read very proper scientific sex manuals. Our children experimented freely. We find ourselves somewhat sheepish, embarrassed at how little we know—even after forty or fifty years of marriage!

We have found ourselves living in a time when many people are very confused by all the choices they have to make. A time past all illusions of human perfectibility: violence, noise, pollution, a population that has exploded and crowded us together in cities that are becoming increasingly unlivable.

In my childhood, I never heard the word "pollution." I know now that many people in many places were being injured by new chemicals, new synthetic materials, but it would have been unthinkable to have believed a time might come when all the earth and all the oceans could become too damaged to support human life.

We certainly learned, with the death camps of Europe—and more recently with the boat people of Cambodia—that all our scientific progress, our belief in rational intelligence, had in no way changed the human potential for bestiality.

Most of the major changes in society came after World War II, a time of enormous expansion, an explosion of technology and industrialization. Psychologist Dr. Sigmund Koch studied the extent to which we tried to use what new psychological insights were available to us in planning for our future. He points out that although a momentous decision was made after the war to cover this entire country with enormous highways from Maine to California, no one considered what would happen to American society. This move caused the destruction of thousands of villages and towns, the gutting of neighborhoods; it changed American family life forever. It led to gigantic shopping malls and millions of fast-food stands. It led to more and more instant suburbs without a history, apartment houses built like rabbit warrens where anonymity was far more characteristic than neighbors knowing each other.

One of the things I dearly love (we must be of an age) is Russell Baker's column in the Sunday *New York Times Magazine,* where he wrote about the demise of Main Street:

Main Street is dead. Dead as the Bijou Theater with double-feature programs that changed three times a week. Dead as the dry-goods store that used to sit at the intersection of Washington Avenue. Dead as the trolly car that used to clang down the middle from the First National Bank all the way out to the Bosky Dale Amusement Park. Dead as Sinclair Lewis. . . . Without Main Street it [is] hard to distill America into a handful of simple truths. Main Street was where the Fourth of July parade was held, where you got the mortgage for your first house and bought the presents for your child's first Christmas; but more than that it was the center of things. . . . It was the product of an age when the country had a center that held. When you stood on Main Street, you could tell yourself, "This is the center, the point on which all things converge," and feel inexplicable but nonetheless vital comfort that results from knowing where you stand in the world and what the score is.

Television has surely created a dramatic change in our lifetime. We judge political candidates not on what they stand for, but on whether or not they are good salesmen. We are assaulted, brainwashed into wanting things we don't need; we crave to be like "everyone else," and most of all, we see many of our children and grandchildren bound to the tube almost every waking hour. Still, television can bring exciting new ideas and adventures into people's lives.

The women's movement changed us, too. One of the things that bothered me greatly in the early days of the women's movement was the stereotyping of what was demeaning to women. It appeared at first that homemaking and motherhood were to be viewed in this way. In the course of good human relations at home and at work, it seemed to me that *no* work need be viewed as either respectable or insulting if done because of useful common goals. I was duly shocked (and overjoyed) when I was asked to write an article for a businesswomen's newsletter about how destructive women's attitudes have become in the office where they feel demeaned by fixing a cup of coffee for the boss! I think what's happened is that there are now more women bosses and they are developing a different perspective; getting a job done, together, is again becoming paramount.

I go crazy with the necessary "hims" and "hers" in writing, but I have tried to be reasonable. When I wrote a children's book and mentioned a mother feeding chicken soup to a sick child, and a father taking a kid to a baseball game, the editor insisted on reversing the male and female roles. It seemed mighty silly to me, but again I cooperated. I still think that mothers distribute more soup and fathers more baseball tickets, and this doesn't trouble me, but it's not worth fussing about.

However, I drew the line at a children's book in which a child was named "X" so as not to be saddled with sexism! Ridiculous! It's been comforting to observe that while many of the sound and sensible aspects of the women's movement represented necessary social reform, there is a growing awareness (once again!) that little boys and girls are truly different!

And while in some ways many of us felt threatened by the new open freedom about sexual behavior and sexual relationships, many people are grateful for the ways in which their own lives have been changed. One woman, seventy-three, said, "If it hadn't been for the sexual revolution, I would have missed a love affair with a young man that rejuvenated me completely at the age of sixty-nine!

Change is neither bad nor good in the abstract. We need to evaluate what seems strange or uncomfortable; we need to check to see if we are being stiff-necked, inflexible, rigidly unwilling to see the advantages of some changes, or whether the changes we don't like at all really *do* represent hazards we can't tolerate. For example, a change I will never accept is now a common attitude toward difficult children. I despise the term "Tough Love" in talking about young people who are in trouble and desperately need some kind of reassurance that the world is not as bad as it appears to them to be. Getting tough is just one more simplistic answer to a complex problem, and it is a change that affects a basic value in my life.

Sometimes, however, I start out shocked and then change my mind, such as my great discomfort at the way our teenaged children began dressing in the 1960s. I was brought up to believe that one never appeared in public without wearing (among other things) a hat, stockings, a girdle, and high heels. That's how I traveled with a tiny baby in the early 1950s.

Re-examining my first shock and revulsion, I discovered that being comfortably dressed helped a lot in feeling friendly, getting along with strangers, traveling in comfort, and in general focusing more attention on what one was doing rather than on how one looked. Now I love to travel in slacks and wear my comfortable walking shoes so I can walk to an opera or a play and get the exercise I need. Once in a while I miss the glamour of people getting dressed up, but not enough to want to go back.

Some changes worry me terribly, such as the greater problems for young children whose parents divorce and the changing of the very nature of family life.

Some changes annoy me momentarily but aren't important enough to fuss about. Unfortunately, I think, I got too easily accustomed to hearing words that would have inclined my grandmother to wash my mouth out with soap. But I've learned to tolerate colorful language so long as it doesn't interfere with decent human relations—when it isn't used as a violent attack on another person.

Some changes I will *never* adjust to; I don't try—I just do what I can to run away as often as possible. I adored New York City through all of my childhood. The city had grace and charm and beauty; it was the mecca for all the creative arts; the theater district was my Garden of Eden. Watching the destruction of anything connected with childhood memory hurts. There is bound to be a sense of loss when places and things—and most of all people—disappear from our lives. A building I lived in at Seventieth Street and Columbus Avenue has been condemned, and I can't bare to look at it. When I was a little girl I went to school opposite the Sheep Meadow in Central Park. That's exactly what it was then, a place for grazing the sheep that lived in the sheepfold, which has now become a fancy restaurant, The Tavern on the Green. In a recent issue of *New York* magazine, there was a picture of the sheep grazing near their enclosure. It was a scene out of my childhood; I loved to be taken to see the sheep. The picture felt so much more familiar to me than the restaurant, even though it's been there since 1934. My memories are those of a six- or seven-year-old—far clearer than when I grew up and ate in the restaurant. Part of hating change is that it destroys one's personal history. I hated the tearing down of the Old Met and S. S. Klein's department store. I hate Bloomingdale's for no longer being a nice comfortable store in which my grandmother, my mother, and I knew exactly where everything was.

I guess each of us feels best about those changes we helped to bring about in some way. I am happy about the changes that I took some small part in bringing about; the greater understanding of children's needs, the way parents and children are so much more able today to talk to each other about feelings, the greater awareness of how we need to help children deal with such crises of life as divorce or the death of a parent.

Alvin Toffler wrote about "future shock" and the more I think about it, the more it seems to me that the older we are, the harder it may be to deal with change. We have a past history—younger people don't. We have to change, at least in enough ways to live in the changing world. They see the changes as a normal course of events.

As I examine what changes I love, which ones I hate, when I'm glad something continues to change, when I'm glad when some recent change is given up, I realize I'm really creating a self-portrait! Changes that leave a sense of ourselves intact don't bother us too much. If they fit in with our image of who we are, we can accept them; when the changes challenge our identity as we've lived it all our lives, we get upset.

Changes in other people's attitudes toward us are often

hard to take. We have considered ourselves mature, wise, experienced, and when someone very young treats us in a patronizing way we feel angry and frightened. Perhaps we once wielded a good deal of influence in our families and in our work, and now fewer people are interested in what we have to say. Younger people seem, very often, to be indifferent to the past that was ours—where we were and what we did during World War II, what happened to our families during the Depression; what it was like to see the first "talking movie" or to hear that Lindbergh had landed in France. We begin to see a glazed, faraway look in the eyes of our audience, and are shocked to realize that *we* are boring—just the way we once thought our parents were!

Larry, as a research psychologist, searches throughout history for insights related to his own. He finds that in every stage of human history, somebody had some of the ideas he is developing, refining, re-creating with the greater knowledge available in the present. He is constantly shocked and amazed that younger students, writers, "scientists" content themselves with a five-year search of the literature in whatever field they are investigating as if nothing important could possibly have happened before that! (This can be quite annoying when one's own research goes back over thirty years!) However, I always know that Larry has found a new treasure when he comes home and tells me about someone who, in 1804 or 1927—or 2000 B.C.—was on the same track he's now on. When young people dismiss history, they lose the grandeur of the human experience, to say nothing of repeating the same old mistakes over and over again. Perhaps few things hurt us more than having our own history dismissed.

Having grown up in more formal times, I find instant

intimacy hard to get used to, but I see its advantages and appropriateness in this fast-moving, mobile society. It's still a shock to call someone on the telephone whom I've never met and never spoken to before—especially someone who sounds much younger—and hear them call me Eda.

It's hard to adjust to changes in ourselves and the way others see us. I thought my mother was old at forty, my grandmother ancient at sixty-five. Now I know children see *me* that way and it blows my mind! Walking on a street one day with my eighty-eight-year-old father, two young men passed, looked at us, and I heard them say, "That's where we'll be in thirty years!" I cringed.

When I was younger, I thought older people were very intolerant of young people. Now I find that if I'm not careful I get very angry and impatient with teenagers—and sound just like my elders. The young people seem rude, fresh, indifferent to others' rights. They drive fast and push people on buses and don't hold the doors open for the passengers behind them. I have to remind myself not to lump all teenagers together, but to judge individuals, as I always did in the past.

Younger people could argue, with plenty of justification, that I don't give the present and the future a chance. I feel more and more out of touch with the worlds of creation—art, music, theater. Two years running I actually despised the plays that won Pulitzer prizes. I find modern music cacophonous and grating. With every blast of rock and roll, I feel one more brain cell shriveling and dying, and long for Glenn Miller, Rodgers and Hammerstein! It takes a lot of courage, but I must even admit I like representational art better than modern abstract painting. I am ashamed to admit it, but the Calder sculpture in front of the Vivian

Beaumont Theatre makes me think of a defecating giant! I'm sure that my resistances are wrong some of the time, but I can't believe I'm entirely wrong. I don't think I'm wrong when my attention dissipates immediately when confronted by characters on a stage who are so ugly, so without redeeming human qualities, that I wouldn't tolerate them for a moment in real life.

Fortunately we have choices where change is concerned. We don't have to capitulate on every point. I don't have to go to a modern opera if I don't want to. I don't have to change my opinion that some contemporary artists are talented wallpaper designers. I don't have to accept any social attitude or behavior that really upsets or displeases me. And that, I think, is the key to how we deal with social change. We need to try, to taste, to give new experiences a chance, and then we have this wonderful new freedom to say the hell with it. Or we have the equally valuable freedom to say, "How lucky I am to have lived long enough to experience such new and wonderful things!"

Outside changes in the environment are child's play compared to the changes that are taking place inside each of us. We look different, we feel different, our social life changes, our work life may turn into retirement, the children (maybe!) are leaving or have already flown the coop, we may be divorced or widowed, we may be caring for older parents, our energy level is changing.

I surely believe in making the most of life, but I also believe that we can burden ourselves unnecessarily if we assume a brave and cheerful front at all times. When I suddenly look in the mirror and see an aging face, or when I see the tired lines, the shadows, under Larry's eyes, when inside my head I still feel as if we are a young couple, it is a painful and surprising experience. Like Russell Baker, in another of his wonderful *Times* columns, I want, I need, times to feel grouchy about the things I cannot change, for as far as I'm concerned, even if Larry and I both had face-lifts, I'd still know we were sixty-four and sixty-three. Baker wrote: ". . . if I can have an uninterrupted three-day grouch two or three times a year, life seems a little more tolerable. For those three days I refuse to smile or cheer up."

What I and most of the people I've spoken to feel most grouchy about are the physical changes that are occurring. I vividly recall how bored and annoyed I used to be, listening to my mother and her friends talking about all their ailments, as they got older. I swore this would never happen to me. As with so many other things I didn't understand, I have surely eaten my words on that subject.

I was wearing a cast on my left arm for several months. I was in constant pain from what seemed to be a complicated ailment in my wrist. Many doctors, many different diagnoses. One day I walked into a room where there was a woman I hadn't seen in some time; she asked me what was wrong with my arm. Another woman, one I had just seen the week before said, "Don't ask her, it's very boring!" She said it with a laugh, but the ghost of my poor mother appeared before me and I knew I was over the hill.

One day I got on a bus in New York at Seventy-second Street and Broadway. Two women who hadn't seen each other for a long time met unexpectedly. One asked the other, "How are you feeling? I hear you haven't been well." The second woman replied, "I'm not going to bore you with that story. I hate people who talk about their medical problems." The first woman seemed to accept this statement at face value, and nodded. The second woman went on, "Except I've got to tell you, you have to watch out for doctors, or they can kill you." There followed a monologue of her illness and her struggle with the medical profession which continued until she and the other woman left the bus at Eighth Street and Fifth Avenue—a ride, in midday traffic, of about an hour. The listener had rolled her eyes despairingly at those of us sitting on the opposite side of the bus in exactly the same way I had when my mother and grandmother would discuss all their physical problems, and I am now mortified to discover that I and many of my contemporaries are doing exactly the same thing.

There are a number of similarities between adolescence and old age. In both cases there are physical changes over which one feels no sense of control. The teenager gradually becomes aware that a child's body is becoming a man's or a woman's. There is simply no emotional preparation possible for this dramatic change; it feels funny and awkward—and because it will lead to new roles in life, it is very scary. The older person, less vigorous and energetic, with lined face, gray hair, wrinkles, who is going to flab all over, getting tired earlier in the evening, having more trouble sleeping—partly because of having to get up to go to the bathroom at night—unable any longer to eat heavy foods without paying a price in indigestion, becoming increasingly aware of periods of diarrhea and constipation, feels completely alienated from this changing body. And the roles one must play, as this process continues, are more frightening than those faced by the adolescent. The teenager faces sexual activity, going to work, marriage, parenthood, all potentially frightening, I grant, but a person noticing aging processes faces the possibilities of becoming a chronic invalid, depending on others, suffering senility, and playing the definite and unavoidable role of a dying person.

When I mentioned this parallel to Henry, age sixty-seven, he laughed and said, "And what's even worse, they have the energy to take it and we don't!"

Whenever I asked the question, "When did you start to feel old?" almost invariably the answer had something to do with changing health. A man of seventy-three who traveled all over the country giving lectures, who chopped wood for his stove, who could walk miles over his land in New England, who shoveled snow, who read more than any man I know, wrote one simple line on my questionnaire: "I became old when I had a stroke." He also said that while he very rarely thought about old age before, he "now thinks of it often." When asked what he felt about people eighty and over, again his succinct reply was, "Lucky if healthy."

Another man said, "If you fall and break a hip or a knee at seventy-five, you know that healing will be a long, arduous recovery, and the dependence on others reminds you immediately of what is soon to come as a reality of life. If you have a serious accident involving broken bones and all sorts of other complications at twenty-five, you may of course suffer greatly, but you know you're young enough to heal completely, and while you may be impatient with temporary helplessness, it never occurs to you (unless the accident causes paralysis) that you won't recover fully."

It's true. When I hurt my knee I was only too delighted to use a four-pronged cane. I knew I'd need it only for a week or so. My father, who uses a regular cane all the time, would have nothing to do with the four-pronged variety.

An example of how our fear of change interferes with adjusting to it is sleep patterns. Everyone tells us we need less sleep as we get older, but there is a great deal of anxiety among older people as they begin to sleep less than seven to eight hours a night; it *feels* as if something is wrong.

We have in our neighborhood an unusual pharmacy that sends out a newsletter to its patrons—a terrific idea, I think. One issue included this report on sleep:

A newborn baby sleeps 16 hours a day. A 4-year-old, 10 hours, and young adults average 8 hours sleep a night. As we get older, our sleep patterns change even more. This is especially true when we're past 40 or 50. In those years, we often find that people need only 3-5 hours sleep. So don't worry if you don't get 8 hours sleep a night. Sleep habits are almost as individual as handwriting. There's no medical necessity that everybody get 8 hours sleep. . . . The unbroken, sound sleep of youth is a thing of the past for most elderly people. This is a normal change with age. It's neither good nor bad, but the change worries many people when it shouldn't.*

No matter how well we try to take care of ourselves, there comes a time when we become aware of having less physical energy. We just can't garden as long as we once did, we can't walk as far, we can't stand shopping in crowded stores where there is no place to sit down. The thought of cooking for a dinner party strikes us as a horrendous burden. If we have been very active most of our lives, the loss of vitality can be a great shock and very distressing. But we can learn to deal with these changes, as we

*Brandt Pharmacy, Sandor Rogers, ed.

put them into perspective and view them in relationship to our total life experiences.

Physical changes are obvious, easy to recognize. Sometimes the more subtle changes, the ones that come upon us slowly, almost imperceptibly, are the most difficult to see and to adjust to. For example, loose connections become lost connections. It comes upon me slowly and then I am startled; people I saw all the time in my thirties and forties—people whom I thought of as close friends—I may never see again. Most of the relatives I saw in childhood have died, but there are still uncles, aunts, and cousins with whom I feel a deep kinship but whom I almost never see— except at funerals!

When I was much younger, we and our friends saw each other very often; somebody was always giving a dinner party on Saturday night. I still like most of those people, but it seems to be too much trouble to make the effort to make a date—we don't drive at night anymore (can't see well enough) and we get tired more easily; I'm now accustomed to going to bed early most nights since I've gotten into the habit of starting to write at about five A.M. Socializing just doesn't seem as important as it once was.

A few old friends call once in awhile, and I feel nostalgic for our mutual past and feel a sense of loss, but it doesn't last. It seems too much effort to re-establish old connections. Part of this is surely due to changing interests and activities. Many of our old friends were in some way related to work we were doing at a given time. What we once may have had in common (such as raising our children) is no longer there to hold us together. And yet, sometimes, sitting in a theater or a restaurant, looking at two or three young couples out on a date together, I feel a sudden longing to go back to that stage of my life.

It doesn't last long! The truth is that as we get older we are far more selective about how we spend our time; being alone becomes more attractive. With a sense of time running out, there are fewer people we want to spend that precious time with.

About ten years ago Larry and I went to Florida to visit his mother. I couldn't get over the fact that she had no food in her refrigerator. She had been, in the early years of our marriage, the Jewish Mother of Us All, with homemade matzo ball soup, homemade gefilte fish, homemade tsimmis, homemade everything, and about nine courses at every meal. I was shocked; I couldn't understand what had happened to her. She simply said, "I've done my share of cooking, that time of my life is over. I eat a big breakfast down in the restaurant in the building, I have a sandwich by the pool for lunch, and we eat at a cafeteria every night." Was *this* the woman who had taught me how to make a noodle pudding?

Today I understand perfectly; I'm reaching the same point. I have about three dinner parties a year—usually on birthdays or holidays. I enjoy cooking in New Jersey, where I have a tiny house to write in, but where the kitchen is part of the living room and looks out on a lake and the view is beautiful all year round. But it wouldn't bother me at all never to cook another meal, despite the fact that I was a gourmet cook in my thirties and forties. Like my mother-in-law, "I've done that already." And as we get older, food ought to become simpler and we should eat much less of it if we want to live a long time. Rather than cooking a fancy meal for eight people on a Saturday night, Larry and I now prefer to get into our bathrobes and eat a Lean Cuisine frozen dinner while watching the evening news.

OH, TO BE 50 AGAIN!

Many of the people I talked to said they were making new, younger friends; that they were bored with some of their peers who had stopped doing anything interesting with their lives. Ralph told me, "I'll give you an example; George was a really interesting scientist doing some unusual research. I liked hearing about his work. He was automatically retired at sixty-five, and it bores me to death to listen to him talk about golf."

Once in awhile an old friendship, long given up, resurfaces and turns out to be just fine. Another person told me, "I met Sue on a bus. My wife and I hadn't seen her or her husband for over forty years! Somehow we just lost touch after the war. I was really glad to see her and because I knew Sue and Dave had always been interested in good causes, I spontaneously invited them to a party we were giving to raise money for the ACLU. They came, we liked each other all over again, and they are new friends."

Some old friendships remain because those friends have virtually become relatives. I am still very close to three women I've known since I was six years old. We never lost touch, and it is really as if we are sisters. The relationship would continue, I think, even if our interests had become quite different—and to some degree that has happened—but there is a feeling of being able to be totally relaxed with certain old friends. Doris told me, "I have known Janet for fifty years—we were teachers together. There are some things we can't stand about each other, and yet we enjoy traveling together; it's the feeling of familiarity. We're both widowed—I suppose in a sense this is like a marriage—comfortable, familiar, even if you drive each other crazy with certain habits!"

There may sometimes be a feeling of painful nostalgia

for a relationship that was once vital, essential, but has been outgrown. We need to remind ourselves that a change in friendships doesn't necessarily mean loss. As I get older and become much more discriminating, I am more aware of who are the givers and who are the takers, the whiners and the stoics, I'm more aware of the tyranny of the weak, the shyness of the blusterer. I have learned something important about myself through each relationship, and on the whole know the changes were necessary, constructive. But I must admit to a recurring fantasy in which Ralph Edwards would come up to me and say, "Eda LeShan, this is your life!" and for at least one half-hour I could see all the people I've ever known!

I have found it valuable to go back and renew some old friendships, even very briefly. I find it necessary to travel a lot for my work and it gives me the chance to pick up on old relationships. Sometimes it's wonderful; I hadn't seen Catherine for almost ten years, but we discovered we had both been growing and changing in many of the same ways, and we could pick up where we had left off without a moment's pause. On the other hand, Jean saw me on TV and called the station to arrange to have lunch at the airport. It was a disaster! She hadn't changed one iota since high school, and we found nothing whatever to share except a few old and worn-out memories. Friendships change, but what is most important is to make the changes mean something in terms of our own growth. Sara said, "What you have to watch out for as you get older is that you don't choose your friends on the basis of 'who will listen to my troubles?'"!

Our family life is another area in which very dramatic changes affecting our feelings may occur. We may be recently divorced or widowed; our children may just have left the nest—or they may have suddenly and unexpectedly returned. We may have suddenly found our roles reversing with elderly parents who are now beginning to depend on us. Along with the pleasures there is surely a certain shock to discover that one is now old enough to be called "Grandma" or "Grandpa"!

For those who have remained married, all kinds of changes are occurring, and one often hears the refrain, "I married you for better or for worse, but not for lunch!" More couples being thrown together more of the time— maybe even all of the time. There are couples who are genuinely, profoundly bored with each other but don't have the energy or the courage to do anything about it. There are also couples who are surprised to discover the return of an earlier passion that was watered down years ago by diapers and report cards, kids walking in at inappropriate moments, and chicken pox and drug scares. Suddenly the house is quiet and empty; even matinees are possible again. If retirement has meant doing what you want to do when you want to do it, that's an encouraging setting for thoughts of lovemaking! Married life may mean quiet despair, constant bickering—or, with all the accommodations and growth of many years, the best time of your life.

It is possible that there has been a gradual diminution in sexual feelings, a serious problem if it is one-sided. Most of us were taught as children that passion will be replaced by a warm glow of friendship as the years go by. A writer who lived from 1850 to 1928, Jane Ellen Harrison, wrote: "Life does not cease when you are old, it only suffers a rich change. You go on loving, only your love, instead of a burning, fiery furnace, is a mellow glow of an autumn sun." Because of my age and the world I grew up in, that sounds far less strange and upsetting to me than the gerontologists, the sex therapists, who now announce exultantly that we can still be cavorting madly at the age of ninety!

Flexibility seems to be the name of the game. We need to learn that it is important to keep our options open. We have to accept changes we can't do anything about—but we don't have to like all of them. We may decide that something we thought might be the ultimate disaster in our lifetime may actually have certain advantages. Or we may need to allow ourselves to feel our regrets, our anger, our sadness. Trying to repress such feelings only makes them stronger. We are not only allowed to change our point of view—sometimes it just happens. I remember that at the time that Helen Hayes's husband, Charles MacArthur, died, her devastation was evident quite publicly, so I would guess it was even greater in private. She and her husband had suffered the terrible tragedy of losing their beautiful and talented daughter Mary to polio, and one wondered how she would deal with the ending of a long and exciting marriage relationship. In her recent book, she wrote: "This is a great time of my life, the best in many ways. I can do what I want, when I want, go where I please—as often and as long as I like. I'm accountable to no one and no one need check in with me. The world is my playground, my workroom, my stage, and my responsibility in a small measure, too. What I like about the eighties—mine and the century's—is that this decade is so full of change . . ."*

*Helen Hayes with Marion Gladney, *Our Best Years* (New York: Doubleday & Company, 1984).

When we accept the changes we see in ourselves we can begin to make vital and exciting new choices for ourselves. The woman who has spent her working life teaching nursery school may want to "retire" to taking courses at an adult education center, build up her association with grown-ups; a man who has worked in a scientific laboratory for thirty years and is forced to retire may discover he'd like to take a course in poetry. Someone who has had to slap meals together frantically for the thirty years in which she's been raising five kids might love to take lessons in gourmet French cooking. Charles told me, "Inside I've always been a serious political person, very concerned about being a citizen of this great democracy. But working eight hours a day and raising a family, I never had time—except once I was PTA president for a year. Now I'm slightly disabled and work only part-time; I've joined a political club and I love it!"

Learning *not* to do the things we don't love anymore is an important way to use our opportunities for change. It astonishes me how often (and how easily!) I now turn down speaking engagements I don't want to accept. I even canceled *six* meetings when I was in great pain (from arthritis in my wrist). In forty years, I'd *never* canceled a meeting; Larry went with me once when my temperature reached 102°.

There are surely many aspects of getting older that arouse appropriate anxieties and fears. If we deny these feelings, they become a far greater burden than if we face them. I was fifty-nine when my daughter broke her leg when she was five months pregnant. I took her to the doctor several times while she was in a cast, and of course, this was no small feat; I had to help her maneuver from the car to the doctor's waiting room. Her dependency made me begin to feel very anxious, and I quickly realized that what I was feeling was, "Will it be me next? Will the tables turn and will I be the helpless one that she has to take care of?" Now I take my father to the doctor, and he needs to lean on me.

It is normal to feel anxious about dependency; we have been autonomous for all our adult lives; we are experienced, mature, responsible, independent people—how could we *not* be afraid of losing those attributes? There is no easy answer, but what I tell myself is that even if (when!) I have to have others take care of me, there are two things I will hang on to for as long as I possibly can—my dignity and my ability to communicate my feelings. And most of all, I try to remember that there are still choices to be made, that attitudes toward changes could make a tremendous difference.

I found a wide assortment of reactions to the inner changes of getting older. A woman who has recently had a face-lift, who runs every day, who looks much younger than her sixty-five years, seems jaunty, optimistic, unconcerned; she really doesn't feel she is changing at all. A widow, depressed, lonely, developing some physical symptoms of aging, wrote me: "I have the feeling that I'm pulling away from contemporary life. I'm no longer in tune with the new fashions in dress, literature, theater, art, music—I feel left out and isolated—I don't know how to talk to younger people. I have no common ground with my children—not even with my peers who are still working. Too many friends and colleagues have died off. I miss the exchange of ideas with my contemporaries—people who shared my history and are gone."

Janice, still engaged in the practice of law at the age of seventy-five, told me, "Sometimes people use the things going on in the outside world as an excuse for the failure to face the inside world. If you really make a conscious effort to deal with challenges life presents, change becomes interesting rather than frightening."

There comes a time when the effort to get dressed and go out at night to hear a concert just seems too much. There are fantastic records to listen to. There comes a time when it becomes difficult to hear every word even in the best seats in a theater—but there is *Masterpiece Theatre* on television, where you can sit close and turn it up loud. Whatever the hazards of television may be for children, it is a wonderful resource for older people, with movies, ballet, concerts, plays, and interesting talk shows and also lots of junky silly stuff when we're in the mood.

There comes a time when driving a car becomes a danger to ourselves and others. One of the outstanding services of many senior citizens' centers is the chance to travel by bus, together, without the stress and strain of getting places on one's own. An aunt of ninety-two, while living in a residence for older people, told me, "I saw the cherry blossoms in Washington in the spring and the autumn leaves in New England and I've been to lunch-theaters and Sunday afternoon concerts—more than I was doing when I lived alone in my apartment." She is the same lady who, contemplating the move from her home to institutional living, said, "Well, it's just another adventure."

A woman of eighty told me that she doesn't have the strength to travel much or visit her friends, and most of her friends are in the same boat. "We meet less often, and we talk more on the phone," she said. "I've begun to write letters to my grandchildren, and much to my surprise they often answer me, and I'm subscribing to more magazines, so I can keep up with things at home. I hardly paid any attention to my neighbors in my apartment building when I was younger—I was too busy going places. Now I'm looking closer to home for companionship, and I've met several nice people."

For some of the people I questioned, changes had come slowly and comfortably, with a feeling that there were new advantages in life. Florence wrote: "I have read that the older ages are the happiest years and I think I understand why. I truly did enjoy the years as a stay-at-home home-maker and mother of five children. I have thoroughly enjoyed my years as a paid professional person since they left home. I feel that I have been fortunate to have had opportunities for both careers."

Peter Ustinov seems to have a relaxed and philosophical view of aging. In an article in *Modern Maturity* he makes gentle fun of the Hollywood tension about remaining forever young. When asked if he regrets the younger parts he can no longer play, he replied, "Oh heavens, no, I wouldn't want to go back in my life. I am more at peace now than I have ever been, although I am aware there is a tendency in men of my age, especially in my profession, to pretend to be younger than they are. . . ."*

What he likes is that "I notice as one gets older one can express himself with greater ease because nothing is quite as serious as it was when one was younger . . ."

May Sarton's attitudes toward the changes that occur as one grows older both put me to shame and inspire me to

Modern Maturity (Aug./Sept. 1984).

do better: "One thing is certain, and I have always known it—the joys of my life have nothing to do with my age. They do not change. Flowers, the morning and evening light, music, poetry, silence, the goldfinches darting about . . . I am happy because I feel alive and well and in a constant state of expectation before each day. What surprise may be hidden in today?"*

A remarkable woman, a wonderful attitude—but surely not the whole story of aging and changing. We need to acknowledge the darker side as well. Change hurts sometimes and needs healing.

We owned a house on a lake on Cape Cod. I used to go there to write, but getting there by plane got too expensive, and the trip became more tiring as I got older. However, when my mother died we planted a Japanese maple in her memory and her ashes are buried there. As I got more and more fed up with city life, I thought I might be able to persuade Larry to move up there permanently, and in a wild fit of insanity I allowed an irresponsible builder to talk me into turning a lovely summer cottage into an all-year-round house four times the size I needed. It was a disaster until my daughter and son-in-law said they'd like to live there, and they did for a number of years. Then, for a complicated assortment of reasons, I realized they might not stay there and that we would never go back.

I had to face the fact that in rebuilding the house and planting that tree and many others, I had held on to an irrational fantasy that this would become a kind of family homestead, passed on from generation to generation, and that my grandchildren and great-grandchildren would live

*Sarton, *At Seventy,* p. 174.

there. It was, of course, nonsense; a dream of a world that hasn't existed for more than a century, a cry of hunger for stability in an unstable and uncertain world. It was very hard to consider the possibility of letting go, but I realized that change, even painful change, can have its advantages. From the sale of the house there would be some extra money for our old age, and meanwhile we would have unloaded a heavy burden. It would be more fun to travel, perhaps to help our daughter with her education goals. Somebody else would enjoy the maple, the fruit trees, and the rhododendron that were now so big. That was all right. I would always remember the first time I saw the hill and that house on that lake. The memorial service for my mother, surrounded by our family and friends, was in my head for as long as I lived. Change was not so terrible if I could still look forward to new adventures.

Recently I was talking to a very wise friend about the attitudes grown children have toward their aging parents. I started to mention the daughters in *King Lear* and she interrupted me and said, "Don't tell me that play is only about children and old parents. What it is really about is that people who get old feel they will lose their kingdoms."

What is your "kingdom"? What is mine? It seems to me that if there is something we don't want to lose as we grow older, we need to discover what it is we want our "kingdom" to be, and then we need to figure out how to make it happen.

~~~~~~

The Never-Ending Search for Oneself

I DON'T THINK EITHER LARRY or I knew what we were doing in the early years of our marriage. We had no name for it—all we knew was that we were struggling, often desperately, to understand ourselves and each other whenever we ran into trouble. As we got older, it became a conscious process; if we were irrationally angry, if we were chronically depressed, if we couldn't get on with the work at hand, if our child or either one of us was suffering, there was only one thing to do. It was back to the old drawing board of life, back to searching for causes, back to trying to discover more about ourselves—a never-ending exploration to more clearly define one's identity. In our case, we used the resources of individual psychotherapy, but of course there are other paths for other people—prayer and meditation, group therapy, vocational and marriage counseling, and so on. What we discovered is that there is no way of ever knowing all about oneself, partly because one never recovers all of one's past experiences and feelings and partly because different things become important at different phases of one's life.

While I was writing *The Wonderful Crisis of Middle Age* I

was having trouble crystalizing the idea of the necessity for continual growth and change at every phase of one's life. We were invited to a dinner party where I was seated next to a marine biologist, and I could tell from the expression on his face that he was as distressed at being stuck with me as I was with him; it seemed clear when we were introduced to each other that we couldn't possibly have any interests in common. However, over the years I'd learned an important lesson from Larry; if you *really listen* to other people you can usually find something interesting about them. And so I asked this man about his work—and discovered that he was a fascinating person, devoted to the creatures under the sea.

At one point he asked me if I knew how a lobster could possibly grow when it had such a hard shell. I had to admit that this question had never been very high on my list of priorities. He then proceeded to explain that when a lobster begins to feel crowded in, let's say, a one-pound shell, by natural instinct it knows the hard shell must be discarded and a new, bigger shell formed. The lobster is in great danger during this process, which, as I recall, takes about forty-eight hours. It can be eaten by other fish while it is completely naked and vulnerable, it can get tossed against a coral reef and badly damaged. But there is no alternative; if the hard shell is not given up, there can be no growth; the risk is essential.

I couldn't get this imagery out of my head—I even dreamt about it—and when I mentioned it to the therapist I was seeing at the time, who was trying to help me with my current writer's block, she pointed out quite accurately that this was the symbolic, metaphoric theme of the book I was trying to write about middle age—a time for change, a time for growing. It was absolutely true and everything went swimmingly (sorry!) from then on. The problem for human beings is that, unlike the infallible, instinctual lobster, we don't always know when it is time to "de-shell," to take risks, to make room for new growth. And sometimes, even when we recognize the symptoms (migraine headaches, marital crises, losing three jobs in a row, hitting a child, feeling suicidal) we don't have as much courage as the lobster; we cling to the life we are leading, terrible as it may be, in terror of facing the unknown.

I believe it is necessary to learn that unless we work at becoming more than we are at any given moment, we will die long before they bury us. Trying to stay the same, remain the same person, no matter what is happening, is like becoming a five-pound lobster trying to survive in a two-pound lobster's shell—suffocating, desperate, impossible.

There is probably no time in our lives when the struggle for identity becomes more important than as we get older. People who work with the dying—ministers, people who work in hospices, relatives who are willing to be open with a dying family member—all report the same phenomenon: death is a different experience for those who feel reasonably clear about who they are and have come to peaceful terms with what they have made of their lives. The search for one's special identity can continue until one's last breath—and can make that final experience if not acceptable at least endurable.

As we get older, it seems to me the search for identity often takes the form of cultivating our eccentricities. Person after person in my interviews commented in one way or another that one of the advantages of getting older was that one could be "more myself." Sometimes this involves major issues of belief and faith—ethical principles. Sometimes it is the silliest of things. In my book on middle age I struck a blow for freedom; I wrote that I had grown up in the "bobby sox" era, that I wanted to walk a lot and that wearing ankle socks and sturdy shoes was important to me, and I didn't care if I looked like an eccentric old crone. I received many pairs of socks from sympathetic readers, and now that I really *am* an old crone, and everybody is wearing ankle socks, I like to think I started the trend. But something much more remarkable happened. As soon as I had the courage to do what I wanted to do, *I felt like myself.*

One day a year or so after the book was published, I was standing at the counter in Zabar's, a famous New York delicatessen–gourmet emporium. The place is so popular that we were standing three rows deep, and behind me was an older couple. The woman had recognized me and whispered to her husband, "That's Eda LeShan, and she really *is* wearing socks!" Before I could enjoy my fame, she added, "And she looks *awful!*" I discovered once again that when you are really "doing your own thing," it doesn't matter at all whether other people approve or not—as long as what you're doing doesn't hurt or exploit anyone else.

How much more important it is to allow ourselves the luxury of eccentricity where it may really count. Almost everyone I talked to about getting older commented on the "pleasure of speaking my mind." One woman said, "When people are rude about holding doors open on a bus or in a store, I tell them the whole of civilization depends on how *each* of us acts toward each other person." A man told me, "I *argue* more! I'm cantankerous. If I see someone wearing a button for the election of someone I think is an SOB, I try to engage that person in debate!"

As for myself, I never let a child's stroller pass on a rainy day, that is "protected" by one of those plastic covers, without telling the parent to watch carefully to be sure that the child is getting enough oxygen. Ten, twenty years ago, I would have been embarrassed to interfere; now it doesn't bother me. I think most of us begin to feel freer to be ourselves just because we *are* getting older.

What is important about eccentricity is that it really means doing what we think is *right* without regard to whether others approve or not. That could make us excellent citizens if we follow through!

Old age really is our last chance to evaluate, our last opportunity for self-examination, self-assessment. When we are able to figure out where and when we sold out, when we let other people's needs interfere too much with our own inner development, what we love and what we hate, we are setting the stage to be most authentically and truly ourselves for whatever years we may have left. And nothing can be more invigorating than an inner declaration of selfhood.

It's not an easy task at any stage of life to figure out what is special, unique, about oneself. So much of what we become is a reflection of other people's expectations. From the time we were little children, so eager for love and approval, so dependent on our parents, so eager to please them, we have unconsciously assumed that what they taught us we should want for ourselves must have been right. After all, they were the grown-ups, all wise and wonderful, we thought then—how could they possibly lead us astray? Most of us grew up believing it was more important to be good than to be ourselves; more important to find a secure profession at which we could make a good living than to be happy in our work; more important to please others than ourselves. To some degree every child "sells out" for love. We might have been dying of shyness but we played the piano when Grandma came; we might have hated arithmetic but we believed the nonsense that if we didn't work hard to get A's, it would ruin our adult lives. At the very worst, our childhood need for love and approval might have turned a potential ballet dancer into a manufacturer of men's suits, a potentially brilliant judge into a despairing housewife. If, as we have lived our adult lives, we have been plagued by depression, by chronic illnesses, by feelings of rage or hopelessness, chances are that a long time ago we decided to be good at the cost of being ourselves.

There never really was such an equation and that's what we have to learn now if we never learned it before. In the child's mind, being good meant becoming whatever it was one's parents' dream might be. Hopefully most of us have already discovered that this was never true. The more one fulfills one's own dreams, the more decent, civilized, compassionate one can be in one's dealings with others. When we spend our lives trying to satisfy other people's unfulfilled needs, we learn sooner or later that nothing will ever satisfy, nothing will fill the bottomless pit of their demands.

One of the reasons we are often afraid to take a look at our own needs is that we are afraid we will become mean and selfish and irresponsible. How could it be otherwise if we resent the things we have to do for others? The truth is we are only resentful when we are psychologically malnourished, when we are giving too much more than we are getting.

Jim told me that he played the Fairy Godmother Game

(described later in this chapter) and *all three* wishes were that he didn't have to go to see his mother in the nursing home three times a week! He felt guilty and ashamed of his response, but finally mentioned it to a friend, a social worker who worked in a senior citizens' center and whom he thought might understand. The social worker said, "Sure, that's perfectly natural. Your mother happens to be a very bitter old lady who is a bottomless pit. If you visited her three times a *day* she would still say you don't come enough. How about visiting her once a week, and trying to make it a quality time together by letting her know you know what some of her disappointments in life have been? The other two evenings you go out with your wife or go take a course—you're always complaining that you've never had time to take that evening high-school course in carpentry." Jim felt greatly relieved. On the next visit to his mother, he said, "Ma, I know this place makes you sad and angry and you've had a hard life with many disappoint-ments." Then he just listened sympathetically for two hours. At the end of the time, he said he'd be back in one week. She smiled for the first time in many months and said, "It helps a lot to talk to you." Jim told me, "Some-thing very deep had happened—I can't really define it—but I felt different, and my mother knew I was really there for her. And it stayed that way as I felt I was giving as much as I could and was also taking care of me."

As we get older and some limitations begin to present themselves to us, we begin to get some notion of how we see ourselves, what values we have—which things matter because of our own attitudes or the attitudes of others. One woman told me that when she can no longer drive a car, she will stop feeling like a person. Another said, "If I ever lost my money, that would be the end of me." Don told me, "Education was the most important thing in my family. If I ever felt I was going to pot intellectually, I would feel I would rather be dead."

There is a sense of shock when your vision of yourself is suddenly destroyed. In her charming book *Full Circle: Rounding Out a Life,* Martha Munzer tells a story about her sister who was riding in a train one day sitting opposite a youngster of about seven, ". . . one-tenth her own age. He couldn't take his eyes from her face. . . . My sister learned the reason when he blurted out, 'Lady, your skin doesn't fit!'"*

And then there are the identity shocks that come from within. A friend of mine told me, "I don't remember the exact day it happened, but it was before I was sixty. I passed a mirror and had a flash thought—'That's how I'm going to look when I get old.' I couldn't synchronize the internal feelings of a young woman with my actual image."

We define ourselves through parental expectations and the reactions of other people; we define ourselves by sudden new perceptions of our own. And we define ourselves by what the culture tells us rather than what we feel internally. In Chapter One I mentioned the man who had just climbed a mountain but who then felt old because a woman asked her son to give him a seat. By whose definition was he defining himself as old? Surely he couldn't have believed that anyone really old could climb a mountain!

One woman commented, "What makes me feel old is

---

*Martha Munzer, *Full Circle: Rounding Out a Life* (New York: Alfred A. Knopf, 1978).

that people don't listen to me, they don't value my opinion. If I enter a conversation among younger people, they listen politely, and the minute I'm finished they turn away." My reaction when I heard this was, frankly, "Well, screw them!" Why were our reactions to the same situation so different? Frances is a woman who, it seems to me, has never fully realized her own potential. She was married to a successful, dominating man and remained in his shadow; since his death she has done nothing to change her life. I, on the other hand, have had more than my share of successes and triumphs, and if I feel I am boring someone, I'm more than pleased to go off and enjoy my own company. All of us react in terms of how we see ourselves. It isn't the situation but the person who is experiencing it that makes a large part of the difference.

Because this is true, it is important to strengthen our image of ourselves—and change it if necessary—so that we aren't constantly buffeted about by the new experiences that come inevitably with getting older.

There are many different ways of exploring who you really are or want to be, all involving varying degrees of introspection. At this stage of my life I find it helpful, for example, to reflect on which activities are likely to make me forget about the fact that I am getting older and which activities remind me most often and most depressingly of the aging process. When I'm riding on a carousel, I feel eight years old; when I'm being fitted for special inserts for my shoes in order to minimize the pain from arthritic spurs, I feel old; when a sentence or a paragraph goes really well, I am without age at all. When I'm hugging (or being hugged by) Larry, I am never more than thirty-two, but when I am doing something for somebody else that I don't want to do and feel exploited, I am the oldest living woman left in the world.

When I asked other people when they thought the least about getting older, they listed such things as when they are swimming, watching birds, playing with grand-children, going to the theater or the opera, watching foot-ball or baseball on television, traveling, cooking a gourmet dinner, and listening to music. When I asked about the times they thought the most about aging (aside from ill-ness), almost all the answers had to do with things they felt they had to do but did not enjoy; housework, listening to a boring friend, being very good and helpful to others too much of the time.

Several people said that their "social life" made them feel old. Proof that we can change once we begin to exam-ine such activities was expressed by psychologist Richard Worthington, who wrote that he and his wife used to suf-fer through large social gatherings that never had any real appeal for them. "Now we do our best to avoid them," he wrote. "Just too time- and energy-consuming and usually boring as well. We enjoy stimulating conversation but only in small groups now."

I feel most myself when I am doing something creative, or expressing love or being playful and childlike. I can't be myself at all clearly when my feeling of activity and energy is curtailed or when I regress to being that perfectly good little girl I once was and whom I have spent most of my adult life trying to appease. When do *you* feel wonderful? When do *you* feel terrible?

A "game" I've been playing with myself lately is to very quickly, without any time to think, write down a series of memories—the first ten that come into my mind. I don't think one can give any great analytical significance to such a task—or should!—but it's amazing how quickly one can see certain clear threads of importance. I just made a shortened form of such a list:

1. Nighttime high-school trip
2. The day I found out my brother had polio
3. My three aunts, my mother, and I having the giggles at a family gathering
4. Chicken pox—father reading poetry
5. First trip to Williamsburg with Larry

Even these five memories tell me a good deal about who I am and what I'm feeling right now. The high-school trip was my idea of what education ought to be like. A wonderfully imaginative teacher, Helen Kay, took us on an all-night trip through Manhattan, to learn how much goes on while everyone else is asleep. We went to a bread factory; the West Side markets, where the butchers stood around fires made in garbage cans to keep warm; we saw fruits and vegetables being auctioned off, went to an all-night diner, talked to some truck drivers, traveled the deserted subway home at five in the morning. This was in 1939, when young people had few such adventures, and I believe I thought of it now because I feel this is a time in my life for doing unusual, interesting things that I've never done before. It was a reminder that I learn best and most by doing and always have.

The day I found out my brother had polio was a terrifying day. I was standing in the living room, looking into his bedroom, and heard the doctor ask him to bend his neck. When he couldn't, my mother ran into the living room crying. There was a long hospitalization, a lot of terror—for him as well as for myself because I might catch it. It was a terrible time. I believe I thought about it now because physical disabilities have been creeping up on me and I am scared to death that this will change my sense of myself. A large part of my sense of identity has been that I have a great deal of energy, am very active and independent, and am terrified of dependence on others. I think I would feel "paralyzed" as a person if I couldn't continue to be very active.

Number three is that I identified very strongly with these women in my life and had wonderful, happy times with them. Only one is still alive. A very large part of my sense of identity is now dependent on memories rather than actual relationships, and I never stop mourning the losses, but I try to keep them internalized, part of what "me" means to me.

Number four is a memory of my father and me sitting on Riverside Drive. He is reading Tennyson's long story poem "Enoch Arden" to me to help me to keep from scratching while I am recovering from chicken pox. He was a wonderful poetry reader and I loved to listen to him as a child. This one is easy! If anything is really attacking my sense of identity, it is the reversal of roles with my father. Can I still "know who I am" as increasingly and inevitably I will have to become the parent, the caretaker?

And finally, number five is more of number one; the wish for more new adventures. The very first trip Larry and I took together, while Larry was still in the army, was to Williamsburg, where he'd gone to William and Mary College. I had never seen a colonial town and found it fascinating. I have always loved theater, and this made me feel as if I had become part of that time and that place. In order to maintain the part of my identity connected with the drama of adventure, I need time for more of it.

I asked Larry to do the same thing, and the first two memories on his list were walking on the beach and the first time he took out a library card! (The very *essence* of the man!) These quick stream-of-consciousness memories not only tell us something of what we have been, and what we are, they can also indicate to us the things we need to keep doing or feeling in order to be most ourselves. Larry will never have any identity problems at any age as long as he can be near the sea and a very good library!

Larry has been an excellent role model for me; he is certainly the most "himself" of anyone I know. At one time he was going to give a speech to a church conference in Colorado and I was out of the city when he was to leave. I suggested by phone that it might be wise to wear a suit and a tie, but he didn't agree. (He owns only one tie, which he wears exclusively to funerals.) Instead, in very cold weather, without a topcoat, he arrived at La Guardia Airport wearing baggy old pants, a heavy sweater under a beat-up old sports jacket, a very large multicolored wool scarf I had knit for him, and a French beret. He had asked for and been given a first-class ticket, since it was a long trip over a quick weekend and he wanted to be very comfortable while traveling. When he walked up to get his seat assignment at the first-class desk, the agent said, "Sorry, sir, this is just for first-class passengers." Larry—and everyone who heard the story—loved it. *He* knows who he is at all times, and wears his eccentricities like a badge of honor.

Many people can arrive at a deeper sense of selfhood and their innermost feelings through meditation and fantasy trips. Any good librarian can help you locate some books to read on these subjects, and there are many courses given. What you have to watch out for are the crazy cults and the not-so-crazy groups led by very smart businesspeople who have learned to creatively exploit people. The criteria that I would use in dismissing any mind-exercise group would be, does it supply its leader with mansions, Rolls-Royces, and bank accounts in Switzerland, and does it have a theme and a set of rigid rules and principles suggesting very strongly that *this* guru has found some final answers to universal problems. The more thoughtful, responsible classes in meditation, body awareness, and mind stretching can usually be located through reputable community agencies such as a YMCA or a church or temple group or a university.*

There are hundreds of mind games you can try on your own as well. One example is the Fairy Godmother Game, in which you make believe that such a person has entered your life and will give you the three things you want most in all the world. If you write down your wishes quickly, without thinking about it, you may be in for some interesting surprises. One woman who tried it said she thought she loved her busy social life but the first thing she wrote down was, "To be alone." One man told me that all his life he'd thought he hated the stressful nature of his work—that he thought he was really meant to be a bum and a beachcomber, but was surprised to see that he wrote down, "To

---

*One good book I would recommend for background is—not surprisingly—*How to Meditate,* by Lawrence LeShan (New York: Bantam, 1979, 9th printing).

keep on doing just what I'm doing, to take some courses in the computer field, to go dancing again."

Another "game" that can really shake you up is to tell yourself you have six months to live and to ask yourself what you'd like to do with that time. Would you go on living as you do now? If not, it may be very important to listen to the alternatives that occur to you. If you would become an artist or take a trip around the world or change to a completely different life-style, these may be messages you need to listen to. You may not be able to live out your fantasies, but you could go to more museums, take an art course, do some traveling, wear more comfortable clothes, and entertain more informally.

Another often useful exercise is to pick a time in your life when you were unhappy about something. It can be either as a child or as an adult; you felt helpless, frustrated, angry, sad, or guilty. Pretend that you are now getting into a time machine and going back to that time—some particular moment. You are yourself now—a mature, experienced adult. You get out of your time machine and move into the scene; what would you do? Would you feel compassion? Could you help? Would your feelings be the same as they were at that time, or would you now be able to be more helpful? Such a challenge may help you to see if you have made much progress in knowing how to be kinder to yourself, more creative in solving problems, more understanding and less guilt-ridden. If the answer is no, then it is clear you need to do some work in changing your self-image.

One exercise that I find very helpful at times when I feel caught in a web of depression and unhappiness—when the stresses of life seem overwhelming—is to sit down and pretend I am writing a letter to the child I once was. You might try this. What would you want that child to understand? What might you want to explain? What misconceptions might you want to undo? As you talk to this inner child you may discover some unfinished business about your sense of identity that needs your attention now.

Another often helpful question to raise is, suppose you were really your own very best friend; what would you give yourself for a birthday present? A woman who answered that question by saying, "Enough money to start my own catering business," went to a bank, got a loan, and did just that. A perfect story? No; she found the work far more exhausting than she'd anticipated, kept it up long enough to pay back her loan, and sold her business at a slight profit. "At least I haven't spent the rest of my life wondering if I'd really missed my vocation," she said. Fantasies need not be turned into literal realities; they simply point out some interesting aspects of ourselves that need nourishment.

Asking these questions of yourself does begin to provide the habit of exercising the search for oneself, of contemplation and reverie, in trying to get in touch with real feelings. We need to think about what we are doing at any given time to elicit what is most true and unique about ourselves. For one it may mean going back to school and exploring new fields of interest; for another, it may be psychotherapy; for another, more time alone to walk in the woods or along a beach; for another, taking up a new sport activity.

Going over picture albums, reading old letters and diaries, is another way of getting in touch with oneself. When I look at my high-school report cards, for example, it is immediately clear that I am a person who will never understand or be interested in the sciences, but that literature, history, art, and drama are "my things" and always have been. The difference between then and now is that then I was made to feel a failure because of what I was and am, and now I can revel in my individuality, my interests, quite comfortably. One of the great joys of my life is that I never even have to learn what "software" or DNA or $E = MC^2$ is, and nobody is going to give me a D. But even more important, no matter how long I live, I'll never satisfy my interest in the subjects I love.

The more we think about our lives, the more we become sensitized to who we are and how we are affected by the events around us. Elizabeth told me, "On rare occasions I get a visitor who is interested enough in me to come this long way to visit me. A few months ago Bill came—he's doing a biography of a mutual friend and he responded to me with real interest. I came to life—I swear I felt ten to fifteen years younger and looked it too. I always liked Bill and it took me back to happier times when I felt more like myself than I do now." I asked Elizabeth if she could think of anything she could do to reach out to other people which would make her feel the way she felt when Bill came to visit. She said she'd have to think about it. A few months later she wrote to tell me she had gotten herself a volunteer job as senior-citizen editor on a local newspaper, reporting events in her town for older people. Now she was interviewing others. "I feel like myself most of the time now," she wrote. "I can't do too much, I get tired; but while I'm being a reporter, I feel younger and know who I am."

A sense of identity often comes through most clearly in what we are doing; sometimes we only need to examine what we are doing in order to get a deeper sense of our inner priorities. When one woman says to me, "I wake up every morning dreading the day; I know that there is not one single thing that I am going to do that I want to do or that will make me feel good; I feel like a mule, trying to climb a rocky mountain, being whipped all the way, unable to go any faster," I know that this person is surely not living a life that in any way expresses her special needs. An opposing view was expressed by Claudette Colbert in an article written during the time when Ms. Colbert was appearing in a play (at the age of eighty) in London with Rex Harrison, which stated she'd been acting for sixty-one years. She commented, "Once in a while I hear myself saying, 'This is probably the last play I'll ever do.' But then I say, 'Bite your tongue, I don't want it to be.' My mother lived to be ninety-four. I've always thought she died because she was bored."*

In much the same vein, a seventy-six-year-old paleontologist was telling about his work—I think he was a dinosaur-foot-tracker—on the CBS television program *Sunday,* and when asked if he ever planned to retire, he said, "I'm trying to taper off, but things keep coming up."

When we begin to examine our lives in our later years, and when we find a need for change, we are faced with having to make up for lost time; we have to have the courage to take risks. As one smart woman put it, "It ain't fair to get old before you be young." It is more than likely that you will find that some of the things you want to do or be are not part of mainstream thinking, and you have to decide which is more important at this moment of your life—

*Rebecca Morehouse, "A Theatregoer's Notebook," *Playbill,* Vol. 2, No. 12 (1984).

to "fit in" and please others or to strike out on your own. A friend wrote me on her sixty-fifth birthday: "I'm very ambivalent about my looks. That's always been important—- I've spent a lot of time being slim and pretty and well-dressed. Now I'm aging, I'm getting sort of lumpy in places I used to be svelte. Part of me is nervous and uneasy and then there's another part of me that really wants to say the hell with it and get on with the business of whom I am on the inside."

Someone once sent me an anonymous article in which an older woman, reflecting on her life, talked about the things she would "dare" to do if she could live her life over again. She wrote that she would dare to make more mistakes, and that she would be sillier; she would take more chances, eat more ice cream and fewer beans. She had lived sanely and sensibly all her life and was having some second thoughts, including living much more in the moment instead of planning so far ahead. She concluded, "I would start going barefoot earlier in the spring . . . I would ride more merry-go-rounds. I would pick more daisies." We each need to find out what daisies we've missed picking.

There is one area in the search for our fullest selves in our later years that is completely misunderstood. My theory is a very comforting one—but I also think it is valid. It has to do with what we remember and what we forget.

I can remember every detail of the dinner party conversation I had with a woman I met two years ago and whom I now meet in a theater lobby, but I have no idea of her name. But when I heard that Janet Gaynor had died, I remembered almost every detail of the part she played in my life when I was seven or eight years old. "Aunt" Lillie, a lady I adored—one of my mother's best friends—took me to a movie, my first. I remember we walked up Columbus Avenue from Seventieth Street where I lived to Seventy-ninth Street, then we turned west and walked to Broadway. Aunt Lillie was tall—a dancer—and took big steps and I was running most of the way. I always laughed a lot with her and I always knew I'd have an adventure, a wonderful time. But I was totally unprepared for the *movies!* It was absolute magic. I can recall vividly Janet Gaynor, feet spread apart, arms up in the air, singing "Sunny Side Up." I discovered romance that day. She and Charles Farrell became my idols and filled my fantasy life for months thereafter. Aunt Lillie bought me the sheet music and my mother played the piano and we all sang "If I had a talking picture show of you-oo-oo."

The older we get the more vivid and clear becomes our long-ago past and the more hazy what we did yesterday. I walk from one room to another, only to arrive at my new destination without the slightest idea what I was coming to get or to do. But I can tell you the names of my teachers from first to sixth grade without hesitation.

We need at this time in our lives to begin to distinguish between memory and remembrance. Memory is all the facts, all the data of our daily lives from beginning to end. Just think of how we have overloaded our poor brain cells with all that we've had to remember for sixty, seventy, eighty years! Twelve times seven (I call my husband if I need to know things like that), what red and green traffic lights mean, what's a pound or a pint, the price of a bus fare (from five cents to a dollar in my sixty-three years), the streets of the city I live in, the dates of the Revolution, the Civil War, the names of the presidents, on and on and on. If you have moments of terror over what you are forgetting, I suggest you try to make a list of all the things you know and remember. It would take weeks—months—to accomplish such a feat.

We feel as if we are becoming senile old idiots because we can't find our glasses (hanging around our necks), can't remember a telephone number we've been calling for thirty years, forget to buy light bulbs three days in a row. The truth is, we are refining what is worth remembering when the overload gets too much to handle!

Make a list of the things you forget most often. Chances are almost every item will have to do with the minutiae of daily living. Next time you can't remember someone's name, think of the things you *do* remember about this person. You remember that her sister died in a car accident; you remember that her husband is an alcoholic; you remember that her daughter is a very successful lawyer. What you do remember is *everything important about her.* What we are beginning to forget are the unimportant details. I don't mean to minimize the annoyance and frustration we have to endure. It's a damn nuisance to look for your watch for fifteen minutes, and then see it's on your wrist, or have to call ten people before you can find out who played opposite Bette Davis in *Now, Voyager* and lit her cigarette so romantically. (Don't bother to call anyone; it was Paul Henreid!) People my age and older find themselves frequently frustrated and angered by such occurrences. We find ourselves asking the frightening question, is senility setting in?

The answer is that unless there is a great deal more wrong with us than just forgetfulness, we are simply becoming more selective in what we remember. If, instead of getting furious at ourselves and being frightened by what we interpret as decay and decline, we could, for a few minutes, think of what we have had to store in our brains, we would be overcome with self-appreciation and self-congratulation that we do as well as we do!

Memories of the past help us to find the strong sense of personal identity we crave. The older we get the more we need to know about who we have been, what we have done, how we have become the unique and special people we are. One of the apparently quite natural developmental tasks of growing and changing during the later years is to reorganize one's memory files, placing the most important things about us front and center and relegating unimportant facts and details of daily living to a position of secondary importance. A friend told me that her elderly mother forgot how to make scrambled eggs and never could find her house key, but could go through a family album and name every relative over a seventy-five-year period. An elderly man who often forgot his address and had to carry identification on him whenever he went out remembered the addresses of the first tenement apartments he and his family had lived in when he was a young child and they first came to this country as immigrants.

During the earlier periods of our lives it was absolutely essential to remember all the facts of daily life and to teach our children how to survive in the real world. The full focus of our attention was on the present, on daily survival. Of course to some degree this is still true, but not to the same degree. We don't have to get the kids off to school, travel to work, shop for dinner, go to the PTA meeting, do the laundry, discipline the children, and discuss the family budget all in one day anymore! And we can be resourceful when forgetting gets to be a real problem. I have lists all over my desk; my big lists have little lists of their own; on busy days I write out my schedule hour by hour. I leave notes for myself around the house; I keep all the important phone numbers (especially my own!) in my wallet—and that goes only in one compartment of my pocketbook, never anywhere else. Once we begin to understand that our forgetfulness is simply the discarding of details in order to get in touch with the essence of ourselves, we find clever and creative ways to help ourselves. I know which friends I can call who remember which things I forget; I don't struggle anymore to remember a word or a name. I try to let it go, knowing that sooner or later, if I relax, it will probably come to me. When I'm writing, I leave blanks where I can't remember a name or a word and fill them in later—but this is all after having learned that the struggle was only making things worse. I am learning, slowly but surely, that *remembrance of things past* is the necessary work of my brain as I get older, so that I know more clearly each day just what makes me, as a person, as special and unique as my fingerprints. My memories are different from anyone else's in the world.

Until two or three years ago I could go up and down escalators without a thought. Then, in an airport, with a small suitcase and an over-the-shoulder bag, I suddenly became very frightened of falling—the steep incline scared me for the first time in my life. Ever since, with or without baggage, it's been the same, and I recently recalled that I stopped being able to go on a swing about fifteen or twenty years ago—it also, quite suddenly, had made me dizzy. It was a shock to now recall how long ago this feeling of instability had started. The subject came up when Larry offered to travel with me on a book tour, since almost every large airport now has steep escalators. I was greatly touched by his concern, but then he said, "I hope this inner-ear deficiency never extends to the carousel." My first reaction was one of horror that there are some things one must endure and accept about getting older but that other things are simply not to be tolerated; that if a time came when I couldn't ride on the carousel in Central Park—something I have been doing regularly since I was about seven years old, and which Larry takes me to whenever I feel blue and/or on my birthday—I would feel that my identity as a human being was being destroyed! I don't know what I'd do, but I do know that the sense of lost identity I see among the very old in nursing homes must have something to do with the loss of those things and people and activities that were essential to a sense of "me."

What will I do if I get dizzy on a carousel one of these days? I will go and watch the children go round and round; I'll call up my cousin and talk about how we used to try for the gold or silver ring when we were children—but I guess most of all I'll *remember*. This is the advantage of getting old, remembering the early events of childhood that tell us who we are. As long as I remember the exquisite joy, the childlike exultation of those rides, I will know who I am.

There is another aspect of remembrance that has a more profound meaning, going far beyond the issue of personal identity. While we may be forgetting some of the details of daily living, and some peripheral facts, we aren't remembering only the past. What we are remembering are matters of universal importance—things that have to do with the quality of our lives. We are thinking more about loving; we are remembering those experiences that make us feel part of nature, part of the larger universe—a magnificent sunset, a mother bird feeding her babies. We look more closely into the heart of some exquisite flower. We are capable of becoming more reflective, more contemplative. *Being human and being part of a larger universe* is a natural and necessary developmental task. The more successful we are in distilling what is really important about life, the more accepting we will become of our mortality. We are moving slowly from the specifics of daily living to the larger issue of the meaning of our lives.

Perhaps nothing is more important to a sense of self than the values by which we live; how we treat other people; the hopes we have for a peaceful world. If our values are different from those we see becoming paramount in the culture, it's all too easy to develop the notion that we must be wrong. I often feel like an alien, as if I must have landed from another planet. Everything I believed in politically hasn't been part of my world for over twenty years at least; I grew up in a world where no one talked about the private lives of public people and I wish that were still true; I know much more than I want to know—I need some illusions in my emotional diet. I feel old-fashioned, out of step in a hundred different ways. It is exceedingly difficult to keep in touch with what I still believe, to make modifications in my values where I see a good reason to do so, and to hold on to what seem to me to be deeper truths for all time than the world I find myself living in. I have always considered myself deeply religious, profoundly moral, but because I grew up in an environment in which this was all internalized and not institutionalized, I am terribly alienated from and frightened by the strong waves of fundamentalism I see engulfing this country.

I find it impossible to listen to rock music, watch MTV,

give a damn about daily rates on money markets. I am bored by porno movies, I don't know the names of any of the baseball players, who, I gather, are known to every citizen except my husband and myself. In the Alan Jay Lerner–Burton Lane musical *On a Clear Day You Can See Forever,* there was a song called, "Wait till We're Sixty-five." A young man is trying to convince his fiancée that they have a wonderful future together because of the way he has arranged for insurance and pension benefits. If they can just stay alive until sixty-five they will have a "Guaranteed income, house with a view, doctors and nurses, surgery too . . . ," everything completely paid for from the time they are sixty-five until they die. Nothing to worry about ever again. His future bride is in her early or mid-twenties, and when the play first appeared, most of the audience laughed and thought this was all ridiculously unromantic. I keep thinking about that song and how American values seem to have changed. Today's young people seem to be as completely preoccupied with financial security as the young man in the play. We laughed at such a preposterous preoccupation with money and security just twenty years ago. I'm still back there, somewhere—and doubly wounded by the accompanying loss of compassion for the weak, the troubled, the impoverished, that seems to me to be rampant in this land. How do I hold on to what I believe? My values are essential to my sense of self.

Speaking at a lecture, May Sarton, at seventy, said this was the best time of her life. Someone in the audience expressed great doubt and May Sarton explained, "I am more myself than I have ever been. There is less conflict. I am happier, more balanced . . . more powerful . . . I am better able to use my powers."*

*Sarton, *At Seventy.*

Choreographer George Balanchine, when asked about his creativity and energy in his seventies, commented that it is indecision that is tiring. When you know what you want to be doing, you have more energy.

Once we have accepted the ambiguous feelings of aging, once we have acknowledged the changes in the world inside ourselves—once we are fully engaged in the search for our fullest identity—we are ready to move on, to use our powers, to make choices, to control our lives for all the future we may have at our disposal.

~~~~~~

Choosing the Future

AUTHOR JAMES MICHENER, BEing interviewed on a television program,* was asked if there have been any changes in his work schedule as he is getting older. He said he was working as hard as he ever did but "I don't kid myself. I know I need an afternoon nap now, wherever I am, whatever I'm working on." He added that he still feels capable of coming up with "three great ideas, any day," and that's because he still loves what he's doing and isn't in any hurry.

That seems to me to be a pretty good summary of what we need most as we get older; to hold on to what gives us the greatest pleasure, and to do so while accepting the need for eventually slowing down. For many of us this may be one of the hardest tasks we've ever faced, and most of us come to the choices we have to make with little or no preparation.

A woman I spoke to said—only half in jest—"I may hate you forever for making me think about my future!"

*Interview with Heywood Hale Broun, *Sunday*, CBS-TV (Nov. 11, 1984).

We come to our later years almost totally untrained for the kind of thinking that is now required of us. I don't know of a single grade school or high school that offers courses in introspection, and very few colleges give credit for work in meditation. I'd like to see these skills cultivated from kindergarten on into graduate school—and they would be if we really understood how vital these skills are to planning at any stage of life and most of all when we want our precious time to count the most.

The value of introspection, meditation, or prayer is not only that it can help in the process of self-discovery, but that beyond that it may help us to have the courage to be innovators at a time in our lives when we may be retiring from the work we've been doing for a long time, when we may need new interests and sources of inner gratification, and when we may very possibly have to be quite resourceful about finding new ways of earning money.

Two examples of what seem to me to be the true measure of initiative and creativity by two obviously introspective and thoughtful people are these: an article in *People* magazine* told about Arlene Simon, a determined woman who had decided that her particular "turf" was not going to suffer the destruction of so much of the rest of New York City on the part of real estate developers and others with no interest in maintaining cohesive, stable neighborhoods. She's created a full-time job for herself and *does* fight city hall—very effectively. Also there is Cynthia, who lives in an apartment complex in a housing development in a large midwestern city. She is a very energetic black lady who was forced to retire from a civil service job at sixty-

*"The Empress of West 67th Street," *People* (Nov. 5, 1984).

five. Her building is now mostly made up of older people who have lived there since just after World War II. Many are handicapped and alone, and none of them has much money. Cynthia wanted something to do and she wanted to supplement her pension and her Social Security benefits. She also didn't want to have to do any traveling. Two months after she retired she put up a sign in the mail room; she would deliver anyone's mail for twenty-five cents a day, and she would go shopping in the neighborhood for one dollar. She told me she's having the time of her life. "I'm doing social work," she said, "and at a price my neighbors can afford!"

Despite the general lack of training for making choices, and lack of planning on the part of many people, we all know some people who seem to have made a wonderful adjustment to the later years. They looked forward to retirement, knew exactly what they wanted to do, had planned for years where and how they would live, and they have good health and enough money to enjoy their lives. Let those of us who envy them get on with the business of struggling with the more common dilemmas of our world! The large majority of us do *not* have such smooth sailing. Often we may have some of the attributes of the happy life we dreamed of, but one or more parts are now missing; there's enough money for the dreamed-of travels, but one's partner is suddenly gone; we got the condominium in a warm climate, but have just had bypass surgery that was not very successful; we put all our savings into the house in the retirement community only to discover we are bored to death and miss the grandchildren. Dorothy told me, "I knew retirement was going to drive Lester—and me—crazy when I found him alphabetizing my spice shelf!"

Of course, by the time we have reached our sixties we surely should know that life is far from perfect at any stage of living; if we have dreamt irrationally of "all that changing" with retirement, we are, of course, doomed to disappointment. On the other hand, with careful and honest self-examination and a willingness to deal as creatively as possible with the realities of our lives, there surely can be many years of at least partial fulfillment ahead of us.

We have to watch out for two dangerous assumptions that often creep into our thinking, at least unconsciously. The first is that our goals for ourselves are unattainable and the second is that they will never be accepted by others.

One man I interviewed, Russell, said, "Muriel and I are just too old to move—it would be too much trouble. We're stuck here forever." He and his wife want to sell their house, which is much too big, too expensive to heat, and too hard to take care of; they want to move to a small garden apartment. Their grown children are willing to help. There is no rational reason why this goal isn't obtainable, yet something makes it *seem* impossible. Maybe it is their sadness at giving up the place of all their memories. Often if we can face the mixed feelings we have about a situation, we can discover that although we feel ambivalent, we do want to change our lives, in spite of some pain.

Stella, widowed four years ago, wants to take a trip around the world. She said, "Since Sam died, I couldn't even think about it, but it was a dream we both had for such a long time, and now I'm ready; I'm ready to go for both of us. I feel it would be a memorial to him. Maybe after that I could get on with my life." But Stella is sure that her only son and daughter-in-law would be furious at her for spending so much money on herself. "I'm sure they would feel I should help them financially and that I was being a foolish spendthrift. I don't want to make them angry; I may need their help if I ever get sick. And they wouldn't understand at all why this was important to me."

I had a problem with interviewing; I often got confused about my role (as an investigator) and turned into the family counselor! In this case, I suggested that Stella sound them out—tell her son she was thinking of such a trip and see what his reaction might be. She later told me that her son thought it was a wonderful idea. Stella said, "He told me he'd been very worried about me ever since his dad died—that it seemed I would never stop grieving, and taking a trip was a very healthy sign." Of course, sometimes it may very well be true that others may not approve of what we do. I asked Stella what would have been so terrible if Martin and Sue had been angry. Couldn't she have told them how she felt? Wouldn't they have gotten over it? Didn't she have a right to live her own life? Hadn't she suffered enough deprivation? Too many of us were taught as children that the worst thing we could ever do is to displease others. We should now have discovered, through the struggle for our sense of identity, that this teaching was untrue and very damaging. At long last we can begin to say, "I need to do this even if some of the people I care about don't understand or get angry."

Nobody can tell you what decisions to make for your present and your future. (If anyone tries, throw them out!) When *you* feel the need for expert advice you can choose to find it, whether it be a financial expert or a marriage counselor or a psychotherapist or a nutritionist or a real estate broker. All decisions should still be entirely your own. What you can learn about yourself and your needs should be matched with your feasible options. I couldn't possibly recommend any particular way of life, for two reasons; one is I don't know you personally, and two, I'm not an expert in any of the areas in which your choices and decisions must be made. What I would like to do is examine the areas in which these choices must be made and to suggest attitudes that may help you make constructive choices.

Anne Morrow Lindbergh, in her speech at Smith College, also talked about the fact that when she was a freshman at college she was always in a muddle trying to decide what was the most important thing to do each day. At that time of life opportunities seemed limitless. It's true for all of us that when we are young we want a kind of smorgasbord of life—we want to taste everything, try everything; it seems almost impossible to deny ourselves a vast assortment of experiences. Mrs. Lindbergh comments, "But now, at seventy, the need to decide on priorities is far more intense. Time, energy, and perhaps money are even more limited. We face deadlines—not of examinations or term papers, but our own limited years of life. How to choose?"

First of all by declaring our uniqueness, our individuality; by understanding that what may be a good choice for someone else may be all wrong for us. Secondly, by preparing for mistakes, for failure. Failure is the way we learn!

Most of all we need to see the rest of our lives as a series of new beginnings in which we remain as active and as independent as possible. Getting old ought not to mean giving up. Helen, at seventy-two, said, "They say stress is a killer. But I think no stress is equally deadly. If your days just slip by without any highs and lows, without some anxieties and pulse-quickening occurrences, you may not be *really living."* One of the characters in Neil Simon's play *Biloxi Blues* says, "If you have no problems, the day is over by eleven A.M.!"

In questioning people I found that one attitude in particular seemed to interfere with a couple's beginning to make plans, and that was when each partner sensed that their timing, their readiness for change, might be out of synchronization—that their needs were different on different time schedules. Kenneth, at sixty-eight, is eager to retire, travel, play golf, have more fun. His wife, Nancy, is only fifty-nine, has a wonderful job, isn't the least bit inclined to retire. Or Carol can hardly wait until John retires; the kids are grown and gone, she's ready to move to a smaller apartment in a warm climate. Husband John is a workaholic; there isn't a chance that he will retire voluntarily for another five years, at least.

These are not insurmountable problems. My friends Sara and Fred are doing just fine. He's sixty-five, thrilled to be rid of a job that he found more exhausting and debilitating than anything else. He's always painted as a hobby; now that's his work. He loves puttering around the house; he doesn't mind doing all the shopping, is enjoying learning to cook, is happy he can relieve his wife of many chores, says he's so busy he can't possibly do all the things he wants to do. Sara has a very exciting responsible job as the head of a large social agency and can relish it now more than ever, with fewer household demands on her time. She makes this concession to Fred's retirement: she has told the board of her agency that she has to have both a winter and a summer vacation now, so that they can travel together.

Nancy's husband, Kenneth, who is waiting around for his wife to retire, needs to get busy filling his own life with interesting activities he never had a chance to pursue. Some retired spouses with wives or husbands who are still working find this a fine time to go back to school, with or without goals for completing any special degree. Carol, who knows her husband has no intention of retiring, needs also to build a life of her own. What many women in this situation have done is join with other women to take trips to places their husbands aren't too interested in seeing, or they may go back to school, or take exercise classes or find volunteer work that gives them new interests. Instead of feeling defeated by such issues as differences in needs, we need to see this as a challenge that allows us to find new satisfactions in our separate lives.

When we think about the future, most of us who aren't there yet think about retirement. Even thinking about it seems shocking, and acceptance of this likely occurrence may be a long and arduous process. What to do if it is mandatory and we don't feel ready? What to do about taking an early retirement we do feel ready for, if it may mean financial sacrifice? And most of all, what are we retiring *from*, and what are we going *to*?

For many people the word "retirement" is synonymous with getting old and, unfortunately, for many it seems to connote an ending—a loss of control over one's life. Quite the contrary; there are still many choices to be made—we still have a great deal of control over our destiny. It seems to me that a lot of the depression that often accompanies the approach of retirement from work might well be avoided if we could look upon this time of our lives as an opportunity for new beginnings. But it is not at all a simple matter to arrive at such a positive attitude.

One of the people I questioned said, "I wish I knew how

to plan for retirement. It seems to me it was easier to plan for a career than to plan for 'old age.' I know it's necessary, but I am unaware of the right formula. Because of that, I sometimes think I'll end up as a hobo, friendless and alone!" If retirement from our jobs is still some time away or if we find ourselves unhappy after retirement has taken place, we need to "tune in" on that self we have hopefully been cultivating and do some planning, make some choices.

The problem about retirement for many people is that whether they have liked their work or not, it has been their center of identity. One man in a senior citizens' center once told me, "For fifty years I was 'Harry the Tailor.' Now I'm nobody." Other people in the group protested. They said, "You're also Harry the grandfather," and "You're also Harry my friend." Harry was quite startled by this idea that he might be a person even without his tailor shop.

Many people die soon after retirement. When that happens, it may be because that's all they felt they were—the person in the job. A friend told me, "We were all so terribly shocked. The superintendant in our apartment building died *two weeks* after the tenants had given him a farewell party after twenty-seven years of service. He had appeared to be in excellent health. He was a super super," she said, "available to us any time of the day or night. I guess that was his whole life." What we need to think about is not retirement *from* but retirement *to* what?

Catherine told me, "I began to feel old when I had to retire; I'd become hard of hearing and found I could no longer teach school. I was not prepared for retirement. When it happened and my daily routine was broken I felt old and useless for awhile until I took stock of myself and began to develop new interests."

A friend of mine, who lost her college teaching job when cuts were made in student loans and fewer people could afford to go to college, became seriously depressed. She was sixty-eight at the time, quite seriously crippled by arthritis, had already been forcibly retired from another job at sixty-five. She could afford to live quite comfortably in retirement, and I couldn't understand her distress until she said, "I'm a product of the work ethic; I've learned to think I am nothing without a job." She realized, she said, that she was going to have to "tackle my whole value system, learn a new set of values to live by." Retirement makes us feel as if we are giving up not only a job but a sense of who we are.

The fear of inactivity is a serious problem for many retirees. They have always been so busy—what will they do with the quiet, with not having to get up every morning? People who are used to being surrounded by others all day long at their jobs are terrified of loneliness.

One of the things we need to remember is that no matter how old we get, there is always *something* that can enrich our lives. Eighty-six-year-old Selma, who had a stroke and is in a wheelchair, told me, "I can still read. That has always been one of my greatest pleasures, and thank God my eyes still work!" Ninety-four-year-old Elsie, almost totally blind, told me, "There's still the radio. I listen all day and learn a lot. I love all the talk shows. Especially when people call in and tell their troubles to a doctor. I'm glad I'm not them!" A seventy-eight-year-old woman told me, "I was always very active. Now I pace myself. I still dance and swim, and walk, but *very slowly*! I do more reading and think about what's going on in the world. Fortunately I am compassionate and have a sense of humor, so people of all ages still like me."

Initiative and creativity can make an unwanted retirement more than endurable.

A few years ago Larry and I took a one-day bus trip around the Isle of Wight, off the southern coast of England. There was an elderly couple sitting just behind the bus driver, and they and he seemed to know each other intimately and kept up a running conversation. The couple were more than eager to embellish and expand on the driver's tour-guide speech, and on one of our stops, we got into conversation with them. They were in their late seventies, and had lived in the town of Cowes for thirty-two years. The man had a hunched back and great difficulty in walking; his wife told me he'd been badly wounded in World War II and had had seventeen operations. Before the war he'd been a bus driver and now, each spring, they begin a weekly tour around the Island, which they continue to do until late fall. The man told us, "I may not be able to drive the bus, but I can still talk to visitors, tell them about our home, make them feel welcomed. It's something I look forward to all winter."

The search for meaning, for seeing our lives as useful and purposeful—feeling that the world would be a poorer place without us—is a fundamental necessity all through life, but never more significant than when we begin to get old.

Whether we take an early retirement or never retire, or retire and get another job or work as a volunteer, or go on with an education or sit happily on a fishing pier all day, the central issue is to "know thyself," to examine our dreams and needs.

Long before we have to make decisions about work or retirement from a job, we need to think about what gives us the most pleasure and also what would make us feel most anxious, most frustrated. I know I am ready for a much more "vegetative" life. I want to spend more time in the country. I want to stop doing work that exhausts or depresses me. I might continue writing children's books because that refreshes me. I am getting in touch with the child inside myself and that is always joyful and satisfying. But when I look back at the work I've done, I feel a deep sense of satisfaction and a feeling it's time to quit.

On the other hand, I know Larry will be working until the day he dies. It is his greatest joy—as necessary for him to be in search of some new truth as to breathe. It has taken a lot of hard work to feel so sure of our choices, but each of us knows, somehow, when a choice is right.

Much as I value solitude—and I craved it during my younger days as well as now—I know there are many people who feel most fully alive through their interactions with other people. A retired friend who is restless and unhappy told me, "It's different for you—a writer thinks and imagines and talks to herself by writing. All my life I've been an outside kind of person—I need companionship. I like being with people. I can't change my nature now. I have to find a place for myself where I can go on relating to other people."

I learned an important lesson from Beverly Sills, who was asked on a television program how she felt about having given up being a great opera star—didn't she miss the performing? She smiled and said, "I've done that already! Now I want to help create a great national opera company." For many years I have looked back with a good deal of pain and regret on some of the high moments of my life that ended. For example, for three years (from 1970 to

1972) I was moderator of *How Do Your Children Grow,* an educational television program on which parents discussed many aspects of child-raising. Looking back I think it brought into focus my best talents, and a few years after it ended, I began to feel terrible regrets. Several times I've tried to think of ways of reviving it, and when people have told me they remember it, I have felt sad instead of happy. When Beverly Sills said "I've done it," that hit a nerve.

I knew instantly that she was right. In order to go on using one's most creative human capacities, you have to let go of what has been—be glad for whatever glory there has been in your life, savor every moment and then look forward to finding new ways of expressing yourself. If I were to be challenged to do that program again now, the truth is, I really wouldn't want to, after all. I'm fifteen years older and the stress would be too great. I've learned to relish the memory without any regrets.

Multiple "retirements," or never retiring at all, are the answers for some people: A widower who became seriously ill after his retirement told his doctor, "I have nothing left to live for." The doctor asked him if he'd ever had any secret longings, and he said he had always wanted to take a trip around the world. Since he expected to die anyway, he took all his life's savings and went on a world cruise. He came back thoroughly refreshed and quite healthy and decided to try a new career as a travel agent. That was six years ago, and he's about to retire again. "I think I'll try something just a little less taxing, this time," he said.

A woman who moved from New York to Florida said at first, "I worked hard all my life and now I'm going to rest." After two years of resting and becoming increasingly bored and irritable, she went to work in a department store modeling clothes for senior citizens. Then she became a very successful fund raiser for a charitable organization. "These last five years have been the best years of my life," she said.

The late Dr. Hans Selye, the medical researcher who did more than anyone else to make us aware of stress, said at the age of seventy-two, "I have nothing against retirement as long as it doesn't interfere with my work."

Albert Myers, president of Myers Brothers Department Stores, retired in 1979. He received an engraved gold clock on which his name was misspelled! He recalls thinking that if that could happen to the *boss*, it must be even worse for ordinary workers who feel shunted aside. Researching the issue of retirement, he found that more than 70 percent of the men and women approaching retirement were doing so without making any preparations. According to an article in *People* magazine, Myers "refused to go quietly to pasture." He developed a chain of travel agencies, started a hot-air balloon company, and formed an organization to help people over sixty live full and successful lives. At sixty-seven he wrote a book (with Christopher Anderson) entitled *Success over Sixty* (Summit Books, 1984). Myers has a number of what seem to me to be sound rules: plan for retirement a long time before it comes. List the things that have mattered the most to you at various periods of your life and select the ones that are most important to you. Concern yourself with finding not the most lucrative job but the one that will give the most personal satisfaction.

People who continue to work, at least on a part-time basis, can sometimes be intolerant of those who prefer to take it easy. Psychologist Richard Worthington told me, "I play golf with individuals who find meaning not so much in the golf, per se, but rather in the companionship, the sharing of everything and anything, even the joys and frustrations of the damn game. Some of them hold tenaciously to the past instead of being alertly alive to the only time which truly exists—the eternal now. But the poor bastards have so little self-appreciation that their lives have become increasingly narrowed and circumscribed. Golf saves them in more ways than one. Bad shots, for example, do provide small surges of adrenaline and cortisone that keep them toned up."

Some people seem quite defensive about their right to be lazy, to take it easy, to do nothing at all, if that suits them! A typical comment was, "I waited all my life to sleep late and go fishing and play bridge, and people look at me suspiciously, sure I must be miserable. I've never been happier in my life."

Another point of view was expressed by U.S. Congressman Claude Pepper, who said, "Life is like riding a bicycle. You don't fall off unless you stop pedaling." Which merely proves that people are different, and need different things from life. But a 1981 Harris poll indicated that 75 percent of people under the age of sixty-five want to keep working when they retire. Despite the fact that there is very real discrimination against older workers, 25 percent of retirees do continue to seek full- or part-time employment.

Some people who feel their work is their reason for being need to "work until they drop." I interviewed musician Mitch Miller when he was seventy-three years old. I'd seen him in a summer concert, conducting an orchestra in a classical program and ending up with a rip-roaring "Sing Along with Mitch" which had the audience dancing in the aisles and screaming their joyous response.

Mr. Miller gives eighty-five to ninety concerts a year in thirty to thirty-five cities, usually as conductor of a symphony orchestra, sometimes as oboe soloist, sometimes doing a live "Sing Along with Mitch." I visited him in his office in New York. On the wall was a cartoon from *The New Yorker* in which a couple are telling their troubles to a therapist, and she's saying, "As nearly as we can figure, our troubles seem to have started when 'Sing Along with Mitch' went off the air."

He has several explanations for his vitality and ability to work at a schedule that could knock out someone half his age. He says it's partly genes—his parents lived and were healthy into old age, and then he said, "How many people are privileged to work at what they love all of their lives?" His energy also comes from his orchestra and from the audience. There is a love relationship, an immediacy of experience, which energizes him and he says there is no letdown afterward. The experience is so real and so satisfying that he is exhilarated, not exhausted by it. Another factor is that he says he loves a broad range of music—he's ready to listen, anytime, to jazz, to country music, rock and roll, modern music—he is fascinated by invention, innovation, is always learning, continually seeks new musical experiences. He told me, "It helps a lot to reach an age when you no longer feel you have to accommodate yourself to others anymore, when you speak your mind and are comfortable taking the consequences." He wants to keep doing what he's doing "until I drop."

Sometimes one is catapulted into thinking of retirement unexpectedly. Jean wrote:

I had a terrible scare—I suddenly got amnesia! It must have been a small stroke. I was in the hospital for about a week. My memory came back in about three hours, but you can't imagine the terror of not remembering what year it is, or your children's names. After that happened, I began to think more about retiring than ever before.

One of the things I think about doing when I retire is getting more exercise. I get up at 5:30 A.M. to do twenty minutes' worth, but I would love to go swimming for an hour every day. I would also concentrate on more nutritious food. We eat out so much now because it is so easy, and it isn't good for us at all. A retirement project will be to develop family albums with all the thousands of pictures my husband has taken through the years for each of the children.

We may have to make adjustments to the unexpected, and we may also find that even the most careful and sensible planning can go awry. A friend of ours retired from a job in the city at the age of fifty-five and moved to Arizona, where he bought some land as an investment for his old age. He continued to work on a part-time basis until at seventy he had a stroke that left him paralyzed. The land investment was disappointing, too, but not disastrous. He says, "I can live, but I'm not sure I want to, this way. I thought I had everything figured out, that I'd outsmarted all my friends."

Planning too little can leave us totally unprepared for retirement; planning too much may leave us angry, disappointed. We need to constantly remind ourselves that our lives have always been filled with unexpected events and this does not change.

Perhaps the hardest task of all is to know when to retire, and when not to. Peter is a minister of a large congregation in a church in upstate New York. He is eighty and he talks about retiring only because he wants to hear people tell him not to. But he's having a hard time getting that response. His sermons are confused; he meets someone who has been a member of his church for forty years and says, "How's your mother?" when he officiated at her funeral ten years ago. At a wedding he forgot the name of the bridegroom. When he visits the Sunday-school children, they can't control their giggles because his stories are all mixed up. A member of the church told me, "We don't know what to do. He is greatly loved, but he is also hurting a lot of people now. We try to encourage him to write his memoirs, but he is really too confused and I guess he knows it. We will have to forcibly retire him, but we all wish he had known it was time before this happened."

On a visit to London an Englishman told me, "My father comes to the factory every day. My mother packs his lunch as well as mine and that's the high point of his day. I need to see other people, do other things during the lunch hour, but I eat with him as often as possible because there is nothing he can do anymore, and since he started the business I can't tell him to stay home. But it's terrible to see him sit there all day, staring into space." In a publishing company, the entire staff is praying for the former director to willingly leave. When he sold the company there was an agreement that he could stay on as long as he wanted to; now everyone regrets the agreement. He is treated with derision and pity, but never the respect that was once his. He's given "busywork" like a child, but is unable to let go; he is too anxious about finding any meaningful alternatives.

We all fear that we too will not be aware when we need to be. How can you tell when the same thing is happening to you? Write down what you consider the main requirements for your job—what makes you feel good about what you are doing. Hang the list on the wall, and as soon as any item seems in jeopardy, begin to make plans for retirement. Or while you're still thinking clearly, ask a coworker who is younger, or a partner, to give you a letter you will now write to yourself but leave in his or her custody, to be returned at the appropriate moment. Or start to cut down slowly, relegating some responsibilities to others gradually so that the changes can be made over a long period of time.

Recognizing inappropriate times for retirement is as important as retiring when it's time to do so. We need to feel very sure that we aren't overreacting to a temporary depression or unusual fatigue after a bout with the flu. If we quit precipitously, too suddenly, we may regret it. But that's not the end of the world. There are always alternatives and often better ones. A bank manager took retirement at sixty-three, expected to love it, hated it, but also realized he'd done it because he had come to hate his job. He'd been relatively happy as a teller, taking care of people's money, but had suffered horribly when he became important enough to have to turn down people's requests for mortgages or loans for a new business. He went to the president of the bank and asked if he could come back as a volunteer to train cashiers. His course was so exceptional and so successful that he was offered a part-time job that suits him just fine. A woman who had to have a serious operation felt so weak afterward that no matter how much her doctor reassured her, she was sure she'd never be able to work full-time again. She quit her job as a buyer in a department store, then recovered completely and was miserable at having made too hasty a decision. Her house happened to be full of plants—her husband described their sun porch as a year-round jungle, and suggested that she might put her green thumb to good use. For her next birthday he bought her a small greenhouse and she went into business selling plants. Her background gave her all the skills she needed and she now earns money working at what she had always considered a pleasant hobby.

Attitudes are what matter most; attitudes and the willingness to allow one's imagination free reign, without being afraid of the risks involved. For those who retire from one job and then find they want to find another, there is certainly no question that older people are discriminated against in the job market. But instead of passively accepting this reality and assuming there is no answer to it, we need to think more creatively about ways of circumventing rigid and inflexible attitudes often based on meaningless stereotypes.

One way used successfully by some is to take a volunteer job (or create one) in the not entirely unrealistic hope that if you are really making a contribution, it may turn into a paid job, if you need the money.

Another approach is to think about the needs of the particular community in which you live. If your area is like most in this country, the older population is increasing and will need more special services. Many men and women have started new careers by setting up home-cleaning services, for example, hiring younger men and women who need part-time work. They may advertise that they specialize in helping older people; they may contact social agencies that provide services to the elderly. While some communities have "meals on wheels" programs, they often have long waiting lists and sometimes the food is not very good. One couple in their late sixties prepare one meal a day for about fifty people at a reasonable price, delivering lunches in their station wagon. The margin of profit is small, but it is a beginning, and they are planning other services they might add. Boutiques, specialty gourmet shops, and crafts shops are always interested in considering new articles to take on consignment, from jars of your homemade jams to hand-knitted sweaters and carved wooden birds.

Those who are highly motivated and take the initiative can usually get work. And if they focus on what they are interested in doing, they may end up enjoying the second job more than the first. An elementary-school principal went to a local nursery school and talked to the director about the fact that so many children now live in single-family, usually fatherless homes. He convinced the director that a male role model was badly needed, and he offered his services as a "grandpa"; he got the job. A handsome but somewhat heavy woman of seventy-two walked into a dress shop in Miami Beach and convinced the owner that he needed a woman to model large-size dresses and wait on customers who could identify with her—who, she pointed out, constituted a large part of his clientele. She got the job. In general, it seems to be easier to take on small businesses where one can make a personal impression.

However, there is no denying that the pressure of the cult of youth is what we feel and see all around us. The question is do we have to accept a verdict that we find ridiculous, when we still feel vigorous and competent? The answer is a resounding No! There was an experiment during World War II that made it quite clear that much of the apathy and depression of old age comes from reflected attitudes. There was a serious manpower shortage during the war, and one enterprising psychologist decided he might be able to help the war effort by recruiting older people for jobs in New York that were being vacated by young men who were going to war or to work in defense plants. He had noticed a great many older men and women in his own neighborhood who stumbled out of their apartments each day only to sit staring into space on benches in the middle of Broadway, day after day, greeted a friend perhaps, and then shuffled back home, appearing to be in very poor health and barely keeping themselves alive. He began talking to groups of them, invited them to a community center to discuss possible job opportunities, and spent a number of weeks in discussion with them about how they saw themselves. He managed to mobilize the life force in many and helped them go to job interviews. The end result was that the majority were able to go back to work, did an excellent job according to all follow-up studies, and many continued to work after the war was over.

There are hundreds of similar examples of what happens when people stop judging themselves by society's standards, and are strong enough to fight for what they know are their real resources. There are, for example, nursing homes where the patients lie in bed, drugged, doing nothing, waiting to die; they have accepted the staff's judgment that there is nothing more in life for them. There are other nursing homes with similar populations, in terms of age and illness, that are beehives of activity, because the director genuinely believes his patients are still able to go on living meaningful lives.

For those who feel their lives are full and satisfying without work, fine; for those who feel that work is as important to their sense of themselves as breathing, there is more work to be done than we can find people to do it—

both paid and voluntary. If retirement is followed by a period of apathy and depression, it might be a good time to get some vocational counseling. The minute we open the door and let in the light of new possibilities, the juices begin to flow again. Sometimes we need an outside, objective opinion about whether we are going through a normal period of mourning for the ending of one part of our lives, or if we are grieving because we need to go on working.

The worst trap we can get ourselves into is thinking that how we look is the only key to getting a job. There's nothing wrong, of course, with being presentable. We can be attractively clean and neat and carefully dressed. But unless we're headed for show business, face-lifts and hair dying won't help unless such things give us confidence we would otherwise lack. *Attitude* is really far more important. In some jobs, the boss actually may be more impressed by maturity. The manager of a fast-food restaurant told me, "I'd rather have one little old lady with white hair who shows up every day than ten teenagers who show up whenever they feel like it!" (I had asked the question because I'd noticed how many "mature" men and women were working there.) Many businesses have long since discovered that their over-sixty-five workers are far more reliable than younger people. The manager of a shoe store (where I also saw many older salespeople) told me, "First of all, the salary isn't enough for a young person supporting a family. Secondly, people with young children are out a lot when their kids get sick. Thirdly, they're always looking for something better and don't stay very long. The older, retired person is glad to be working, more contented, has fewer outside problems."

A most important alternative to working is returning to

school on whatever basis seems most satisfying. Because of the increase in the population of older citizens (and the economics of keeping colleges from bankruptcy!) there is tremendous interest now in providing adult education for older people. As we live longer and there are more years available to us, we can get an education we never could have before. As psychologist Dr. Richard Worthington put it, "[education] leads to a keener appreciation of both our inner world and the outer, more nutsy one!"

A woman who was always a housewife reflected that people who had careers and higher education seem to do better in the later years. She said, "They can identify with their respective professional groups when they retire." She felt that they were more likely to keep up with new developments in their fields. She decided to start taking courses herself, mostly in art history, an area of special interest to her. She hopes to eventually become a volunteer guide at the local art museum.

A particularly imaginative and meaningful innovation is what is called Elderhostel, an organization through which colleges and universities are now offering courses during vacation and summer recesses to older people, when their regular students are away. Elderhostel* publishes seasonal catalogs, with a wide variety of courses that take place mostly during the summer, or during relatively long winter vacations, mostly at colleges, but some at various religious seminaries. The staff is almost always the regular college staff. The catalog not only describes the courses, but also the facilities—the type of campus, whether much walking

*For further information and a catalog, write to: Elderhostel, 100 Boyleston Street, Boston, Mass. 02116.

or climbing stairs is required, the sleeping facilities. Courses are given all over the United States as well as in Canada, Mexico, South America, and Europe. The tuition covers food and board—everything except travel expenses, and one-week courses in this country are still usually under $200 a week. (There may also be some scholarships available.)

One man told me, "I just came back from a two-week course in contemporary drama at a small college, where I slept in a dormitory room. It made me feel young and gay just to look at the sexy posters in the room I was borrowing briefly!" Retirement doesn't have to require changing one's nature. It means finding new avenues to fill old needs.

When I was in high school, I took a course in ceramics. I have some pretty good sculptures as a result, but I never really kept it up afterward. I'd love to take a course again, when I retire. Both Larry and I are very curious about many things, and look forward to pursuing some of our yet undeveloped interests. Larry says he may try for a degree in archeology, a field he thinks he might have gone into if it hadn't been for a terrific psychology professor he met in his freshman year of college.

There are inexpensive courses, free courses, home-study courses at many levels in hundreds of fields. Usually we can find advertisements of these in local papers, but probably the best source of information is to write to your state education department asking for a list of resources in adult education.

Any discussion of retirement raises the issue of finances. There is something unique about our generation when it comes to finances—we are "Depression kids." Most of us carry deep inside us the anxieties of our parents, a profound insecurity about money. Even for those of us who have prospered, earning more money in a year than our parents may have seen in a decade through the 1930s, there has always been a vague feeling of doubt and uncertainty.

With few exceptions, most older people slowly but surely come to realize they are going to have to live on less money than they have become accustomed to. For many this is a terrifying blow. It reawakens old terrors of childhood that we have spent a lifetime trying to put to rest. There is no simple "cure" for such feelings, but once we can begin to acknowledge that at least part of our fear is irrational, we can begin to deal with the reality. It may help to make a list of all the expenses we *don't* have anymore! The orthodontist, the piano teacher, the summer camp, the college tuition; we need fewer clothes, we entertain less; we should be eating more simply; people won't (or surely shouldn't) expect expensive gifts from us anymore. Assuming we have reasonable financial assets, we need to recognize that in spite of inflation, in spite of cuts in social programs, in spite of whatever unexpected business losses there may be, it is possible to plan for a simpler, less extravagant life in which we can be comfortable, and that there need be no loss of self-esteem in ending our lives less wealthy than we were at the height of our working lives; in fact, it's really quite logical and appropriate, and worthy of our best planning.

Next to health, everyone I questioned felt that it was impossible to have a serene and happy old age without financial security—which means, of course, that most older people are in trouble! When we were young we thought that Social Security benefits would be stable and satisfactory and provide a major part of our income. Now we live in terror of cuts and new exemptions. People who are totally dependent on Social Security live in abject poverty; people who have supplementary pensions and health insurance programs find that even with the greatest care they have a very hard time making ends meet. Many older people find that their children deeply resent the possibility that they might be called on for financial help—that they loudly proclaim a poverty that the parent knows is not real. Other old people swear they will die of starvation before they allow their children to help support them. A real problem that receives too little attention is the horrifying spectacle of children taking control of an elderly parent's money in ways that are quite underhanded and exploitive. If there is one thing that makes life pretty terrible for older people it is surely the problem of money.

There are no simple answers. For those of us who are still working, it is very important to get expert financial advice so that some of our current resources are being put aside for later years. On the uncertain chance that one can learn from "negative input," this is what one of my correspondents, a successful doctor, had to say:

I am essentially a creature of the moment; I am a hopeless idiot when it comes to financial matters; I am reasonably good at my profession and the idea of retirement never enters my mind. That is for other people, not for me.

I have lived all my adult life on the verge of bankruptcy. I have never managed to save a penny. When I have enough in the bank to pay next month's rent (now mortgage and maintenance) I think I'm rich. I immediately take a vacation, buy a load of books, a new coffeemaker, a few records, and maybe even a sweater (cashmere, of course). Now I am faced with a dilemma. I've forgotten about office rent, salaries, insurance, laboratory, towels, supplies, and the fact that I have to eat. God forbid I get sick in the middle of all this. Solution: I borrow money. Unfortunately the bastards demand interest. I never quite take that into account. Now I ask you, how the hell can anybody prepare for old age when you live a life like that? Obviously, "financial security" is something you read about in the advertisements. I don't think I'll ever be able to thank Paine Webber. But I wish I could.

Some of us have tended to be overgenerous to our children as they start their nest-building, and we have to re-orient our thinking; the more we save now, the less likely we are to be a burden to them later on. We need to think long and carefully about our assets, and whether or not it may be wise to sell some property and make other kinds of investments, for example.

I have always hated thinking about money; I go crazy listening to all the financial advisers on radio and television but I know my attitude is wrong: this is a time of life when we need to give careful attention to our financial resources.

Now, while we are still young enough to do it, we might begin to be thinking about selling valuable jewelry, paintings, and antiques. It has taken me a long time to face up to this idea—years, in fact. For example, Aunt Lillie, whom I adored, brought two hand-embroidered silk kimonos back from a trip to China in the 1930s. They are quite magnificent, but unless they are properly cared for they won't last much longer. My daughter doesn't want them, and I could probably get from $500 to $1,000 for the pair of them. My choice is really to hold on, but then they will be ruined or lost after my death. I ought to sell them now and invest the money. I'm going to find out about selling them although I can hardly bear the thought. Most of us have many more things than we use or need, but these objects are full of memories. If members of the family want them, and we can afford to be generous, fine; otherwise, I think we have to internalize our memories and let go. I'll never forget Aunt Lillie's hilarious stories about her travels in China and Japan, or the vivid colors of the kimonos, or how much I loved her. Of course there are some things that must go with me until I die; my job now is to begin to distinguish between what is too precious to part with and what can become expendable.

I know that if I had to, I would be quite capable of taking any kind of job to supplement my income—a check-out lady in a supermarket, saleslady in a K-Mart—anything I could get. I'm very lucky in having skills that will probably always be salable if I need them—at least until I collapse! By this time there is also the comfort of a certain amount of income from all the many books I've written that are still in print. And assuming that as a writer I still have all (or most!) of my marbles, I can go on working, since writing doesn't require great physical activity.

A housewife can try to sell her pies in local stores; a retired foreman in an automobile plant, if he has to, can pump gas. It's not impossible if we don't feel that we lose our pride, our sense of identity, by doing menial work. A widow of sixty-seven told me that she was grateful that when she was a child her father, a coal miner, had made her feel that if you did your job well you could take pride in anything you did. She is still healthy and works as a housecleaner for a small cleaning firm. "I don't mind at all doing the same work for other people that I do in my own home, and by working three days a week, I add enough to my income to eat out once in awhile and even go to a movie."

A woman of eighty-six, living in a nursing home, understood very well the plight of others. She wrote: "I don't think about money at all because I know I have it and it's being carefully taken care of. I can buy what I want but I really don't need or want anything. God help people who haven't got what they need."

Rich and poor, everyone I questioned agreed that financial security is unimportant if you have it, important if you don't. And not only for material comforts. Almost everyone related money to freedom, independence, the right to go on making one's own choices. Poverty was seen as a kind of helpless imprisonment. Dr. Marvin Meitus wrote:

Financial security is very important. Being in the field of medicine I can see how the lack of financial security can create major problems. People who are not healthy and lack financial security certainly can become worse in a situation when health care becomes extremely expensive and beyond ability to afford. The population that is growing older are very much aware of this, as evidenced by all the discussion regarding Medicare and its benefits.

Actress Pat Carroll wrote:

Financial security at any age is important, simply because it frees your worry beads for more important concerns. An older person should not be burdened with the mundane. As you get older, you don't NEED so much, you don't WANT so much, for by sixty or seventy, you will have learned how little the material things you had really mean. I have always loved cars, and have had some marvelous ones, but for the life of me, I can't remember what any of them looked like! Clothes have never meant anything to me, but faces from the past, like treasured valentines, keep popping onto the screen of my memory, and THEY are important.

A television producer wrote: "Economic security seems as important to me as having my health. It is simply a matter of having options. I'm in mortal terror of having to be dependent in my so-called 'golden years.' I am sure this is why there are so many suicides among older people."

A woman who had recently retired from teaching and whose husband now worked as a once-a-week consultant to his long-time employer said, "We're *saving our money*! We have finally finished paying for our children's education—and before anyone asks us to help the grandchildren with their education, we're saving every penny we can without really depriving ourselves. It's a national disgrace that so many older people are living in terrible poverty. I do what I can to help change government policy."

A major problem for older people is the number of con artists ready, willing, and eager to cheat them out of what money they may have. Old people are considered the best possible target. Dr. Richard Worthington wrote: "We are constantly importuned by people who offer us anything from limited partnerships to outright scams. This is something all older people should be alerted to, and I'm sure you will come across many case histories. Certainly, we have plenty of them here in California. Oldsters are indeed preyed upon and must watch their *p*'s and *q*'s."

We should be aware that as difficult as it may be to get

private or government aid, there are resources available to us, if we are persistent in our investigations. It may take several months and many telephone calls to get meals on wheels in some communities or to make a landlord provide more hot water, but a real nag will eventually get the necessary attention. One elderly man told me that he was practically freezing to death one winter when he read in the newspaper about money being available for heating bills for old people. He said, "I was sure I would die of hypothermia until I went after this program. I wasn't exactly able to keep my apartment as warm as I used to like it, but at least I knew I could now survive the winter."

In big cities, especially, the bureaucracy can be terribly discouraging. It costs money to visit social agencies, or to call them; if you are sick, you feel there is little you can do. If need be, ask a relative or a friend to call the local hospitals and see if any have home-care programs, a much-needed innovation that helps people who can't leave home and also saves the hospitals a great deal of money, since outpatient care is much less expensive than care in the hospital. If you belong to a church or temple or any service clubs or professional organizations, these may either have sources of help or know about some. It's not only a good idea but necessary to do this kind of investigatory work before we get too old and sick and tired to do it.

It's not the end of the world if we have to ask children for help. It may make them feel good to do it. Many older people live with their children out of economic need and it can work. As in all else, attitude is far more important than actual circumstance, except in the most extreme cases of abject poverty. If we still feel a sense of dignity and pride, if dependency doesn't rob us of our sense of identity, being poor may be something we can accept with a certain amount of grace. In many cases there aren't any other choices—except, of course, to work both individually and in groups for a more compassionate social policy when it comes to the care of the elderly.

As a society we seem to be failing miserably in exerting the kind of militancy we need. We have enough nuclear power to wipe out the planet in a matter of minutes, but our children, the handicapped, and old people are expendable, according to the national policies the majority has supported. We need to use all our inner resources to plan for ourselves, and just as important, we need to look at the larger picture and see the part we must play in changing attitudes toward those who are least able to help themselves.

Financial planning gives us a view of our priorities. Which is more important, new clothes or a trip? Eating in restaurants or going to the opera? Buying a book (we could order from the library) or a sweater we desperately need for the winter? Buying unnecessarily expensive Christmas presents for grandchildren or taking them to the zoo?

I know one old lady who made a risky and very brave decision. At the age of ninety-two, Harriet began to "feel her age." She was living alone, and became very frightened if she felt dizzy or weak. She had a limited amount of money, enough to ensure her life if she continued to live alone or went into a nursing home, which would absorb all of her savings. Instead she decided to stay in her own home and hire a companion, someone who would stay with her all the time. Her children found a marvelous woman, full of the zest of life, warm and loving. This woman brought Harriet back to life—made her begin to use makeup again, to buy new clothes. They began going to museums and theaters together, they went to restaurants, they went on several trips, including a trip to Israel. All of this was extremely expensive. Harriet was well aware that in about two years' time she would have used up almost all of her money. But for the first time in many years, she was feeling wonderful, was glad to be alive, and looked forward to each day's adventures. She said, "In two years I'll be ninety-four. I'll have to go to a real cheap nursing home, I know that, one that will just take Medicare. I don't kid myself—it will be bad if I still feel good and giving up the life I have right now will be a terrible thing. But at least I'll have wonderful memories to look back on, and it's a gamble. Right now I'm alive and I want to live; if I'm lucky, I'll die when the two years are up."

Even when we may have enough money to live in relative comfort after retirement, money may still be an issue in our lives because we probably grew up thinking that if we did something for nothing it was worth nothing. It is not easy to convince older people, who are part of a generation in which the work ethic was so strong, that volunteer work might very well prove to be the most fulfilling of any time of one's work life. What I find terribly sad is that so few people with time on their hands make the effort to find ways in which they can be helpful to others and, in the process, regain a sense of their own worth. A friend told me, "My mother was a kindergarten teacher for over thirty years. The day-care centers in New York desperately need volunteers. She'd be wonderful. Instead she sits at home, doing nothing, grieving over my father's death two years ago, only gets dressed to go shopping for food or if we go to see her. I know she needs to be needed, but I can't get her to move."

Depression after retirement is one major reason that so many people seem paralyzed to move on. Sometimes the depression is so serious that there must be therapeutic and medical intervention, and fortunately for us, there are now many useful, successful drugs that can be prescribed in conjunction with counseling or psychotherapy. In the end, only we can make the personal decision necessary to help us feel most alive, as our lives change. The healing powers of "doing good" are not to be underestimated. A seventy-four-year-old woman who works for the Fortune Society (a New York agency devoted to counseling ex-convicts) teaching reading and writing and math skills to almost completely illiterate ex-convicts told me, when I thanked her for her wonderful contribution to doing something truly constructive about the crime rate, "Eda, there is no way I could ever repay my students for the joy I get when they get the high-school equivalency diplomas, or even go on to college, or get good jobs. I feel a sense of exhilaration that I never thought would be possible at my time of life."

The truth is that at every stage of our lives we need a sense that our lives have meaning and purpose. When we are young, this feeling may come from earning a living and raising a family, or from a career that serves the needs of others. When those roles are gone, we have to find new ways of feeling good about ourselves. I know a retired schoolteacher who tutored children for many years after her retirement. When she had a stroke and had to be in a wheelchair, she arranged with a local school that two of the children with the most serious learning disabilities be sent to her home one afternoon a week for tutoring. I know several other teachers with similar skills, in near-perfect health, who are lonely and discontented, who make no effort to do anything to be of service to others. What they say is that they hated teaching and that it's the last thing in the world they want to be doing. One has been a bird-watcher for the last fifty years, developing considerable expertise; might she not feel much better about her life by going to a nearby museum and offering to take older people on short, untiring bird walks in the park? The other former teacher says now that if things had been different in "her day" she would have gone to medical school. Hospitals and clinics are always searching for volunteers. Older people surely have every right to take it easy if that is what gives them genuine pleasure. I'm talking about people who are unhappy and need to do something about it.

We also have every right to keep searching for the right volunteer job. It is perfectly true that many volunteer jobs are dull and may simply repeat what perhaps we have hated doing all along. It's true that typists and letter-stuffers are necessary in every organization, and there are people who don't mind routine jobs. If you hate it, keep looking until you find the right niche. If you don't find one, make one.

There is a scandalous waste of wonderful talent of older people in this country. Some agencies and organizations are trying to do something about it, but when the chips are down, we have to take matters into our own hands. What unmet needs do we see in our local communities? Which national problems concern us most? Are there pressure groups that we think are doing an important job that we'd like to work for?

One senior citizens' center in the Midwest was in danger of closing for lack of funds. The center had a bus service; it served lunch to its members; there was a staff of recreation and rehabilitation experts. The director had done a won-

derful job of setting up excellent facilities and hiring a terrific staff, but the budget was exploding, and the local
charitable organizations that supported the center were
getting very worried. Then one of the board members had
an idea: let the senior citizens do the cleaning, the cooking,
and help to raise funds, through various crafts fairs, perhaps even undertake to put on an original musical they'd
been talking about. They could even become assistants to a
smaller professional staff. Eventually the psychiatric counselor trained a small core of assistants to lead group therapy
sessions under careful supervision. Costs were cut by a
third, but even more important, a lot of people who spent
most of the time complaining about either their medical
problems or the fact that their children and grandchildren
didn't come to see them often enough found themselves too
busy (and too happy) to remain preoccupied with their own
problems.

What matters most in volunteer work is whether or not
it makes us feel good about ourselves, and this can happen
no matter how much we may once have earned. The head
of a hardware chain volunteered to teach shop in a youth
center in a ghetto area of a large city; a college professor
volunteered to help black students with limited educational
resources, but excellent potential, to study for SAT exams.
The former head of a large chemical plant volunteers his
service at a local high school for an after-school science
club. None are demeaned by their work; all feel they may
be making a greater contribution than ever before.

Sometimes adversity points us in the right direction. A
woman I know is unable to see two of her grandchildren.
When her daughter divorced their father, she agreed never
to see the children again, and their father, in anger and

bitterness, has forbidden the children to see their maternal grandparents. Instead of wallowing in self-pity (she has no contact with her daughter, either) my aunt has been working very hard with other grandparents on the issue of grandparents' rights in divorce cases. She's gone to court about seeing her grandchildren and lost; she's appeared at congressional hearings and on TV and radio, been interviewed by newspapers and magazines, and is now in touch with hundreds of families all over the country in similar circumstances. When I asked for her comments about aging, she wrote, "Involvement in important issues and efforts to bring about meaningful changes have diverted me from an indulgence once succumbed to, can lead to feeling old and helpless." (Her diligence paid off; she has recently been allowed to see her grandchildren.)

Volunteer work can also help to maintain a comfortable and familiar balance. One wife was terrified that when her husband, a school principal, retired, he would be moping around the house all day. She was greatly relieved when he offered his services to a therapeutic day-care center for disturbed children, where he gives the loving attention these children crave.

Sylvia wrote:

I really didn't start planning until it was forced on me by losing my job. The state and federal funding which covered my work at the college was dropped very suddenly, and I went into a deep depression. The way I came out of it—it took about six months—was by *structuring* my life with volunteer work that I knew was just as useful and important as the work I'd been paid for. Structure and being useful give me a reason for living. I also more consciously cultivate friendships with both older and younger people now. That broadens my perspective and enriches my life in many ways. As soon as I started working, I began to feel better.

This is probably the most important and crucial issue related to retirement: to understand that work can now be what we do in life to give us a sense of meaning and purpose. There are some very lucky people who have careers which meet this basic human need, but most do not; we work to survive. Retirement can be the beginning of joining that fortunate group who have always worked for pleasure, fulfilling their own deepest needs and also being of service to others—two basic requirements for good mental health.

We need to make choices about living arrangements that will best meet our unique needs and wishes, but none of us will ever get it all! We will have to make compromises in housing, just as we have surely done all along. (How many of us commuted to work from the suburbs for our children's sakes?)

Some people decide to remain in the house that is too big even when the children are gone and the heating bills are too high; the mortgage is paid off and they would rather live among their memories. Others can't wait to sell and move to a small apartment in a warmer climate. Some people need to cling to their belongings, others sell everything, buy a trailer, and travel. Our options are, of course, influenced by our health, our family connections, and our finances, but we still need to realize there is plenty of room for variety, for choice.

As I write this, Larry is sixty-four, I am sixty-three. We plan to soon launch an intense search for the Next Move.

There are long waiting lists at most adult communities and so we want to get started now. I have already bought the books available from AARP (American Association of Retired Persons) which give information about housing possibilities,* and we are consulting older friends who have already made plans or may now be living in such a community. We have already decided that while there are disadvantages in so segregating ourselves, we will just have to be creative about keeping ourselves active and busy for as long as we can, and remain as private as possible as well. The advantage that we feel is important is that one of us has to die first, and we will feel better if we know the other will have a support system. We also don't want to depend on our daughter for nursing care, although she would give it lovingly. We will feel less anxious about later dependency if we know it will be handled by professionals.

The plan horrifies many of our friends. They think we are crazy! One friend said, "I don't approve of older people congregating in communities for older adults only. We need young people, and they need us. They help keep us on our toes—and occasionally we can express some little measure of wisdom that may be useful to them, thus enhancing our self-regard." We all have to do a lot of soul searching and try to figure out what kind of planning makes the most sense to us. Is there some place we learned to love on our travels? A place where we felt more at home than anywhere else? Do we love the changing seasons, or do our aging bones require sunshine all year round? Do we want

*National Continuing Care Directory (American Association of Homes for the Aging, 1984) and Planning Your Retirement Housing (American Association of Retired Persons, 1984).

to be near enough to children and grandchildren so that they can remain a vital part of our lives? Will there be opportunities for work of some kind if we want it? In looking for an adult community, Larry and I have to keep in mind that 1) it must be near a very large library for him, 2) it must be near the ocean for both of us, and 3) it must be close enough to a city so that we don't get a case of the bends from a sudden deprivation of "cultural advantages"! We also need to think about privacy as well as a community of like-minded people. We have to investigate bus and train connections. We have to find a location that meets both our needs, as must all married couples. If you are alone, you need a home where you feel safe, where you can be close to family and friends if they are a necessary support system.

Mitch Miller told me that at one time he bought some land in a beautiful resort area where a group of very fine apartments were to be built and where there would be every possible kind of services for older retired people, from a first-class golf course to a spa, to a nursing home and hospital—supposedly all the good things of life and the safety factors all built-in. He finally went to see the property when he was in the area. "I took one look at the place and that was it," he said. He knew immediately that this was not a way of life that could ever suit him. We need to do a lot of looking and questioning, and trusting our instincts.

What may well hold us back from making decisions is the fear of failure, and that's entirely understandable. If we make decisions too impulsively, too hastily, it may cause devastation at this time in our lives. One person I interviewed told me, "When my husband died my son convinced me I couldn't stay alone in my apartment—the neighborhood was getting too dangerous. So I quit my job, took early retirement, and moved to a small apartment in the same suburb of Philadelphia where he lived. There was just one small problem; I didn't know how to drive, had no car, had to wait for my daughter-in-law to drive me anywhere I needed to go. I missed my old neighborhood and I was bored to death."

Fear of failure is understandable, but not an excuse for not making choices! Giving up is the real danger. The lady I just mentoned called a taxi service, and went to see the rabbi at the local temple. He arranged for her to be picked up by a driving school's car. She learned to drive, got her license and a car, and became active in the temple. "Once a week I drive to the old neighborhood, go shopping to *my* butcher and *my* bakery, and see my old friends. I even drive my daughter-in-law places when her car is at the garage!"

Marian was able to learn the skill she needed for suburban living. If she hadn't, there were other alternatives: a senior citizens' group with bus service, taxis to a railroad station, the development of friendships with people who could drive to restaurants and movies.

What I found as I talked to people in different adult communities was that there was almost always an enormous range of possibilities for individual differences. Irene loved taking the bus trips offered by her adult community, but she found many of the people very boring and too focused on their health problems so she seldom ate in the dining room, preferring her own small kitchenette. Franklin, very lonely since his wife's death, living in the same adult community, ate every meal in the dining room, went to every lecture offered, went to art classes, swam every day in the heated pool. Madeline, a retired school principal, also living in the same place, active all her life in "good works," got herself elected to the local town school board, and was also chairwoman of several in-house committees. Florence, with a large family spread all over the country, still feeling well, always an avid traveler, was away a great deal of the time and was not interested in developing close friendships, except with one or two other people.

The single person who prefers to go on living in a neighborhood where crime is increasing must make the concession of not going out alone or at night; the widower who wants to keep his house may have to take in a couple of boarders to make ends meet; if we find the perfect place to live, it may mean fewer visits from grandchildren who now live farther away. Whatever decisions we make, there will be compromises, but by our time of life that should be no surprise.

Along with considering where to live, we are usually also making choices about *things*. One woman told me, "I think more about getting rid of our many possessions and easing the responsibilities of our home than my husband does. He is still in a collecting mode." I look back in wonder, now, at all the years of accumulation—the souvenirs of trips, the lamps, the furniture, the kitchen utensils that seemed so essential. Those years of collecting and acquiring were the years when it never occurred to me that I wouldn't live forever!

We seem to choose to be nest builders in our twenties and thirties and forties, and then to begin to get rid of nonessentials in our fifties and sixties. A friend in her seventies told me, "Once you get so old that people you love begin dying, you know how little value *things* have."

Now I have had the painful experience of having to dismantle the homes of two dead relatives. I also see my father wrestling with the painful problem of what to do with my mother's files, the books and articles and stories she wrote, her lecture notes. She was also a writer and an educator. How can I let the memorabilia of her life be thrown out? What can I do with the collections of my lifetime? Do I leave it all for my daughter to worry about some day or do I try to begin getting rid of things now? It's not easy; most of our paintings are by friends. They are many and large. Would my daughter, Wendy, be able to absorb them into her life? Would any library want my files and child development library?

One of the painful realities of getting older is realizing that practically everything we own will last longer than we will! I'm forcing myself to accept that fact. I'm thinking and planning; what I can't or don't want to sell, I want to give away—as much as possible before I die. I need less and less for myself as I get older. I've begun to give away jewelry and other things I value as birthday, anniversary, or Christmas presents, to younger relatives and friends, acknowledging that these are not new, in the hope that a souvenir of me might be appreciated. One thing is for sure: we have stopped buying anything but absolute necessities. If the refrigerator or the stove or the car or the television set don't work, we'll get them fixed, we won't buy new ones. A few years ago I had to put up a fence at our home on Cape Cod. The fence man told me that if he varnished the fence he could guarantee it would last thirty years. When I said that was a matter of no consequence to me, I shocked myself more than him!

On the surface this chapter may appear to be all about

the specifics of planning the way we will live as we get older, but the truth is that the specifics fall into place as you figure out who you are, as you explore the possibilities creatively. We can get facts and information from the outside world. What nobody else can give us is the courage to use these for our own growth. I think we all have much to learn from people who have had the courage to "do their own thing" all their lives and continue to do so as they get older:

George Burns, being interviewed on *The Merv Griffin Show,* said he fell in love with show business when he was seven years old, and would be in it until he no longer had any choice in the matter. He said, "I'd rather be a failure at something I love than successful at something I hated. I love it more now than ever. You have to fall in love with what you are doing."

A woman active in YMHA activities wrote, "When you reach my age, you've learned to sweep away the nonessentials and get to the point. It saves time—and time is precious now . . . a woman named Thelma Ruble put it like this: 'I'm not living on borrowed time. I'm living on given time.'"

Martha Munzer wrote:

As time closes in, I feel that I've indeed had my life—friends both real and literary, family, work, play, adventure, and abundant good health for adding zest and for helping to cope with periods of sorrow and grief. Also that there's some life to live, no matter how much or how little, in the ever-present now. And "now" means, if it means anything, not only to connect but even to disconnect just a bit—to simplify, to reduce life to its essentials, to take a good hard look at its bare bones . . . There is only so much I can do in the time of my life. I know my choices are limited. No one can take on all the problems of the world ... As of today, I tend to feel that my well-loved mentor, Henry James, gave the wisest reason for living one's life through to the end, no matter how great the misery. He wrote: "Life is the most valuable thing we know anything about and it is therefore presumptively a great mistake to surrender it while there is any left in the cup."*

I kept asking Larry to give me his definition of old age, and he kept telling me he had to think about it. Finally, one Sunday, reading the *New York Times* Travel Section, he said, "I think I've found my definition of old age. It's GREED! I want to see more, do more, travel more. I want more of everything!"

And finally, the point of view that best expresses my own goals was a comment made by film director-writer-actor John Huston, in a television interview: "I don't like getting older. I had to give up smoking and I like to smoke. If I have too many drinks, I wake up at night with something unpleasant going on in my stomach. I saw a ship once that had foundered on the rocks. It was being pounded to death by the waves. The funny thing was that smoke was coming out of the funnel—there was still fire in the boilers. I guess that's how it is with me. There's still fire in my belly. It's still fun."†

---

*Munzer, *Full Circle*.
†*Sunday*, CBS-TV (Sept. 30, 1984).

~~~~~~

FIVE

In Sickness and in Health

IT IS VERY RARE TO FIND absolute unity when you question people about their feelings on any subject, but it happened; every single person with whom I discussed aging said that health was the keystone—health was the difference between a bearable or an unbearable old age. A colleague, describing the vitality of her ninety-year-old father, said, "There are no young people or old people. Just healthy people and sick people."

After we are sixty or sixty-five, any illness seems connected with aging and the loss of autonomy and independence. Lucy, aged sixty-four, told me, "Health is *all important.* So often the body betrays the spirit, which is really young. With good health one can function, remain independent, vital. The opposite is dreaded. When I become sick now—if I just get a virus for a couple of days—I immediately panic about not being able to take care of myself."

Any indication of physical weakness becomes a reminder, a screaming siren, of what we are beginning to fear as we get older—helplessness.

And then there are the diseases that we've heard all our

lives *are* a sign of aging. Somehow it never occurred to me that I could possibly get arthritis before my late seventies; at sixty I was already suffering from arthritic spurs in my heels and arthritis in my knees, making the long walks I'd loved a thing of the past. By sixty-two it was in my wrists, just as I was about to begin writing this book. *Panic.* I had to suffer the trauma of relinquishing a manual typewriter that had been my steady companion through more than fifteen books—it was like an extension of my own body— and learn to use an electric typewriter. Three machines were returned to the store because I was so intimidated by them. Then I had a wonderful idea; might there be an electric typewriter that *looked* like a manual typewriter! I found one! It was love at first sight. I can type again, but always the underlying horror of aging through illness remains uppermost in my mind. And terrifies me, for what might happen next?

I have always been frightened of being sick. It has been my nature to be very independent, very active; illness leaves me helpless, at the mercy of others' care. Now it scares me more than ever because when I was younger, even though I may have railed against being sick, I knew deep down I would get well. Now each illness seems another part of general deterioration. It is, I think, my far greater awareness of mortality, and my fear of becoming dependent on the care of others.

Almost everyone who tried to recall for me when they first began to feel old described situations in which something happened to them physically. A woman said, "The day my feet hurt so much that I knew I'd go out and buy space shoes was the day I knew I was old." Two other typical comments from people I talked to were: "I've learned a lot about aging since my body began to speak to me," and "I never thought about getting old until I had a stroke at seventy-three. Now I think about it all the time."

We are not only frightened of the signs of aging in and of themselves; we are frightened—as well we might be—by all we have seen and heard about the lack of health care resources for older people—the skyrocketing costs of treatment despite Medicare and Medicaid, which we hoped would prove to be compassionate programs giving older people dignity and security and now seem most frequently to have become programs giving physicians and hospitals license to charge astronomical fees.

Any kind of physical incapacity or illness interferes with the person we have been, changes our sense of our identity. Pat Carroll told me, "Knee surgery and resulting partial incapacity made me feel older, if not downright OLD, for I felt limited, restricted in my previous method of expressing life through physical activity (tennis, running, dancing, et cetera). I have always looked forward to aging as another one of life's roles to play, but a role you can shake off . . . the arthritis, the fading eyesight, the creakiness doesn't go away, even with renewed physical activity."

My Aunt Edith wrote:

As the youngest of four siblings, I didn't think about getting old much because they had so many years on me that as long as they were around they made me feel like the "baby." Now that my two sisters are gone, my stiff knees, aching arthritic joints, and assorted physical deficiencies have made me aware that I am an old lady. My hair had already turned grey/white but I convinced myself that early greying was a family syndrome. Getting down on the floor to play with my grandchildren and having to roll over to get up clinched my delayed recognition.

We come upon images of ourselves that simply don't fit; they are shocking, and awaken new anxieties.

In a shoe store recently I saw a woman in her sixties looking at her feet in the mirror. She was wearing orthopedic walking shoes. She told the salesman "These are my mother's feet. I'm not ready for my mother's feet."

May Sarton wrote:

. . . yesterday when I was hurrying to get to an appointment on time I fell forward on the stairs and wrenched my shoulder. It shook me, because it brought vividly to mind the hazards of living alone. One feels fragile. And I realize the anxiety is never far away . . . On a deeper level than the mundane fact of a possible fall or heart attack I feel sure that after sixty everyone has death in the back of his or her consciousness much of the time.*

It was especially shocking to discover changes in people I'd known for over thirty years. Ellen and John were two people who were so energetic, so uncomplaining, so "up" all the time, that they were sometimes a little wearing when I happened to be feeling tired or depressed. In a recent letter Ellen wrote:

I began to feel old—something I haven't given too much thought about before now, because of John's problems with angina, even after his remarkable recovery from heart surgery. It

*May Sarton, *The House by the Sea: A Journal* (New York: W. W. Norton & Co., 1977), p. 26.

gave us a jolt. Then all of a sudden I have developed miserable arthritis in my knees for which there seems to be no cure. Then suddenly my eyes have gone blurry which makes reading more difficult. I've known for a long time that I had retina deterioration but it has not been serious until now. The eye doctor reassured me that I wasn't going blind but can't do much to improve things. So the combination of eyes and knees suddenly threw me and made me feel old. I don't like it at all and hope I can be braver about it.

How can anyone speak of "the prime of our lives" when we are sooner or later faced with such age-oriented physical problems? There are, of course, thousands of people who remain in wonderful health well into their eighties— even their nineties. We know they do because they are *news!* For every George Abbott who can still be directing and producing Broadway musicals in his nineties (as well as dancing with his young bride in nightclubs) and all the elderly stars of Hollywood, TV, and Broadway who seem to remain eternally young, there are most of the rest of us who are getting tired more easily, beginning to notice new wrinkles, and visiting doctors more often. What we must guard against, however, is the tendency to assume that every illness is related to the process of aging. We have to really work at keeping our sense of perspective. It certainly infuriates me that arthritis keeps me from taking long hikes, but as I walk the five blocks I can walk and I see a four-year-old child with severe cerebral palsy in a wheelchair, I am ashamed. How lucky we are if we only begin to have some infirmities when we are in our sixties or seventies! Not in a "Pollyanna the Glad Girl" attitude (probably only our generation remembers her!) but in order to remind ourselves that aging is not synonymous with illness and disabilities.

When I asked Peggy about when she began to feel she was getting old, she replied, "Curiously enough the first time I really felt I was growing old was when I was quite young. I wasn't even forty and I had a hysterectomy. Although my youngest child was eleven and I had no intention of having more children, the loss of the capacity was perceived by me physically and emotionally as aging. Any loss is experienced as a small death." We have to remember that this sense of loss can come at any age and that it is usually connected with some kind of change in one's sense of identity.

We need to understand first of all that health-illness-health remains a continuum even when we get old. We may not be able to recover from some of the illnesses that now beset us, but we can often surmount their effects to a remarkable degree. We may feel really rotten, but unless we are terminally ill, we can feel better again.

A courageous lady wrote me, "Although I am seventy-three, I never felt old until I was diagnosed as [having] MS this year and told I would be in a wheelchair the rest of my life. Then I felt 110. However, I found I still have a mouth and a mind and can still attend and make contributions to most of my favorite organizations. I no longer worry about age except when I am clumsy and drop or lose things. Then I chide myself that I'm climbing back to 110."

A sixty-five-year-old woman said, "In spite of my crippling arthritis, which started when I was fifty, I feel about forty so I am discomfited when kids treat me with respect and people my own age give up their seat to me on a crowded bus. I tend to look around for the old lady. Can they mean me? For fifteen years my body has been older than I really am, so I should be used to all this, but it always comes as a surprise."

We need to understand the absolutely miraculous self-healing powers each of us possesses. If you think about it, look what happens after even the most serious surgery; after several weeks of pain and misery, we begin to get better; we can walk; we can sleep without medication; our muscles begin to work again. What happened? The doctor didn't "cure" the incision—he didn't do anything to our muscles, except force us to keep moving.

Even in old age, self-healing still takes place. Best if there is little anxiety and stress; best if we have interesting and useful lives; best if we feel loved and can love others. There is every evidence that self-healing is most powerful in those who want to live the most. When we bring this power to the battle for wellness it can make an enormous difference at any age.

It's important to understand the meaning of the term "psychosomatic." It is *not* that we make ourselves sick in our bodies by what's going on in our minds! What it really means is that we are finally coming back to an understanding of human beings that was around through all the ages of history, that there is simply no separation whatever between body and mind—it's all one completely bound package. That is the concept behind the term "holistic medicine"—that we are whole. In recent years there have been some fascinating new studies which confirm this belief. One example is a study at Mount Sinai Hospital in New York where they did daily chemical analyses of blood and urine on men whose wives were dying of cancer. They found very dramatic changes in the men's body chemistry that made them far more susceptible to illness.

Recently we heard about a woman with an incurable terminal cancer. I sent her Larry's book dealing with the emotional aspects of cancer.* Her husband, who never let her see the book, read it himself and then told me, "It doesn't apply to Constance in any way, shape or form. Her attitude is wonderful." What he was saying is that a psychosomatic theory of cancer meant that she had given herself the disease because of a neurotic mind. Nothing could be further from the truth. Cancer is a disease indicating that the body's immune system isn't working properly. That system reflects all kinds of changes—among them, underlying psychological stresses. Medical, surgical, and chemical treatments can encourage reactivation of the immune system, but in the long run, the inner emotional climate must change—it can't be left out as something separate and apart. There are no physical diseases and no emotional diseases. There are only breakdowns in the body's way of protecting itself from harm, and treatment must be as total as the reasons for the breakdown. When we get sick, at any age, we need to view ourselves as persons dealing with a maladjustment. Some of this is due to an aging body; some of this may be due to poor nutrition; some of it may be due to dangers in the environment; some of it may be due to genetic tendencies, or sitting next to someone with a cold on a bus. And some of it has to do with the emotional stresses of life which change the chemical and hormonal balance of the body.

I hope you have read—or immediately will read—the

---

*Lawrence LeShan, *You Can Fight for Your Life* (New York: Evans, 1977).

two astounding books by Norman Cousins,* who designed his own holistic treatment for two near-fatal diseases. One ingredient was laughter—looking at old movies and television shows of comedians who always made him laugh. There is growing evidence that the chemistry of the body changes to promote wellness when we laugh!

At the University of California at San Francisco measurements of autonomic-nervous-system functions were taken in relation to facial expressions. The autonomic nervous system regulates involuntary physical functions such as heart rate, blood pressure, and respiration. While there are no final data as yet, the investigators report that frowning and smiling probably can cause definite changes in bodily processes. †

This doesn't mean that a "stiff upper lip" helps to cure an illness. It does mean that when we are sick we need to examine the whole nature of our life experiences. Wellness and illness are experiences of *a person,* not a bunch of separate organs, and when doctors forget this, we need to remember it. The era of specialization in medicine is certainly a necessity (in terms of the ever-growing amount of information and the new skills required) and can help to save lives—but it's not enough. During a period of time when I was seeing an internist, a hand specialist, and a foot doctor, *I* knew that as a total person, I had been through a serious emotional trauma and that getting well required examining that environment in which my body had gone into a kind of collapse—where my symptoms, painful as

---

*Norman Cousins, *Anatomy of an Illness* (New York: Bantam, 1981) and *Healing Heart* (New York: Avon, 1984).
† *Modern Maturity* (Dec. 1984).

they might be, clearly diagnosable as they were, not really curable by medicine, were like a siren going off, telling of danger, a need for changed feelings and attitudes as well as medication. But sometimes we need a shock to jolt us into this kind of awareness.

I remember the years my mother became preoccupied with what was happening to her body. She developed angina when she was about sixty-six years old, and, from then on, there was gradually one physical problem after another: a hiatus hernia, diverticulitis, constipation. By the time she had diabetes and high blood pressure, she was taking about twenty different pills every day. A woman who had always had a multitude of interests, a talented, vivacious, active woman, she focused her attention more and more on how she was feeling. I found it exasperating and boring. I was impatient and not very sympathetic, until she began to have serious heart attacks. But even then, I was not able to identify with what it meant to be betrayed by one's body.

One day, having felt at the mercy of multiple physical ills for some time, I had lunch with an old friend who is about my age. He'd been working on a project that kept him out of New York much of the time, and we hadn't seen each other for almost a year. He looked wonderful; I felt as if I'd become his grandmother. He plays tennis several times a week, and is thin and very attractive. When I dressed to meet him, I felt as if I were a mortician working on a corpse. In catching up on the events of the past year, I reported all the traumas and stresses, and the resulting disorders with which I'd become afflicted. About halfway through I saw a glazed look come over his eyes and I knew I was boring him just as my mother had bored me. What a shock; at sixty-two I was already so preoccupied with physical disabilities that even the most dedicated hypochondriac could have been insanely happy with my attitude. I have tried since then to protect my friends and relatives—and myself—by recalling George Burns's comment, "Don't ask anyone how they feel, because they'll tell you!"

Another way in which attitudes influence our health or illness is through stereotypical worries. One man told me, "When I reached the age of sixty-five I assumed that was a point of transition. I reduced my exercises by half. I quit playing tennis and decided I would take up golf—'the old people's game.' I began to feel old. I felt lousy! So I increased my exercise back to what it had been and went back to tennis and said to hell with golf, and now I feel fine!"

Hilda, at sixty-two, wrote:

We have friends who are so obsessed with thinking about their health and physical condition that they have little time for anything else. Luckily we're healthy anyway. Some people borrow trouble by reading too many articles and visiting too many doctors. I can remember being thoroughly put off by elderly relatives who only did things because "it is good for you" and never "just because." I swore I would never be like that and I am not health-ridden even now.

A fifty-eight-year-old man told me, "Despite two heart attacks and my arthritis, I eat what I please, in a moderate way, and overdo when the impulse arises. It's better to be healthy than not, but I refuse to spend every conscious moment worrying about what I put in my mouth. The quality of one's days is more important than the number, and I am struggling to get some quality into my deadening routines."

Lee, at sixty, commented, "Excessive emphasis on diet and exercise can be obsessive, bypassing many of the pleasures of life in favor of just trying to live longer."

Feeling depressed can also make us feel old and creates an environment in which illness thrives. All of us get depressed about real-life situations in which depression, frustration, anger, and tears are appropriate and are likely to pass more quickly when we acknowledge our feelings and try to deal with the causes. Severe, chronic depression is another matter altogether, and calls for skillful professional attention and care. I knew a woman who lived, for the eleven years that I knew her, under the constant torment of a very severe depression which caused profound anxiety, marked mood swings, and many physical problems. She refused to see a neuropsychiatrist because she was afraid he would "make" her look at her childhood, and for all her adult life this idea had terrified her. Depression can be relieved by introspection sometimes, but at seventy, her wish not to examine the psychological causes of her condition might well be respected and understood. The tragic fact was that with the wide variety of drugs for depression now available, under proper medical care she might have been given a great deal of relief from her symptoms, with little or no self-examination. It is certainly more constructive and courageous to search for the causes of one's feelings, but for those who cannot deal with that, there are now many forms of relief.

Once again, as in so many areas of our lives, the cult of youth makes it difficult for us to come to terms with our infirmities. This emphasis on youth creeps insidiously into our lives. The older man or woman who looks young and feels young experiences a special kind of exhilaration which is relief and triumph, while those who are showing their aging feel defeated, depressed.

At our best, we accept and accommodate without giving up. A seventy-two-year-old woman wrote:

I have arteriosclerosis of one leg, meaning that at present I can walk rapidly but after two and a half blocks I get a ghastly cramp in the calf of that leg (lack of blood oxygen flowing to it) which means I must find some place to sit down for four to five minutes till pain disappears. It slows down my life considerably. But there is hope in me that collateral arteries will eventually open up and take over. My "angiologist" said it may be two years—so I look ahead. *Avanti!*

In order to remain as healthy as possible we need to consider a number of different aspects of our lives. First of all we need to take care of our bodies through good nutrition, suitable exercise, a sensible vitamin program, and rest. We need to choose: do we want to play tennis or take a quiet walk with the dog? Do we want to take up yoga or go to church and pray? Are we really feeling good on a vegetarian diet or will life become meaningless if we can't have a hamburger once a week? We must also tend to our relationships with others as well as garnering time to be alone; love is the most healing of all powers at our disposal—we need to have it and give it even more than we need a balanced diet. We need always, whatever our condition, to think about work—some kind of activity that makes us feel proud about taking up space on this planet. I once saw an elderly woman sitting up in a hospital bed with a tremendous pile of papers and envelopes in front of her. She had had a leg removed. She had always been very active politically, and since it was election time, she had a friend go to party headquarters and she was stuffing envelopes that had been brought to her. She was continuing to involve herself with projects that interested her, and the meaning derived from a useful contribution to the common good led her to a healthier body and soul.

One important issue we need to think about is that there is no point in trying to improve our attitudes and behavior in health matters unless we think we can live with the changes we think we want to make. A friend once wrote me a passionate letter about the wonders she had discovered at a health spa where she was walking ten miles a day, having coffee enemas, and living on brown rice and soybeans. She lasted two weeks, lost about fifteen pounds, arrived back in New York, and told me, "I hit Grand Central Station and went straight to the nearest drugstore and had a banana split!"

As in all other aspects of aging, we don't have total control over our destinies no matter how sound our attitudes may be. This is especially true in the matter of health care, where outside forces play such an enormous part in what happens to us.

In 1950 Americans spent $10 billion on medical care; in 1984 the amount had risen to $250 billion and was still rising at a terrifying rate. Surging costs for medical care top the list of problems older people now face. Nowhere is the extreme between what helps or hinders clearer than in the matter of hospital care. On the one hand, never before have there been so many miraculous advances in medical technology, which can save our lives. A lot of us wouldn't be around now if it weren't for the amazing progress in medicine. On the other hand, there are facts that can make us fear for our lives when we have to go to a hospital.

One of the major problems is that hospitals have become small cities. The small, intimate hospital is almost a thing of the past. The problem is that loneliness; loss of human contact; the need for human touch, understanding, a sense of attachment to others are each factors that may contribute to our becoming ill, and their absence or presence in our lives can influence our recovery. The modern hospital is designed to accentuate and intensify the very feelings that may have played a part in the illness itself and endanger recovery ten thousandfold as one becomes a digit, an organ, a number in the health insurance files.

Larry and I had an experience a few years ago that clearly indicated the kind of changes that have taken place in hospital care over the past forty or fifty years. We went back to visit the army hospital where Larry worked during a good part of World War II. Other than at the war front, there was surely no place at that time that could have been more depressing than that hospital as we saw the ravages of war, day after day, when the seriously wounded were brought in. I worked at the hospital for awhile and I will never forget the weeks after the Battle of the Bulge especially, when it seemed to me that human beings could not be so broken in mind and body and still survive.

And yet neither Larry nor I remembered the hospital as a desperate, tragic place; quite the opposite. It was a place where remarkable healing took place, partly of course due to an excellent hospital administrator and a dedicated staff, but also because of the layout of the hospital. It was so arranged that every ward faced a grassy open-air area and had a closed porch facing the outdoors. Everything was on ground level, and the corridors led to central recreational areas where ambulatory patients as well as those on crutches and in wheelchairs could meet, have a soda, read, play various games. There was an air of intimacy, friendliness, informality, and relaxation.

The hospital is now a Veteran's Administration Hospital, and the men we saw there were at least forty years older than the ones we'd seen during the war—many were even older. But there was still the same feeling of homeyness, informality; a human-sized hospital. However, we were told that this hospital was soon to be demolished and a nurse pointed out the window. There, looming behind us was a giant sixteen-story building, the new hospital to replace the old, just like all the other new gigantic institutions where surely it would be very difficult to find one's way around and no grass to sit on anytime you felt like it.

But that's not the whole story. When Larry was stationed there he was in charge of one of the very first EEG machines, used to study the brain waves of men with head wounds and other neurological problems. The machine occupied two rooms, with walls covered with flashing lights and dials and a million wires. No matter how ill a patient might be, he had to be brought to this center, and the procedure was a long and complicated one. On this trip, forty years later, we couldn't find the EEG room. We were told that now these machines were so compact they were portable and could be moved to the patient. That's a wonderful improvement, but technological advances ought not to interfere with a warm, caring climate and relationships which are conducive to getting well.

One woman, having had a heart attack, was recovering

satisfactorily, sitting up in bed having a glass of orange juice, when she was suddenly attacked by a nurse who threw her down and started to give her cardiopulmonary resuscitation. When she protested loudly, the nurse explained that the monitor at the nurses' center indicated her heart had stopped beating. "Have you considered checking the *monitor?*" our friend asked. An electrician was called to solve the problem, but that sudden onslaught on a heart patient might well have done her in. There is, in this over-technologized society, a worship of machinery, and we are never more in danger of losing our status as humans than when we are in the hospital. The problem is that much of the training given doctors and nurses encourages them to believe that they are working in a garage, repairing cars, not dealing with far more interesting, complex—and even often annoying and frightening—mysteries of human beings. As a result, we are afraid to ask any questions. The doctor implies very clearly, "If you're good and do as I say and don't ask any uncomfortable questions, everything will be all right." We long for the Dr. Marcus Welby approach of personal caring, a close, warm relationship, and we feel ourselves being kept at a distance.

One patient who was to have an angiogram (in which a thin tube is inserted in an artery, usually in the groin, and pushed into the heart; there dye is released and the heart photographed) said she wanted to talk to the specialist. Her cardiologist replied, "You don't have to know the person who does this. We are all good technicians." The patient answered, "But I am not a carburetor."

If you are too ill to defend yourself, you need a friend or a relative to protect you. Mistakes *are* made. If you are suddenly offered a new pill of a different color and size than the ones you know your doctor had prescribed, refuse to take it until the nurse checks with the doctor. Not every procedure that you are put through is necessary. You have a right to question what is done to you. Larry and I have a friend who is our role model for how a person should act in the hospital. She was in for observation, had asked her doctor just who would see her and what would be done to her. When interns appeared to perform examinations which she knew were not required, she would say, "I'm very sorry young woman, I know you need to practice on patients, but I am old and tired and you will have to find someone else."

If you ever have the misfortune to be lying in a hospital bed and your doctor is making rounds and brings a group of interns and residents of both sexes to your bedside, ignores you completely but pulls up your hospital gown, you will be making a great contribution to the future of medical practice if you say, "Doctor, you seem to have forgotten my name and my age. I exist as a person beyond my colostomy. Please introduce me to your colleagues."

Or, if you are lying in a hospital bed, in full control of your mental faculties, and a doctor invites your spouse or other relatives to come and talk to him in the hall, you can also continue to educate the medical profession by saying, "It's my life and my body, and you will kindly consult me and my loved ones right here!" It seems clear that the more we take control, the faster we will recover. But since I have also said each of us must choose what makes us most comfortable, I must acknowledge that there are still some people who prefer to know as little as possible about what's going on. That wish must also be respected.

Hospitals have become big business. As soon as technological advances began to produce very expensive machinery, hospital costs skyrocketed, and both private and public hospitals were in deep trouble. The manufacturers of the new technology and businessmen in the field of institutional administration have come to view the hospital not as compassionate center for the care of the ill, but as a potentially profit-making enterprise.

We now see a change in the philosophy of a good part of the medical profession. Service to humanity has become secondary to making sound business investments; hospitals become franchises like McDonald's. By increasing hospital costs anywhere from 10 percent to 20 percent, hospitals can begin to reap a profit, making them very enticing to businessmen who are surely not primarily concerned with providing a good health-care system. Presently more than 20 percent of the hospitals are now owned by business corporations, and they are buying up more and more hospitals as these institutions become bankrupt or as government support is withdrawn.

Manufacturers of new equipment, such as the mechanical heart, see a great advantage in having their products tested, used, and brought to the attention of the public. That's why they are willing to underwrite $35 million dollars' worth of research in this one area. Groups like the Hospital Corporation of America, a chain of for-profit hospitals, begin to look very attractive to both public and private hospitals staggering under crushing financial burdens. There is no indication that for-profit hospitals are offering better care or are at present run more efficiently. Many take only insured patients, which will mean that 35 million people who can't afford hospital care will find it more and more difficult to get the help they need—and when they do, it will be in overcrowded, understaffed hospitals for the poor only. We will be going back—as we are in almost every area of human services—to the dark ages, where you had better be rich if you wanted to survive.

Medical school training has also focused increasingly on technological skills. Because so little training is devoted to the nature of human nature, it is much easier to focus attention on gadgets, organs, and laboratory tests. The more attention is focused on tests, the more mistakes occur. One seventy-eight-year-old woman who had just had a mastectomy recovered much more quickly than expected when she and her nurse had a good laugh over a blood test report indicating she was pregnant!

George Engle, a leading specialist in the field of psychosomatic medicine, tells the story of an old man who is lying in a bed next to a man who is dying.* The dying man is naked, lying in his own excretions, being resuscitated, pleading with the doctors to allow him to die with some modicum of dignity. A short time later the man who watched this terrible dying was himself hooked up to a number of life-support machines, and although barely able to move, managed to pull the plug. His doctor found a scribbled note that read, "Death is not the enemy, doctor, inhumanity is."

Because of the new miracle drugs and machines, the attitudes of doctors and health-care workers toward aging and death have changed radically. The family doctor of a hundred years ago knew—expected—that dealing with death was part of his profession. Today, there is at least an

---

*Lawrence LeShan, *The Mechanic and the Gardener: Making the Most of the Holistic Revolution in Medicine* (New York: Holt, Rinehart and Winston, 1982).

unconscious refusal to deal with death, and patients feel they are disappointing the doctor if they don't get well. Certainly it is good to have doctors who want to fight on the side of life, but as we get older, we also need doctors who will be willing to care for us even when we can no longer become totally well, and who will not want to keep us alive when our dignity, our sense of ourselves, is no longer present.

These are all overwhelming issues, but there are other changes that reflect a growing awareness of the need for less emphasis on machinery and more on individual human beings. In West Germany one cannot obtain government funds for a cancer clinic or service unless psychological services are also offered. A major university's nursing school has introduced courses on the power of psychic healing as an adjunct to medical treatment. More doctors are recognizing that patients get better faster if they are allowed— even encouraged—to participate, to take responsibility for getting well. Some of the more humane hospitals now provide patient advocates, and patients are actually encouraged to voice their criticisms and talk about such feelings as being neglected or not being taken seriously. Specialists in two of the most common causes of illness and death, heart disease and cancer, have shown a new readiness to examine the psychological environment in which people live, as well as those unique personality characteristics that seem most common in those who suffer these diseases.

I recently heard of the kind of imaginative project that is indicative of this holistic approach to health care. Students in a nursing school in Pennsylvania are given course credit for working in senior citizens' centers, so that they can begin to have a better understanding of older people while they are still reasonably well and active. *The New York Times* (Oct. 14, 1981) reported that this medical school offers a four-year program of geriatric courses covering psychological and biological aspects of aging in which students attempt to learn how it feels to be old. During the first year the students are sensitized to how older people feel through role playing. They are given tasks in which they will be clumsy, such as trying to write with the wrong hand. Classes are also divided into several groups, each given a different infirmity to contend with. For example, the handicap of arthritis is simulated by taping several fingers and thumbs together. Other students stuff cotton in their ears and try to talk on the telephone. Some are assigned to use a wheelchair. Fading eyesight is approximated with the use of grease-smeared glasses, and halting footsteps by placing beans in shoes. Of course, the difference is that the students can remove the cotton and the glasses and walk away from the wheelchair, but experiencing such an identity they are more likely to learn and to remember a new level of compassion. At this writing there are now over eighty medical schools out of a total of 126 that teach some form of geriatrics medicine. Only one medical school has an entire department of geriatrics and a specialty with the same prestige as surgery or gynecology, the medical school of Mount Sinai Hospital in New York. By no strange coincidence it is directed by the very same Robert Butler who wrote the pioneering book *Why Survive? Being Old in America.**

The department offers education to staff and commu-

---

*Robert Butler, M.D., *Why Survive? Being Old in America* (New York: Harper & Row, 1975).

nity leaders at all professional levels. Senior medical students spend a one-month rotation on a geriatrics service just as they do in all other specialties, working in nursing homes and in- and outpatient geriatric clinics. There is a teaching staff and collaboration with all hospital doctors, and an ever greater clarification of the fact that with the exceptions of pediatrics and obstetrics, every specialist will, sooner or later, find him or herself working with older patients. This medical department is also developing a strong research program in order to learn more about all aspects of the aging process. It is not only an oasis in the desert but a wonderful model for geriatrics departments that must surely emerge in the future.

Another indication of the change taking place in attitudes toward health is the increasing number of hospices around the country. These health centers care for the terminally ill who want to die with dignity, not hooked up to life-support systems, but want to be allowed to talk about dying, to communicate honestly with doctors and relatives, where relief of pain is a central goal. What is most important about such places is that they are helping doctors accept that medical care is valid, essential, for those who are dying—that they cannot avoid human death as part of being a doctor or a nurse. Also in the last ten to fifteen years more and more books have been published on death and dying by psychologists, ministers, and medical doctors showing a new awareness of the limitations of a mechanical view of health care and the need for facing our mortality.

This is in sharp contrast to an experiment undertaken by my husband some years ago when he was working on the cancer service of a hospital. He sat on a bench at the nurse's station with a stopwatch and kept a record of how quickly a nurse responded to a patient's call button. He found a definite connection between the time a call was answered and the condition of the patient. The closer a patient was to dying, the longer the time.

When the nurses were confronted with this, they were shocked. It was a completely unconscious avoidance and not hard to understand. Dealing with death every day takes a terrible toll, and doctors and nurses meet this in different ways—physicians who try to avoid getting personally involved and nurses who avoid interaction with the dying patient. In fact, those who care for terminally ill patients on a daily basis often suffer from "burnout" after a period of time. One has to have a strong belief system to face mortality on an everyday basis. This means that when we search for the "right" medical care, we look not only for the best specialist in a particular field, but for a human being who is willing to share with us the human condition.

It is my very strong conviction that when we take control of our own destinies in relation to health and illness, we can solve some of the problems that beset us.

We need to do as much as we can with what we've got and be able to recognize the times when we need help in order to examine the feelings of despair, hopelessness, fear of dying, anger that separate us from people we care about. The capacity to remain actively in control of our own destinies, no matter how limited that control can realistically be, seems to me to be crucial. There is no area in our lives where the courage to act is more vital than our health, and there is no aspect in our lives where this can be more difficult. We must fight for our lives.

When our daughter was a little girl and she didn't like one of our edicts, she would say, "You're not the boss of me!" At the time it was exasperating, but looking back, I delight in that cry for autonomy and personal dignity, and I feel I must say to you, "You are the boss of you!" If necessary carry a note to that effect around with you, or make a big sign and hang it on a wall in your home. You will surely need it.

If you don't like the manner of a particular doctor, you can change doctors. Trust your instincts; you can't get well, anyway, if you are unhappy with your doctor. My internist retired several years ago and a bright young man took over his practice. I was startled to discover that on three consecutive visits to the new doctor, my blood pressure had reached dangerously high levels. He also was far more interested in writing things down and looking at lab reports than ever looking at me. He didn't seem to hear anything I told him. He couldn't have cared less about my work, my personal life, my past. He recommended more dramatic procedures than my old doctor would have. It finally occurred to me that maybe the reason I was feeling worse all the time was that I didn't feel comfortable with this young man. On my first visit to an older, quieter doctor, my blood pressure was lower.

We need to find a physician who sees us as a whole person, recognizes our differences from anyone else, respects our capacity for self-repair, and knows that this can occur to fullest advantage only when we are full partners. We *can* find doctors who will encourage us to be active partners in our medical care. The newer attitude of hopefully more and more doctors was expressed very well in a letter to me from Marvin Meitus, M.D.:

The patient has to participate in his own treatment. He must *help himself* to get well. Participation is more than taking a pill every day. He must choose a diet, exercise, relaxation, etc. Pretty soon you get patients who are no longer taking pills. . . . The miracle cure is when the patient helped cure himself. . . . It's more important what you don't do for a patient than what you do. . . . When a patient says "What can I do to help?" you are in a new ball game.

One of the most serious problems about current hospital care is that big institutions have to be run by administrators, and even when doctors have a human concern for their patients, they are often helpless. For things to run smoothly the patient, from the moment of admittance, is subjected to a routine whose effect is to strip him or her of all the signs and symbols of autonomy and adulthood. The "good patient" is totally passive and dependent, the one who never questions anything, especially the authority figures. Total strangers who know nothing of one's life history take complete control over when we are to be awake, when we are to sleep, turn over, go to the bathroom, wash, etc. Within a day or two the average patient feels helpless and not too bright.

Our pharmacist gave me a paper he had written on "The Elderly as Seen Through the Eyes of a Community Pharmacist."* His observations clearly indicate why we need to be active. He has found a direct correlation between those who are mentally active and have interesting and meaningful lives and the amount of drugs they take: *very little.* People who go to doctors most often and buy the most pills, and who deteriorate both mentally and physically at a more rapid rate, "dwell on their infirmities to the point where they are the major part of their existence. . . . People who

*Sandor Rogers, July 1984.

lose meaningful work are prey to early illness and . . . depression. Lonely people become most hypochondriacal."

There is no one marvelous way in which to take care of ourselves, to try to preserve our health. Running won't do it; wheat germ won't do it; psychotherapy won't do it; vitamin E won't do it. Beware always of gurus with single messages. When someone says, "I have a chiropractor who can cure *everything* that's the matter with you," or "Your *whole problem* is that you haven't tried acupuncture," I run, not walk, to the nearest exit. Each of us needs to look upon health-care ideas, resources, specialists, as a kind of smorgasbord of possibilities. We need to screen out the charlatans, and this is not too difficult because they are always people who 1) are sure they have all the answers—are, indeed, religious fanatics, and 2) charge plenty for their pseudo wisdom. Beyond that, there's nothing wrong with investigating all possibilities.

Health-food store owners (unless they are bonafide nutritionists) are not good consultants on what vitamins you should take, since they want to sell you every item they carry. Sorrowfully, the majority of physicians are also no help in this department, having had practically no training at all in one of the most vital aspects of good health—nutrition. The only answer is to do a lot of reading and comparing notes, and then experimenting slowly to see what makes you feel good. Larry and I were lucky—our daughter did all the studying for us and presented us with a sane vitamin program. But I thought some of her suggestions were a little extreme, especially for substances that were supposed to improve our memory, so I took less. Larry, on the other hand, followed her instructions exactly and when he began to quote poetry he'd been taught in high school more than forty-five years ago, I decided maybe she was right. I increased my dosage and within six months noticed a marked improvement in my memory. (I am deliberately not mentioning what it was she recommended! You must search out the answers that are right for you. I'm happy to say that the number of carefully trained, professionally responsible nutritionists is increasing rapidly with the growing concern over nutrition's role in good health.)

We may have to try dozens of different exercise programs before we find the one that suits us best. There may be realistic limitations on what we can do and we may need to get advice from a physiotherapist about what's possible, but we are never truly aided in a health program if we hate what we are doing. One thing seems quite clear and that is that whatever we decide is a good program for us, we have to stick to it on a regular basis. You may notice I use the word "regular," not "rigid" or "inflexible." A satisfactory exercise program must be carried out at least three or four days a week (even if it's arm stretches in a wheelchair), but I think someone who goes jogging when it snows, or gets up at five A.M. to play tennis because he or she feels as if a cold is coming on and wants to get a game in before getting really sick, is a little crazy. For those who like such a strict regime, fine. The main thing is to keep moving.

What will ultimately make the most difference in health-care services will be what we, as individuals and through our group associations, do about it. Ever since medical costs began to rise so dramatically in the 1970s there has been a widespread belief that patients have no incentive to economize because of Medicare and Medicaid benefits. The AARP appealed to its members to write letters describing their personal experiences and these were reported in *Modern Maturity* (October/November, 1984). Over and over the letters described outlandish bills, often for unnecessary procedures. After a routine operation, a sixty-seven-year-old woman was charged $15 for a pregnancy test. Another woman found a $75 charge on a hospital bill for "traction." That turned out to be the hospital's term for a small pillow for under her feet. It is apparently not uncommon for people to get hospital bills of several hundred thousand dollars, often seriously in error. A doctor who came into a patient's room, asked her how she was, occasionally shook her hand, submitted a bill for $895. She had no idea why he was coming into her room at all. One man, rushed to a hospital with an aneurism, died less than seven hours later. A few days later his wife received a bill for $4,500 from the surgeon, $990 from his assistant, $1,500 from the anesthesiologist. Seven hours of emergency surgery, $22,526.23. The man's wife will pay only a fraction of that with Medicare and supplementary insurance, but she wrote that she felt the government was getting ripped off. In another case a woman was about to declare bankruptcy (in which case she would lose her home) for a hospital bill of $238,000. After some investigation, she was assured this was a "courtesy bill" and should have been so stamped. Actually her costs would be about $5,000. Most of the respondents said it was almost impossible to find doctors who would accept the amount paid by Medicare, and that they were felt very strongly that doctors and hospitals were taking adventage of government funding.

Modern Maturity offered suggestions on how people can fight back. First is to insist on being informed of costs during the time of an illness or hospitalization. Second, always get several opinions of the necessity for any major procedure. About 20 percent of recommended surgeries are not needed, according to a study at Cornell Medical College. Third, do everything possible to find a physician who will accept Medicare as payment in full. Fourth, check bills very carefully, and turn to the grievance procedures in the hospital when there are difficulties. Finally, patients should feel free to question their doctors at length and to challenge their decisions.

We need to be doing everything possible to fight for medical care that makes use of all the progress in science and technology in a way in which compassion and sensitivity for people is more important than making money. For example, there is no reason that every hospital in any one city has to have all the new machines. A cooperative policy of sharing equipment would save millions of dollars. We need to be political animals, joining pressure groups, meeting with those in power to let them know what the older population will or will not tolerate. There are ways to humanize even the most monolithic of hospital buildings and the most depersonalized services. We need to complain; we need to get ourselves on hospital boards. We need to write letters to newspapers, radio, and television stations. Taking action is, in itself, a prescription for good health!

~~~~~~

SIX

Till Death Us Do Part

IF EVER THE STATEMENT
"All marriages are happy—it's the living together afterward that causes the trouble!" were true, we *know* it by the
time we've somehow managed to stay married for forty or
fifty years! Marriage is the most difficult of all human relationships and it is some kind of miracle if you think about
the task of trying to make a life together. Two people with
entirely different histories, different personalities, very
rarely expert in understanding themselves or each other,
somehow manage to cling to each other despite the normal
and inevitable hazards of being human. I marvel not at the
divorce rate, but at the large numbers of people who seem
to hold on!

Marriage is not only the most difficult relationship, it is
also the most rewarding. At its very best, it can mean that
two human beings, seeing what is best and worst in each
other—all frailties, all weaknesses revealed—still seek for
each other's fulfillment. Under such circumstances, marriage becomes the metaphor for what it means to create a
civilized society. There is no challenge more difficult, and
even the best of us are bound to falter at each stage of our

lives—perhaps never more than in old age. It often seems like some cosmic ironic joke that having struggled through so many years together, and feeling we've "made it," there can now be an accumulation of old problems that have never been dealt with seeping up to the surface while we face new problems and fears about getting old.

There are timeless, universal challenges that need to be explored in any marriage relationship at any age if we are to try to make the most of this potentially remarkable institution. Then there are specific practical issues. Though every marriage has its unique history and requires its own solutions to problems, it seems to me that at the same time there are many common bonds among us, one of them being that in a marriage of long duration, some individual distinctions become blurred. Many years ago, there was a cartoon in *The New Yorker* of an elderly couple sitting in a restaurant; the man is saying to the woman, "Which one of us doesn't like shad roe?"

If we have lived together for forty or fifty years, and have worked very hard at growing, one of the lucky consequences may be a level of friendship that is so strong, so profound, that one no longer experiences feelings of jealousy or rivalry or insecurity. Blow-ups—always inevitable—are now recognized by both partners as normal irritations of life and rarely last more than a few seconds.

There are also the long marriages of quiet defeat or bitterness in which no one wins an endless war, where neither partner has been able to accept the need for constant growth and change, for risking self-revelation, for openly facing the hazards of genuine communication, the never-ending task of self-exploration. Instead, a couple may live together for more than fifty years, quietly enduring a marriage that offers little gratification, no hope of dreams ever coming true.

Sometimes the awareness of time running out may lead to the first real signs of discomfort and distress. A young woman told me, "I can't understand what's happening to my parents. I don't think I ever heard them fight when I was a child, never a cross word. Not much loving that I ever saw either—I thought they were just too private, not demonstrative. They had their fortieth anniversary recently, and all of a sudden they act as if they can't stand the sight of each other."

When I asked for a description of their earlier years, Joan told me, "My mother took wonderful care of me and my sister; she was a full-time homemaker. My father went to work, came home tired, had supper, watched TV, and went to bed. Once in awhile we did something as a family, like going to the circus, but mostly we were with one parent or the other. They went out together once in awhile to a dinner party or a family birthday party, but I can hardly remember their ever having anything resembling a 'date.'" It is possible to go through the motions of being married without ever achieving a genuine relationship and then regrets may come too late—or so the couple thinks.

A friend described a visit to her sister and her husband; she told me, "Marie and Joe don't talk to each other at all. Each talked to me separately as if the other wasn't really there. 'Pass the salt' is the level of their communication. It was weird but no surprise. It's been that way for twenty of their thirty years together. They never changed. He was the high-school football captain; she was the prettiest cheerleader. They got married at eighteen, had two children, and never grew up."

The problem with this kind of marriage is that it is a tragedy for these people not to have explored the limitless possibilities of one's self or to develop a changing relationship that can continue to offer sustenance into old age.

Sometimes marriages that have "worked" quite satisfactorily most of the time seem to fall apart in old age. These are the marriages in which we observe great irritability, hostility—what one counselor in a senior citizens' center described as "a man and wife becoming totally allergic to each other." I suspect this often happens when people simply cannot bear getting old. It's hard enough to see one's own face changing in the mirror, but unendurable to have old age confirmed by the loss of the image you remember—the young girl, the young man—you married. Who *is* this decrepit, shuffling, shaking old man who used to toss his son in the air? Who *is* this woman with arthritic feet who can't dance anymore, who showed you how to do the Charleston on your honeymoon? Our partner is a constant reminder of how much of our lives is now past and how little time lies ahead.

Old marriages frequently suffer from old business never resolved in earlier years—old hurts, old frustrations, and misunderstandings. Feeling too tired to change, the anger nevertheless surfaces. One woman's complaint about her husband, after forty-two years of marriage, was "He never gave me a nickname." A man of eighty, after a violent argument with his wife about the date of their eldest daughter's marriage, said, "Never, once, in fifty years, did she show me any respect."

My observation has been that where a great deal of creative energy has always gone into making a marriage work, there can be very profound gratifications in old age.

A friend wrote, at seventy: "Terry and I still retain our senses of humor, love to converse about anything and everything, to laugh and to live with some spirit of audacity, and to enjoy the fact that we are both possessed of endless curiosity about all things. Our times together are the best parts of our daily living; and thank God we have always worked together with (generally) unusual harmony."

I look back on a forty-year marriage that has often foundered and which has required infinite patience, care, and fortitude—a never-ending willingness, a committment to struggle, to learn, to grow. It comes as a lovely shock in one's sixties to discover that it "worked," that the earlier struggles have paid off, and that the love is stronger than ever before, or than one ever imagined it might be! This doesn't mean you never fight again, only that the normal uprisings of anger in all its many forms no longer have the power to divide.

I noticed this on a recent summer visit to Cornwall, England. We took a train to Penzance, where we picked up a car to go to St. Ives. The car did not have an automatic shift, and of course we had to drive on the "wrong" side of the road. What no travel agent had told us was that driving in Cornwall is hard for even the natives. This rocky coastal area is treacherous, with steep hills, tiny, winding streets, and complicated turns. I was certainly not prepared to drive a car with a gearshift I hadn't used in thirty years. Larry, sure he'd have no problem with it, took off like a bat out of hell, missed various English walls by a hair's breadth, lost his way, broke every traffic law while trying to shift gears, and I sat screaming and cringing. In the earlier years of our marriage, such an episode might well have ruined at least two or three days of our holiday. Larry would have been deeply hurt by my lack of confidence in him and furious at my howling; I would have been devastatingly critical of his driving. What happened this time is that as soon as we got to the hotel we both admitted we'd been scared to death and the next day turned the car in and used buses and taxis for the rest of our trip. What has changed is we no longer need to defend ourselves as if there is some terrible danger in admitting human fallibility.

We come to our later years of marriage as friends or enemies; there has been no time in our lives when having a friend was more important. We've been together so long— is familiarity breeding contempt? Do we support or attack each other when we are afraid? It is never too late to look at our marriages and perhaps make them better than they have ever been before.

Some issues that are crucial in every period of married life need to be re-examined and if necessary changed. As I talked to married couples I found that one problem can reach unbearable proportions in old age—when one partner goes on growing and changing and the other doesn't.

A young woman who heard I was writing a book about getting older said, "Oh, I hope you are going to say something about people like my parents. My mother is a lively, outgoing person, always ready to learn something new, go places, meet people, and my father, who is now retired, doesn't want to do anything. He sits around the house, watches television, doesn't read, about the only thing he's willing to do is visit me and my sister and his grandchildren on holidays. My mother is being stifled alive."

I believe that very often the problem of differences in the need for growth and change reach a most unsatisfactory conclusion: one partner sickens and dies.

I worked with a lovely, talented woman for many years. She had come back to work after her three daughters were grown and gone. She'd never had a chance to go to college and I always felt she was far more capable and creative than her secretarial job suggested. She could do just about anything, and her title of "office manager" surely didn't describe her ability to help people with their problems, reconcile differences, smooth out turbulence—solve any problem with which she was presented by a large staff doing a variety of jobs. She had buried herself in housework for so long that her gifts, her needs, had been subjugated to those of her family, although they didn't consciously ask this of her. Her husband appeared to be a simpler person—happy to watch TV and putter around a garden. He had no interest in traveling or in the nature of his wife's work. There was no indication of any strong drive or ambition and he worked at a relatively mundane kind of physical labor. They seemed to love each other, but she was one of the women who suffered in pre-lib days—afraid to fulfill her own energy and creativity.

After I left the agency where she worked, I heard she had had a mastectomy. I pleaded with Betty to get some psychotherapy while she was undergoing the series of radiation treatments. I then heard she and her husband had moved to a retirement community in a western city. Larry and I happened to be out there once and we called her. She invited us to come and see her.

We followed her directions and came to a strange wasteland; it looked like a desert. It was actually a landfill for miles in every direction. Far in the distance there was one small group of garden apartments completely cut off from any other signs of civilization. It looked like a mirage! We drove along a half-built road and realized it was a housing development that was about as far from completion as one could imagine. Outside one door were three or four hanging plants and some cactuses on the ground; Betty had always had a green thumb. I could see some African violets on the shelf at the kitchen window.

Betty appeared at the door, hollow-eyed, gaunt, with a turban on her head. She explained that the cancer had spread and she was getting chemotherapy. Why had she moved to this desolate place? Because Fred wanted to retire; his needs, his interests were simple, and Betty had never considered her needs at all. Here was the ghost of a vibrant, alive, intelligent, exciting woman, dying in a desert, dying of malnutrition of her soul.

When we drove away, I knew it was the last time I'd ever see her; I knew she would soon die. Sometime later I heard she had indeed died shortly after our visit, and Fred had soon thereafter married a woman who had been a housekeeper to a priest for thirty years and just needed someone to take care of.

Janet worked and continued her education all during the years her children were in high school and college. That she was a brilliant student came as a great surprise to her, since she'd been raised to believe she was to be only a wife and a mother. She was so successful, blossomed so outstandingly, that she eventually became head of a college department, an adviser to government officials, and was called upon to travel a great deal. Her husband had fumbled his way through life—a good and decent man who was not much good at anything he tried. He was loving and supportive, but Janet became increasingly guilt-ridden as she found her full powers and he seemed left at the wayside.

Love and guilt—combined with a sense of despair that, after all, she was never to be allowed to go beyond her father's expectations—caused a dramatic change in her general health, lowered her resistance, and affected her immune system. She eventually died of cancer.*

Sometimes guilt and hopelessness are replaced by screaming temper tantrums, abusive insults, or, even worse, terrible silence. Sometimes there are other indications of distress, such as migraine headaches, alcoholism, low back pain, or chronic depression. These reactions are poor "solutions" to a problem when each partner could find ways of satisfying his or her own needs and encouraging their partner to do the same. It is possible to respect each partner's unique qualities and make some accommodations without losing oneself in the process. We need to value change, not to be frightened by it. One obstacle to this process is our common (but ill-advised) fear of hurting each other's feelings. I'm not suggesting that we howl every time we feel frustrated, angry, or blocked, but rather that keeping our feelings too much to ourselves can lead to disaster. At a point in our married life when Larry and I were closer to divorce than we'd ever been, we shared feelings we never had before. Our marriage was deteriorating until it came close to breaking apart—at which point worrying about hurt feelings no longer seemed a primary concern. We each needed additional professional help—to say what we felt, to try to understand how we had each contributed to our problems. I think it would be almost impossible to go through that intense a search for openness without help.

We need to confront each other with the truth if we

*LeShan, *You Can Fight for Your Life.*

want marriage to work, but we need to do it in such a way that it can help, not destroy, the relationship.

In one case of a divorce the man told his wife that he had been miserable for three years, that when the children left home he had felt deserted by her when she went back to an exciting, absorbing job. He felt rejected, unloved, ignored. He had never said a word about it before, but in the course of feeling lonely and isolated he met someone who listened to him and was attracted to him. The divorce might never have occurred if three years earlier he had said, "I'm upset about a lot of things and I wish we could see a marriage counselor or a family therapist together. I'm going to get some help for myself anyway, but I feel our marriage is in trouble and I'd like us to go together." A direct confrontation might have been too painful for either person to handle; by getting help first, it is possible to face the problems without feeling destroyed by them.

When minor issues of misunderstanding come up—such as the fact that you really no longer enjoy playing bridge, or you hate vacationing in a very hot climate, or if you have to have dinner with "that loudmouth" friend of your spouse's once more you're going to scream—you need to say so, making it possible to avoid some of even the little resentments that can build up to major volcanic explosions if they are left unsaid.

Marriage in later years of our lives can be disastrous if we have developed a pattern of using our partner as a kind of target for all our fears and discontents. We didn't yell at the cleaners that ruined a dress; we didn't shout at the teacher who said our child wasn't ready for the next grade; we didn't scream at an unreasonable boss. We waited until we got home, where we felt safe, accepted, and then we took our misery out on an innocent victim—the person we were married to! To some degree this is inevitable; everybody needs a safety valve. A mother once told me that when she told her son to stop yelling, he said, "If I can't yell here, where *can* I yell?"

Now, as we face all the problems and challenges of getting old, we begin to feel less vigorous, and as we see the signs of aging, as we find ourselves beset with all the crushing realities of the future, who can we scream at against the inevitability of being mortal? To whom can we complain about the torments of arthritis, of the frustrations of Parkinson's disease, our embarrassment at not being able to hold a cup of coffee without spilling it? We need to do some very careful thinking about whether or not we want to take the chance of destroying this fragile, this infinitely important loving and caring we have managed to share for forty, fifty, sixty years—to let it disintegrate as we each cry separately against the night. We need to express our distresses, but *together;* not against each other, but *with* each other, hold on for dear life to that dear life we have with us, share our fears.

A problem in many marriages is expecting one's partner to be responsible for making us happy. Whatever our problems may have been, we were mostly pretty sure that getting married would make everything all right. Many of us have placed heavy and impossible burdens on each other. One man I know who had tried desperately to make his wife happy for over twenty years asked her to make a list of the things that would make her happy. He told me, "When we got married, Leslie said she wanted to have money; I worked like a dog until she could have almost anything she wanted. Then it was children, then it was a cruise, a fur coat, a diamond ring. She was always discontented, dissatisfied, angry, and depressed. When finally, in desperation, I told her to write down everything she wanted, I woke up. Every single item on her list was something *I* should do to make her happy. I realized for the first time in all our years together that she had never been prepared to take a look at her own life or take any responsibility for satisfying her own needs. It really knocked me out, and I knew there was no way I could help her."

Both husbands and wives need to understand that when a partner is petulant, demanding, unreasonable, depressed, we have to help him or her face the need to examine inner causes. At one time Larry and I were taking a cruise. In the dining room, at the next table, there was a couple in trouble. She complained about their room and the fact that he hadn't been able to change it. She complained about the waiter and blamed her husband for not complaining about the service. She said she was ashamed to wear her fur jacket; he should have gotten her a new one. She said the orange juice was warm and was furious when he wouldn't send it back. We watched in horror as the frightened, miserable husband accepted the abuse. It was clear she had convinced him that he was the source of all her misery. The waiter we shared muttered to us, "That woman needs a good spanking." I told him I didn't believe in physical punishment but thought the husband ought to tell her to shut up or he was going to leave her. Larry put the issue in proper perspective when he said, "How terrible it must be to feel you need someone else to make you happy! What a sad and frightened person she must be!" Sad, frightened people who lay their trip on a marriage partner desperately need to have limits set and to be encouraged in every way possible to explore the inner resources they never knew they had.

Another serious problem arises when one partner takes on the burden of expressing feelings the other partner cannot deal with. For example, in the early years of our marriage I had to express anger and sadness for both of us because Larry had much more difficulty getting in touch with his feelings. If we were going to be separated when he went on trip I cried twice as hard because he never showed sad feelings. I also got twice as angry at any injustices done either one of us because he hated confrontations of any kind. After many years of therapy and a struggle to free his inner life, our relationship changed markedly. The first time I saw tears in *his* eyes when we were parting in an airport in Europe, I felt as if a ten-ton weight had been lifted from my shoulders; now he could deal with his own sadness—I didn't have to do it for him.

How often we misjudge the marriages we observe around us! We see a hoydenish, scrapping, intense wife and a calm, gentle, soft-spoken husband, and so we judge them. In truth that gentle-appearing man has a great deal of unconscious hostility, which he cannot express; he marries a woman who will do it for him. She will pay a heavy emotional price in addition to being thoroughly misunderstood.

One woman told me, "I wish my mother was alive so I could apologize to her. When my sister and I were growing up she made us furious because she insisted on knowing where we were all the time. Even when we were grown up—even after we were married and had children of our own—she insisted we tell her where we were going, what time we expected to get home. My father never said a word—we thought he was an angel. When my mother died we got quite a shock. Now, all of a sudden, my father expected us to call up every day, report in as soon as we returned from a trip, provide him with itineraries. We realized that *he* was really the anxious one, but he made Mom do all the dirty work for him."

If we feel exploited, burdened by uncomfortable roles that have been thrust upon us, we may need to examine whether or not we may be carrying someone else's baggage, doing someone else's emotional work. It might be a good idea to shake things up a bit: "You're worried, I'm not— *you* call and see how the children are." Or, "I'm angry at what your mother said and I know you are too. It's not fair to make me be angry for both of us." One is unlikely to succeed in bringing about major personality changes, but a new awareness of this pattern of never dividing the feelings or the actions equally when they ought to be, can slowly bring at least some change. We need to remember that passive, quiet people are not necessarily "good people" and noisy, aggressive people are not necessarily "bad." All human beings have many different positive and negative characteristics, but sometimes one person may be doing the emotional work of two.

Some feelings, some challenges, become greatly intensified if we are married and getting old. Fatigue, for example, does increase for many older people, often leading to inertia. Too many people feel that they are too tired, too old, to change. Old angers and hurts cause continuing decay; unhealed wounds fester. New problems seem impossible to resolve. A woman says, "He's home all day now. I hate it but I'm stuck with it." A man says, "My wife has been playing the role of an idiot child who needs me to take care of everything. I never liked it after the first year we were married, but now I can't stand it. But she's too old to change." There are couples who have stayed together through many unhappy years, neither partner feeling capable of escaping. A wife says, "I have been miserable most of my married life, but I'm not trained for a job and I'm not attractive enough to get another man, so there's nothing I can do but bear it." "The only way we'll get out of this rotten marriage is when one of us dies," is the grim comment of one husband.

It is never too late for marriage counseling. There is never a time when we are too old to learn more about ourselves and others, never a time when we can't discover new and better ways of handling emotional distress. Often people who have been married for a long period of time have never really learned how to talk to each other, how to risk the vulnerability of sharing real feelings. Often a third person can help in this process of opening up to each other. One man told me, "After three months of family therapy, I was able to say I was afraid of getting old and embarrassed about lessening sexual activity. I'd been blaming my wife— she was too old for me, she was boring after all these years. I tried having an affair with a young secretary in my office and it was a disaster. Then I agreed to us seeing someone. The day I could say I was afraid—the first time I ever admitted such a feeling in my whole life—I felt so relieved. We both cried. I feel younger and happier than I have for many years. Not younger physically but in my head."

One of the most common anxieties in the later years has to do with one's sexuality. The greater openness about sexual relationships has, on the whole, been helpful to middle-aged and old people, freeing us from unnecessary dark and primitive inhibitions. On the other hand, the pervasive preoccupation with technical skills and the pressure to become more sexually active and experimental than we might naturally be inclined to be have led to a new kind of guilt. As psychologist Rollo May pointed out many years ago, when we were young we felt guilty about sexual feelings, fantasies, and behavior, then the sexual revolution inclined us to become guilty if sex didn't occupy our thoughts most of the time!

While individual choice ought to be at the heart of one's decisions and experiences in connection with sexuality, we need to remember that we are a generation living through a time of transition. At one time any suggestion that older people continued to be active sexually would be greeted with either derision or intense disapproval.

Even more recently, in an article in *Modern Maturity,* Myrna Lewis and Robert Butler, M.D., tell of a time when they were being interviewed on *The Today Show* in 1976 and Barbara Walters warned viewers to remove children from in front of the television set to prevent their exposure to the topic of late-life sexuality. The authors reported, however, that dramatic changes are occurring as expectations change. More and more older people feel free to continue to have an active sex life and are even willing to say so! In the article, "The Facts of Later Life," they stated:

The clinical and scientific knowledge about sexuality is growing. . . . We've known for some years that impotence in men and lack of sexual response in women are not natural parts of the aging process. Both indicate physical disease or disability and/or psychological problems that often can be successfully resolved with diagnosis and treatment. . . . Those who, for various reasons, are not interested in sex, feel freer to say so openly without feeling intimidated. . . . In addition a surprising number of people have broadened their views of love and sex far beyond what they were taught in their youth and they are continuing to change and learn even in very late life. . . .*

Revolutions are all right as long as we don't lose our cool about inalienable individual rights to explore our own needs and, while grateful for the increased freedom, remain able to focus on what suits us, not anybody else. Total monogamy with sex for procreation and almost always in one position was very hard on sensual, creative, adventurous people in the past. A sense that we are only half alive if we haven't tried fifty-seven different varieties of sexual activity, at least several times a week, with wild orgasmic reactions every time, can be just as much of a burden.

In one of his *New York Times Magazine* columns, Russell Baker said he'd always wanted to be as much like other people as possible, and was very disturbed on reading a report that most people had seven or eight sexual fantasies every day. He wrote, "On the day these statistics were published, at least three days had passed since I had a sexual fantasy . . . I was clearly below the norm." He decided that he'd have to do something about it, but his schedule was already so full that there seemed "scarcely a spare moment left to let erotic fantasy romp." After many failed attempts, he mentioned his problem to a friend, who, "wise in psychiatric matters," set his mind at ease by telling him that if he were a songwriter it would be normal to have multiple sexual fantasies, but since he was a newspaper columnist it

Modern Maturity (Feb./Mar. 1985).

was quite normal not to have a single idea for months on end!

A brilliant spoof pointing to the folly of our expecting to have the same needs, the same fantasies, the same performance as other people, as if there were some mysterious, elusive average to be attained.

We need to be open to each other's changing needs, ready to participate in experimentation that is pleasing to both, not afraid of being found wanting—especially as we get older and both desire and performance may begin to diminish—eager always to find new ways of achieving the most important goal of all, expressing love and affection.

If we are clear that giving and receiving love need never diminish with age, we will allow ourselves the freedom to find new and different ways of expressing love. One may naturally experience feelings of regret in nostalgic memories of a more wildly passionate past, but loving can be forever, with a new kind of joy and satisfaction in the ways in which we can continue to touch and hold each other.

We need to focus our attention not so much on performance, but more on remaining interesting to each other and acknowledging our continuing hunger for being physically close. One woman told me, "I like sex better now than when we were young. Now there is less frenzy and more affection and humor and being very relaxed. It's slower, and we talk about love—no more 'wham, bam, thank you ma'am'!"

Sophia Loren, interviewed in *People* magazine, was asked about her marriage—were she and Carlo Ponti separated? She answered: "Carlo and I have been together for thirty-four years. It's not something provisional anymore. It changes, everyone changes. Maybe sometimes there are things more important than passion and love . . . It grows and you appreciate the qualities of the person you are with."

All kinds of hopes and expectations may have died on the way to getting old. We expected to be financially comfortable; now we face inflation and diminished Social Security and Medicare benefits. We expected to stay in the house we have loved; now the costs of heating have become astronomical. We expected to be free of children; now one wants to come home with a baby, another needs money for graduate school. We hardly ever gave any thought to elderly parents because our parents rarely had to deal with this problem. Now we find ourselves having to face the dependency of parents who are living well into their nineties and may demand more of our care than even our children did. Where are the wonderful, long vacations? Where is the freedom we feel we've earned? The loss of dreams, the disappointments, take the form of renewed discontent with each other; who else is there to blame, to get mad at? We often feel torn between the needs and rights of a spouse and those of grown children and elderly parents. "I can't bear to leave my mother alone at Christmas time, so we go to Minneapolis to see her instead of going to Florida, and Jason is in a rage. I feel torn in two," one woman told me. A father said, "I feel the same way my wife does about our having a right to some pleasures now—we worked hard enough for them. But how can I ignore the fact that my son by an earlier marriage may go bankrupt if I don't help him? Where do my loyalties and priorities lie?"

There are no easy solutions to such divided loyalties, such disappointments. It is surely a time for discussion and compromise. Our own needs are important and must not be sacrificed, and yet of course we have to recognize other obligations. What we must keep in mind is that no one else must be allowed, by our own behavior, to think for one minute that we are expendable.

In order to live through the normal frustrations and disappointments of our later years, we can avoid some of the stress by accepting our normal ambivalent feelings. One woman wrote: "I feel that my marriage hampers me, ties me to routines and responsibilities I would rather do without. A husband and wife are accountable to each other. My husband is eleven years older than I am, our tempos are out of kilter. I long to be free—and then, in the next minute, I weep for his infirmities and the years that went by too fast. I guess nobody is ever satisfied."

How much better to acknowledge such mixed feelings than to bury them and allow them to fester, to simmer beneath the surface of consciousness. Acknowledged, one can then try to control the environment—make plans for needed care services and time alone and time away.

The opposite of love is not hate but indifference. Love and hate are both parts of caring and the more one cares, the stronger the ambivalent emotions. What we hopefully learn as we grow older is a kind of inner confidence and self-reliance which takes the sting out of the normal range of emotional highs and lows.

An aspect of the later years that surely brings with it ambivalent feelings is the onset of increasing dependence of a spouse due to a chronic illness. A woman in her late sixties told me, "My husband is a dear man but almost eighty and quite deaf. I have to be responsible for both of us and remember everything for both of us. I guess I'm pretty angry that just at a time when I have enough money to travel and feel free to seek my own pleasure my partner has become more dependent; it's difficult to get away even for an hour." If ever there was a way to destroy whatever pleasures may still be left in a marriage relationship, enslavement of this kind is surely it! Resentment, anger, feelings of imprisonment cannot possibly help. Whether or not one gets any encouragement from one's spouse, it is absolutely necessary to make one's own plans. If there is money for traveling, there surely must be money for nursing and household help.

If there happen to be any old, unsolved wounds in a marriage, that will tend to exacerbate problems of illness and caretaking. Hal and Edith had a good marriage, on the whole; both bright, capable people, devoting their lives to service to others, they had many good and satisfying years and raised three nice children. Sometime during their forties, Hal had an affair with his secretary. He genuinely loved Felice and it was in no sense a casual romance. Edith suspected at first, but never confronted Hal even after she was sure. Eventually Felice found the situation unbearable and moved away. Edith and Hal had never had a confrontation about this episode. When Edith developed severe, chronic heart trouble when both she and Hal were in their seventies, she refused to let anyone care for any of her needs. Even after Hal became somewhat senile, she fired anyone who was hired to help take care of her. She wanted Hal with her every minute, and it became clear after awhile that her dependency reflected a rage that had been held in too long. Edith was paying Hal back for the affair. Their last years together are agonizing, and this might have been avoided if the affair had been dealt with at the appropriate time and their feelings communicated to each other.

Nina's husband developed rheumatoid arthritis when they had just been married a few years; he was only thirty-four years old. Nina then spent the next twenty years in total nursing care. She also developed serious phobias and was unable to go shopping or to drive a car. When her fears became completely immobilizing she finally went for professional help. She began hiring nurses and going on trips with friends; she took up several activities including a bridge club and a lecture series on investments, had lunch out with friends and took tennis lessons. By the time she'd gotten ready to take a cruise to Bermuda, her phobias had almost disappeared. She said, "I found out that Howard was no more or less resentful than he'd been all along. His bitterness at his rotten life had always made him feel angry at me, and I was so miserable, that I reacted badly—I could not even let him know how sorry I was for him—I was too angry all the time. In the course of the therapy I began to tell him how awful I felt for him, and how I wished things could be different. I became a happier person. I'd come home refreshed, tell him stories about people I'd seen, where we'd gone. Because I felt more alive and satisfied, I was much kinder to him; we actually began to feel something for each other again."

We all fear becoming chronically ill and dependent on our spouse, and if we are honest with ourselves, we also fear having to take care of an invalid. Not only the physical care, but the genuine agony of seeing someone we love change. I would hate to have to see Larry burdened with taking care of me, but if I think of him becoming dependent, that is a worse terror because he's always been strong, always been comfortable with my dependence on him. The thought of his losing his autonomy is more frightening to me than the idea of me losing mine.

I've observed such different reactions to this situation. Frances spends her whole life taking care of Bill, who has a heart condition. She watches him like a hawk, cooks special foods, supervises his exercise program, can hardly bear to let him out of her sight. He allows this, seems to have regressed to infancy. He worries about himself, has become completely passive. Frances's self-chosen enslavement has made her husband doubly handicapped. He not only has a heart condition, but he has also become helpless.

There is a small shop in my neighborhood where I've been going quite often for about fifteen years. The couple who own it have been very helpful to me and over the years we became "close acquaintances." They had had a hard life, worked very hard in their store, and it was obvious they were crazy about each other.

One day, I was shocked to find Mrs. F. looking pale, her eyes red from crying. Her husband had been in a car accident, had suffered very serious head wounds, and was in a coma. I dropped in to the shop every few days to see what was happening, and while there seemed to be some recovery, he was still unable to talk and was partially paralyzed four or five months after the accident. Every time I came in, Mrs. F. looked worse; gaunt, exhausted, with dark circles under her eyes. When I said she would get sick if she didn't get some rest, she assured me it was impossible—her work had doubled, and "everyone expected her" to be at the hospital every evening and spend all of Saturday and Sunday there. She has two grown daughters and other relatives, but "he won't try to eat unless I'm there," she told me. As the weeks went by and she refused to consider her own needs, it became clear to me that she was on the brink of a serious physical and mental breakdown. When I finally said, "If you kill yourself, that won't help anyone," she glared at me—the first sign of anger—and said, "Well, then they will just have to manage, won't they?"

No matter how serious one's illness may be, a partner's total self-denial is bad for both. The more exhausted and angry Mrs. F. becomes, the more she will inevitably communicate her feelings to her husband and surely if there is ever to be a real recovery, he will need the encouragement and affection which is now being poisoned by an impossible and masochistic selflessness. I tried to tell her that taking a forty-eight-hour rest period for herself was not going to make matters worse—that she had to demand help from others, that she should just tell everyone else that she needed to go to bed for a rest, or had to get away for a weekend. I could tell from her look that she couldn't do it. Her life has become unendurable and her only way out— as she sees it—is to wait until she collapses completely.

Harry's wife began to suffer from Alzheimer's disease in her early sixties. Harry could afford to retire, which he did so that he could take care of his wife. For ten years he enslaved himself, wouldn't allow anyone to do anything, even as his wife became more and more helpless. He was tired all the time, and his children became increasingly alarmed as he seemed to become more and more depressed. When Harry was seventy-four and his wife needed care twenty-four hours a day, his daughters decided to take matters into their own hands. They moved Harry and his wife to an apartment near a large and excellent YMHA and hired a full-time housekeeper and visiting nurse service. Very reluctantly Harry accepted their urging that he visit the Y. There he found a senior citizens' group, afternoon and evening lectures, and entertainments—a wide variety of activities that interested him greatly. He told me,

"I'm having a new life—the best life I ever had! I take care of Edna at night and on the weekends. She doesn't know who I am anymore, and can barely talk. I still love her for my memories of before she got so sick. But I found out I'm very attractive to the ladies! I've got a widow lady friend and I go to her house to play cards and talk. I took her out to a play. I'm learning things I never even thought about— they have poetry readings and big professors to come and talk about world affairs, and—I can't begin to tell you how my life is now, except it's wonderful."

The invalid has special burdens and so does the care-taker. Miriam, who developed muscular sclerosis in her seventies, told me, "Ralph is anything but a homebody or custodian for me, and I try hard to maintain all my enthu-siasm for his creativity and his continuing professional ac-tivities. I try to attend his lectures whenever possible, and I remain proud of him, but I can read his discontent with my dependence in his eyes, and I wish he were less afraid—or is it revulsion?—to touch me, now that I am disabled. I miss the physical contact, and I know that he can't do more for me than he does. I find it hard to feel deprived in so many ways, at so many levels. Ralph is simply not the man to have to deal with a crippled wife—but while I under-stand it, I feel doubly wounded."

We are so afraid to tell anyone what hurts, what we need. I wonder if it wouldn't help Ralph to grow, to be-come more sensitized, if Miriam could only tell him what she told me. It is more than likely that his physical distance is his way of defending himself against *his* pain over her illness. If Miriam could reach out and ask to be held, it might be that they could begin to cry together instead of separately.

I called a friend whose husband had had a stroke and was paralyzed on one side of his body. "Oh Eda," she said, "it's so terrible! Yesterday, for the first time, David looked at me and began to cry. We both sobbed—I couldn't control myself. I feel terrible that he'll be worse now." She was greatly shocked and confused by my reaction: "Oh, how *wonderful!*" To cry—to share pain—there is no better beginning to recovery.

It might seem from all this talk of marriage that I am overlooking the fact that many if not most older people are single and alone, many through divorce or widowhood. Of course a great number of older people have been living alone for a long time; some have never married; some who became single while still young have never remarried. Those who have been single long before reaching sixty-five or seventy have usually accommodated themselves to this way of life. A typical reaction came from the woman who said, "It was terrible at first. My husband died when I was sixty-four, and I felt my life was over. But my son was wonderful to me, helped me come back to the living, and now, at seventy-four, I've come to love my privacy and freedom. I've made new friends, have new interests, feel quite safe in my home, still travel in my own car—why should I want to start cooking for someone else and doing his laundry and meeting all his needs at this time of my life?" It seems to be true in places where older people congregate that old men are more eager for matrimony or live-in relationships than the women; the pattern of being taken care of by women is well established in the older generation of men.

In some cases the ways in which single older people deal with their feelings of loneliness, the need to share their lives, may lead to relationships that can be just as complex and difficult as an "old" marriage. A father and a daughter may live together, or two sisters. Or two friends who have both been widowed may decide to pool their resources. Sometimes there can be more old unresolved emotional business than in a marriage. I knew two sisters who lived together, one out of anxiety and loneliness, the other who joined forces out of guilt feelings—it was "only right" to help. They repeated childhood patterns of helplessness versus guilt, dependency versus self-sacrifice, all of which were leading to a bitter and miserable life.

While many people are terrified of living alone after a long marriage and may need a long period of adjustment with help from family and friends, living alone is not the horror it might well have seemed in the years when we were growing up. One of the reasons we may dread it is that we have memories of maiden aunts and other relatives who lived with us because living alone was considered a terrible and dangerous thing. For many it's quite different now. There are more support groups, more communities where one can find people in similar circumstances. It is so much easier now to cook for one or eat out. Community activities for single older people abound across the land as the numbers of elderly increase. My impression from those I talked to was that many had found to their surprise that they were enjoying living alone, and that the greatest fear—which is the same as for married people but far more real and intense—was becoming chronically ill and having to be hospitalized without a marriage partner to be protective of them.

People tend to become creative when in need. I found that a lot of planning for such eventualities is going on:

senior citizens' centers where they are working out buddy systems, so that people are on call to help each other; friends who arrange in advance to be available for emergencies; parents who have talked openly and honestly to grown children about these fears and have explained just what they want done in terms of professional help if they can't take care of themselves.

As in all other aspects of becoming old, the single poor suffer the most. They are more likely to find themselves helpless in situations where no one really seems to care what happens to them. It is, therefore, even more important for such people to plan to whatever degree they can by working out mutual help arrangements and by seeking the help of whatever social services there may be for the aged in any town or city long before serious problems arise. I talked with one woman who lives alone in a one-room apartment, has no children, and is trying to survive on Social Security and a small pension. After a frightening bout with the flu during which she felt doubly helpless and alone, she looked up all her community's services for the elderly in the phone book. She called every agency and asked questions about what they might possibly do for her. She took down the names of people she talked to. She got information about the best hospital facilities in her area where home care for the elderly was available. She talked to people about meals on wheels and about visiting nurses, about whom to call if the heat went off. All of this information is listed on sheets of paper on the wall next to her telephone.

Taking action as long as one is able seems to me to be the key to survival. By being prepared, one is not likely to be as overwhelmed later by feelings of great fatigue, of feeling too ill to do anything to help oneself. If the information is already available, it is easier to make use of it when one is in trouble.

There has been a great change in the status of older people who are single because being single is so common and so accepted at all ages now. That is a part of the social revolution of our times which has surely been of help to older people. The women's movement is another source of changing attitudes. Many older women in particular, who now recognize they gave up their own growth, their own potentials, to remain in only partially satisfying roles all their lives, feel a new sense of freedom; now they can develop special interests and talents; now they can take courses, even go to college.

But despite all the changes, those who are divorced often have lingering doubts about what happened. Could they have saved the marriage? Was it so bad, compared to ending one's days alone? Would waiting it out have brought a spouse back? And of course the widowed who were happily married will experience waves of grief and loneliness—a feeling of having lost an essential safety net—for the rest of their lives even if they fill their lives with satisfying activities and relationships. The grief of a lost love, the regrets for mistakes that may have led to a precipitous divorce, cannot be wiped away conveniently or efficiently. As we get older, there should be no surprise in the fact that life is full of pain. All we can do is to make the most of what we have and allow our pain to live and breathe openly, and not try to shut it away. We can do far more with our life situations when we are able to acknowledge the difficulties we face, the pain we must endure.

Another part of the social revolution of our lifetime is

that many older people who were raised to believe in monogamy and fidelity and the unacceptability of having extramarital affairs find themselves in their seventies somewhat surprised, maybe a little shy, about having a "friend" who may live in one's apartment or separately but is definitely a partner. This new pattern is becoming more accepted as older people see the advantages of living alone and in those situations where marriage might mean a financial sacrifice. Many widows have health insurance policies and pensions that would be cut off if they remarried; many single older people want to continue to keep their finances separate because of trusts and wills involving their children. Some of the happiest older people I know have found new companions when they least expected it. When their husbands or wives died, these people were sure that was the end of any romance in their lives. A friend who nursed her husband after a stroke for twelve years is now being courted by a lovely man. They live apart but see each other every day. She looks twenty years younger. A woman in her late seventies began to work for a charitable organization and a much younger man, who worked there too, fell in love with her. He was unhappily married, and they were together as often as possible until she died at eighty-seven.

Terry, sixty-three, wrote:

I was older, much older, three years ago when I was living alone and spending my time after work taking care of my ailing aunt and mother, dependent women in their eighties. As a widow and the chief of our tiny tribe, I felt that the generation gap had closed over me and I was not a niece and a daughter but the youngest of three sisters. All of life had become duty.

Now, living with a lively man only two years older than I, I feel my own age. Not really younger and certainly not older, but definitely better. Let's be honest, having sex back in the repertoire helps. Having, once again, a secret garden of my own helps me carry on my continuing obligations with more perspective and even more energy. But I don't want to give the impression it's all a garden of roses. We are very different and have had a long time to develop our idiosyncracies. There are a lot of adjustments, some highs, some lows. But worth it.

That ability to weigh positive and negative realities is essential to developing new relationships and quite unlike the aspirations of one man who told me, "I'm looking for someone who will be Katharine Hepburn to my Henry Fonda à la *On Golden Pond*." This man is doomed to permanent singlehood unless he can change his expectations!

Whether one is married, or has a live-in or live-out special friend, there is a great paradox in any intensely important relationship in the later years. It seems to me that it has never been more important to cultivate new kinds of separateness—to give each other freedom, space to breathe. At the same time that we need each other more than ever before, separation of any kind now has a new and painful dimension.

If one is happily married, the fear of the ultimate separation becomes more intense with each year. I often feel that I have been too lucky—that it is a rare blessing to love one person for the forty-four years Larry and I have known each other, and that sooner or later "it will catch up with us."

When Larry and I have to be apart—and that is quite often—we both find the partings more and more difficult.

There is a new element of terror that has nothing to do with being alone, but of losing half of oneself. Life is always tenuous; you can get run over by a bus, or hit by a falling rock, or get caught in the crossfire of some street fight—surely we are bombarded daily by the reality of sudden terrors and sudden deaths. But when we get old, there is a new sense of danger. When I hear that an elderly couple has died together in a fire or a plane crash, I find myself hoping it will be that way for us, and then I turn away from such an ending, with the feeling that one of us ought to hang on as long as possible to *remember* the other! What we have to accept is that our feelings are real and must be respected; we must accept our terror or it will torture us in our sleep. There is also the sense that with one of our deaths the marriage will end, too. It has become an entity, almost a living thing. Just at the time when you've gotten all the kinks ironed out, when you are calmer and closer than ever before, you have to begin to prepare for the unbearable.

At the very same time, having separate lives leads to self-discovery, which leads to mutual enrichment. When I was in my early thirties I was seeing a French psychiatrist who often seemed to me to be very daring if not actually immoral! I had been brought up to believe that a happy marriage was one in which the couple was never, ever, separated, except when the wife was in the hospital having a baby. My parents had never taken separate vacations, always went to theater or concerts or movies together, shared all their social relationships. When my therapist said that she thought it would be good for almost every marriage if each person had his or her own apartment, I was shocked, horrified. It took me many more years to realize she was trying to let me know that I was married to a man who needed separate space, time alone. It took many more years for me to realize that *I* could find infinite pleasure in my own company. When I'm in New Jersey by myself, writing, I lead a very orderly life—there is a quiet serenity in keeping the small house in order. I spend quite a bit of time watching birds at the feeders; sunsets are very big with me. I try to listen to my own inner rhythms, doing what seems to come naturally. When the writing really gets stuck I go for a walk. Most days I try to go for a swim at a nearby YMCA. I get up at five in the morning and go to sleep early. I listen to records of old musicals or maybe some Mozart or an opera. I can go to sleep with the radio on without having to use an earplug; if I wake up I can turn on the light and read.

If Larry is with me, I have a sense of disorder. I get up later, there are more dishes to wash, the bed gets more rumpled. He hates listening to records, wants absolute silence while he works. When he's alone in New York, he spends hours and hours in the library, goes to bed very late, smokes a pipe, and stinks up the living room. He loves *Hill Street Blues* and *Star Wars* and James Bond; I hate them. I like comedies, tearjerker movies; he hates them. It has no effect on his work if his surroundings are in a chaotic state of confusion. None of these things is really important. When we are together we adjust, make accommodations, feel no sense of strain. But the separations allow interludes when each of us gets into the center of ourselves, without obligation to anyone else. This is an act of such refreshment that it makes the time together altogether different than it might otherwise be. There are also the separations of business travel, occasional vacations in places the other doesn't care for, visiting different friends we don't especially share in common. We bring back to each other new impressions, new adventures, ideas, observations—gossip!

We need to try to accommodate the basic differences in our emotional levels, in our sources of gratification. When we were first married I was deeply hurt that Larry didn't want to go to the theater as much as I did. For a long time he went with me; I made him feel guilty when he didn't. In the past twenty years I've learned to go alone or with a friend, unless he expresses a real desire to see something. Sometimes I wish he were with me, but many times I enjoy myself more because I know he would have been bored and that would have interfered with my pleasure. I have learned to wait when I feel he has something on his mind. I blurt out my feelings, but he needs time to think about what he feels. I can even wait several days now to find out what's upsetting him! For many years I assumed we both loved the opera. Finally Larry admitted he likes only *La Bohème.* I assumed in earlier years that he liked ballet as much as I did; he never goes anymore. We have faced the fact that we don't like the same people in some instances, and that he feels most socializing is a waste of his valuable time. I occasionally have lunch or dinner with old friends, without him.

As we get older our idiosyncracies become increasingly important to us, and if each partner can tolerate the other's need for being alone to enjoy them, the times spent together are far more satisfying. One woman told me that she felt all the romance in her life was over when her husband said he wanted to sleep in the guest room some of the time because he was getting more restless and wanted to be able to get up without disturbing her. "What I actually found," she said, "was that the nights he *didn't* move out were better than they'd been in a long time."

Retirement can make a dramatic change in a couple's life together, and lead to new irritations because of being together too much of the time. Instead of feeling threatened by a partner's desperate need for more privacy, more space, we need to bring all our creative energies to bear on ways we can give each other time alone, both at home and away from home. Rather than destroying a relationship, it enhances it and offers dramatic refreshment. When a husband or a wife tries to crush out a spouse's need for freedom, the marriage can only deteriorate. Some of us have to remind ourselves many times over that a human being who feels caged is really no bargain as a companion. Many marriages that come apart in old age are those in which one person feels trapped by the other—or both feel trapped and are unable to communicate with each other about it.

One partner is likely to need more space and freedom than the other. We need to sensitize ourselves to our own particular patterns and realize that a need for separateness is *not* an indication that a partner is falling out of love. It means just what it says: "I'm a person who has to be alone or away from intense relationships sometimes." No threat, no rejection—just a fact of life. At one time when I was young and stupid and carried on terribly when Larry needed to take a trip to Greece without me, a wise friend said, "If a butterfly lands on the palm of your hand, you can enjoy watching it; if you try to hold on to it, you will crush it." Fortunately I lived long enough (and worked hard enough!) to want to be the butterfly myself, some of the time. It's unlikely that any couple, considering the range of individual needs, is ever going to need exactly the same amount of separateness, but giving what is needed—and taking what is needed—without feelings of rejection can make our time together so much more exciting and satisfying.

One man wrote me, "I'm lucky to have a wife who is seven and a half years younger and very active. I find myself running to keep up with her! Our marriage is successful because we do certain things together and many things apart. We are independent individuals—more than we ever were before. It adds spice to life."

As a younger woman I was unsure of myself and crippled by self-hatred, feelings of unworthiness. There was nobody there when I was alone. Now there is a person I know and care about very much. The cultivation of oneself and the capacity to be alone, to be separated, enhances each life and life together. It is one of the important ways in which we can nourish a shared life.

One woman told me that she had felt terribly lonely and rejected whenever her husband seemed particularly caught up in fascination with his work life; she felt excluded. "Then," she told me, "I began to seek out my own inner companion, to test myself—what did I like? What interested me? Who was I? I have turned the loneliness into freedom." It is this acceptance and enjoyment of separate needs and pleasures that brings surprise into the times we share.

After many months of each being absorbed in tough work assignments and not having much time together, Larry and I went to England, where he was to give some lectures. We also took a few days' vacation. It was one of the best, most invigorating trips we'd shared in a long time—such mutual pleasure in doing things we both loved—long walks discovering new places we'd never been before. On a walk in Cornwall we kept finding new surprises at every turn in the road. At one point, high on a hill, wandering through a narrow lane, we suddenly came upon a bowling match—people in fancy colored uniforms, a closed-in viewers' stand, flags flying. It was a total surprise. "The reason that walk seems so unforgettable to me," Larry said later, "was that it was like our marriage. I never know what's around the next corner." That element of surprise is most likely to occur when each partner has some separate experiences.

But oh, how hard it is to separate when time together becomes increasingly precious!

Marriage in the later years brings with it a special poignancy. Every separation becomes a metaphor for what is now background music to a happy marriage—the recurring thought that one of us will someday be really alone. There is now, always, a bittersweet quality for us; having worked so terribly hard to make our marriage work for over forty years, we now, for the first time, are truly aware of something never really faced before—one of us will be widowed. It can happen at any age, of course, but earlier by surprise; now it is always background music.

What is far more poignant is what happens to those who are still married but who are hopelessly resigned or bitterly disappointed. For those who have achieved a high order of friendship in marriage, every minute counts; we don't want to waste what we have in pettiness, in details, in the mundane events of ordinary living. For those who are unhappy, every minute is even more important, for there is little time left to search for and reach the dreams of fulfillment that are surely buried beneath the discontent. It is time to nourish the good and work hard to solve the problems that interfere with potential gratifications.

Standing in a hospital corridor once, I saw an elderly woman lying on a stretcher and an elderly man standing next to her, holding her hand and stroking her forehead. I felt shy about witnessing their intimacy—it was as if they were one person in their glances and their touching. I knew that when I got very old I would want to share that holding on for as long as possible—and that in the intervening years I would want to work very hard at keeping our hands touching and our eyes on each other.

~~~~~~

SEVEN

Grown Children: The Dream and the Reality

LARRY WASN'T ENTIRE-
ly sure he wanted to become a father. One of my more
convincing (if entirely inaccurate) arguments was that babies really didn't cost a lot; my second argument was even
more brilliant—that, after all, children leave home at seventeen or eighteen to go to college, and there would be
many long years of freedom from parental responsibility.

Why he has forgiven me for these lies I do not know, but
most of us who have adult children, and are now in our
sixties or older, are only too well aware that parenthood
never ends. In many cases, especially in our generation, it is
more complicated and difficult than in earlier years.

There is, of course, great variation in relationships with
adult children. Sometimes our children grow up to be our
best friends; sometimes there may be conflict with siblings
that goes back to much earlier emotional business in childhood, and we find ourselves caught in the middle of struggles, rivalries, that never ended. Sometimes we are close
and live near each other, sometimes there are great distances, both psychological and geographical.

Most of all, a great many of us find that our dreams of

parenthood in our later years are far removed from some of the realities we face.

Ellen, sixty-three, told me, "I figured it out the other day. We have had more crises with Molly since she was thirty than in all the rest of the time she was growing up. Before, we worried about measles, and being homesick at camp; later we worried about marijuana and getting pregnant. Since thirty there have been two rotten husbands, two small children, and almost total financial dependence on us."

There were very few people to whom I spoke who said, "It's simple and wonderful." (I think there were three such responses out of more than one hundred!) Most of us experience many surprises, much complexity, and relationships that sometimes demand more hard work than ever before.

Dave wrote: "My relationship with my kids is weird in some ways, normal in others. They are still somewhat dependent financially. I take pride in their accomplishments and share their pain in their defeats. I need them to share those occasions that suggest we have mutual roots—like birthdays. Two of the three are in therapy, which has opened up some festering wounds in our relationship."

Pat Carroll wrote:

I seem fairly close to my kids . . . a son and two daughters. None of them married as yet. We are still close enough to fight, close enough to hug and sit by the hour laughing or telling stories or just enjoying each other's company. They puzzle me with their growing pains, because, of course, I would handle their problems much better than they are!!!! Please note the sarcasm. I hurt for them when their plans go awry, I weep for them in their hurts, I laugh with them over the absurdities they begin to see in these silly lives of ours. They are lousy correspondents, but we speak by phone at least once a week, sometimes more. Always a call if they are in trouble, which is comforting, I suppose, but my hope is they will better be able to handle things as time goes by.

There are all kinds of parent-child relationships when children grow up and none are "good" or "bad." People simply have different needs. For one young couple, living in a two-family house with parents may be a wonderful arrangement; in other cases, there can be too many pressures on both generations, living in the same *city*. Some adult children want to keep very close ties; others think sharing every other Thanksgiving and Christmas is just about right. The problems arise when parents and adult children have different needs. One daughter says, "I can't stand having my mother living so near me—she can't leave us alone." Another daughter says, "It's been a great disappointment to me—I thought my parents would be so crazy about their grandchildren, but they retired, moved to Florida, travel, play golf, seem perfectly happy to see the children once or twice a year. I feel so hurt."

Or on the other side of the coin, a grandmother might say, "I don't have a chance to really get close to my grandchildren—my daughter-in-law doesn't want me around." Or a widowed father comments, "My daughter expects me to babysit whenever she wants to go out. I can't seem to get up the courage to tell her I'm trying to make a new life for myself."

Whatever situation we may find ourselves in with either single or married adult children, we need to watch out for the "shoulds" we have inside our heads—the expectations, the goals, the dreams we had, which may be far from the reality. A son *should* call his mother once a week; a daughter *should* be willing to listen to good advice; a son-in-law *should* want to come to our house for Christmas. The best adult relationships are the ones that are most free of the "shoulds." If we can learn to accept what we cannot change; if we can stop feeling threatened, unloved, rejected; if we can get on with our own lives, our children will experience a good deal more pleasure in our company and we will experience far less disappointment.

One of the most common feelings I encountered in talking to others was the feeling that children had become strangers in some way. There was still a great deal of love in the relationship, but as one father put it, "I don't know my son. He is totally different from the way I was at his age—but even more than that, he's nothing at all like the person I thought he would be, growing up in my home."

We have to remember that our children have grown up in the same social revolution that has so changed our lives and the world in general. We were adults after World War II; they grew up in and were far more influenced by a rapidly changing world. They didn't have the rules we had to live by; their choices have been infinitely more complex and difficult. And most of all, I think they suffer from a disillusionment we didn't experience when we were young. We mustn't underestimate what it must have meant to be a *child* growing up with the knowledge of the Holocaust and the atom bomb, with far greater information than we had when we were growing up, of the evil in high places. We believed in the power of good over evil. We had heroes; the few they had were either assassinated or were exposed in a new kind of journalism that no longer allows any public figure to have any private imperfections. They are far more frightened and cynical than we were.

It is not incidental that our generation fought in a war we believed was moral and necessary, and they were caught up in a war of monumental tragic proportions. In an article in *The New York Times,* Edward Tick, who was in college and was never drafted during the Vietnam War, talks about how no one of his generation has yet recovered from the trauma of that war.* Whether one chose to go to prison or jail, or was permitted to stay in college; whether one resisted and felt guilty about those who fought; whether one did go to fight and experienced horrors of such a nature that it would be surprising if they could ever recover completely, all suffered. There had never been a time—or a war—in which there was such a degree of controversy. Tick says of the 17 million men who came of age during Vietnam, "I think that none of us escaped, that none of us feels whole. All our choices—service in Vietnam, service at home, freedom from service . . . failed to provide the rite of passage that every man needs. I want to feel my own strength, worth and wholeness, and I want to belong to my country and my generation. But history got in the way . . ."

In spite of the loss of institutional controls, the devastating social history, the new freedom to behave in ways not sanctioned in our and our parents' lives, we still expected our children to grow up the way we did!

Young people of our generation used to go away to college or go to work, and while we were expected to live at

---

*"Apocalypse Continued," *The New York Times Magazine* (Jan. 13, 1985).

home until we married, we married early because sex wasn't as free and easy as it later became. While some broke the institutional rules, most worried about pregnancy, getting caught, and venereal diseases, which couldn't easily be cured in the days before antibiotics. Most children married early, moved away, supported themselves, and most of all, *stayed married.*

A niece of mine who went to Cornell and lived in the same dormitory that I'd lived in my first year of college couldn't believe my description of how it had been in 1940. No men above the first floor, except fathers helping with luggage; signing in and out every night, with a curfew of 10 P.M. on weeknights and midnight on Saturdays, and the possibility of losing even these "privileges" if you were ten minutes late. My niece lived in a coed dorm, with no restrictions of any kind, and wasn't overjoyed with the coed bathrooms!

The expression "the generation gap" arose out of the realization that our children's life experiences were more different from ours than ever before. For one thing, where earlier generations were protective of parents through keeping much of their lives secretive, our generation of children have forced us to face and accept such things as a free sex life without marriage, or homosexuality. We lived in secretive, hypocritical times, and the change is something I admire. But our adjustment has not been easy, to say the least. When I was in college, the interesting exception was "the girl who slept around." In my daughter's generation, any girl who wasn't sexually active by sixteen was ashamed to let anyone know.

We lived through the Depression—a magnitude of suffering we can never forget, giving many of us a compassion for those who could not take care of themselves. Most of our children grew up without ever experiencing genuine economic deprivation. On the other hand, our children lived through a time of moral crises in the 1960s, which has greatly influenced their lives. A small minority of these children have remained "turned off" by society, but most of us parents have been amazed (and a few of us, saddened) by the advent of the "Yuppies."

Some of the people I spoke to were shocked because their children had become Yuppies. As parents they had been very idealistic, very concerned about social welfare programs, problems of the poor, the handicapped—little concerned with material success. They see their children almost totally focused on "making it," getting rich quick, living the so-called good life.

The truth seems to me to be that the Yuppies are exactly what many parents prayed for in the 1960s! A lot of parents were scared to death, turned off, by what I consider to have been the best generation of young people ever to emerge on the American scene—and which may never appear again. Many parents were horrified by the bare feet and beards, the songs of peace, the turning away from materialism, the willingness to fight for one's beliefs. It seems to me that many of the Yuppies are people who had idealism beaten out of them by the Chicago police at the Democratic Convention of 1968, who were shot at at Kent State, who saw comrades die in Mississippi. Most older people told them they were crazy, irresponsible; they couldn't wait for them to see the light. If you couldn't change the world and make it better, what was the point of trying?

We were rightly terrified by the contagion of drug use. Some of our children paid heavily for this kind of experimentation, and many parents feel very lucky that their children got out of that trap alive and well. There were many young people who were unstable to begin with, who found the freedom of the '60s too much to deal with, who weren't strong enough to make sensible choices. Too many adults made the judgment that all the young people were crazy. Have we ever thanked them for the end of the Vietnam horror? Or for the small progress made in the freedom struggle of blacks? Or for the more relevant subjects brought into university life? Or even for the rich and colorful variations in the way we dress and in our hairstyles? As we spend a fortune on the snob appeal of designer jeans, do we remember that we once threw kids out of school for wearing them—or letting their hair grow long, or growing a beard? There is a common complaint that we don't have any genuine leadership anymore; that we seem to be a nation of people who no longer care what the politicians do, that the ideal of three centuries that those in power must help those who are not (the "women and children first" philosophy) has been so turned around that we don't seem to mind at all when poor children and old people and the handicapped are allowed to suffer. Did our children once try to change the world and did they give up?

I watch the affluent, gorgeously dressed young people in the gourmet shops and restaurants; I see pictures of their apartments—all glass and chrome and black mirrors. And I weep, because I believe that if there had been more of my generation encouraging them, supporting their dreams, they might not have become so lacking in compassion, unconcerned about the major issues of our times.

It is my belief that the small minority of our children who remained turned off by society and the larger group who became clean-shaven and Republican are brothers under the skin. Rather than being self-assured, Yuppies seem to me to handle deep anxiety and depression by living for today, getting as many material comforts as they can get, and refusing to think about anyone else. Many of our children feel lost and unable to deal with what it is like to be in their twenties and thirties and early forties. Marriage has become optional; as a result they find themselves single, young women especially, with no prospects of marriage; it seems that without institutional social controls men are far more reluctant to marry. Life has become so complex that even for those who want marriage and parenthood, the difficulties they encounter are greater than ever before. Safe places for children to play without supervision were taken for granted in earlier generations. Did we or our parents have the kind of fears parents have today? Did most of us desperately need two incomes merely to survive? Did it ever occur to us that our children could be sexually molested in nursery school?

Life is harder for our children and harder for us in relation to them. Whether they express their frustrations and fears or cover them up, they are there. I think we need to face some resentments we may be feeling because we tried so hard, gave so much. All our efforts didn't solve their problems.

Many people in their sixties and seventies feel a special resentment if their children don't turn out the way they expected. After World War II, as we were marrying and having children, millions of us moved to suburbia. Housing was in short supply, we were bound and determined to be "perfect parents," and suburbia seemed just the right answer for the children. Husbands spent half their lives commuting, and with some exceptions, ours was the generation of mothers who stayed home—and whom we later discovered felt imprisoned, bored, frequently quite miserable—as evidenced by their response to Betty Friedan and *The Feminine Mystique.* * Where were those perfect children for whom we had made such sacrifices? Many of their problems stemmed from the fact that they knew we were discontented, that rather than our living our own lives more fully, we expected them to fulfill our dreams. Other parents feel a sense of distance from children who "grew up with every advantage" and who have turned away completely from "getting ahead," who are content to be members of small music groups, barely squeaking by, or cabinetmakers. Typical of this group was a mother who said, "David was a brilliant student all the way through school—his professors all had such high hopes for him—and suddenly, in the third year at Harvard he walked away from everything he was working towards in a degree in architecture. For awhile he became a construction worker, now he helps people build their own houses. He doesn't seem to have any intellectual interests."

When we feel estranged from our children because of some emotional hurdles or because of very different lifestyles, it seems to me we need to do some serious soul-searching. The times our children lived through while growing up may have caused a wide chasm in our relationships, but if we have the courage, the motivation, to rediscover each other, it's so much easier than we think in advance. When we search for common values, whether with Yuppies or their opposites, we can find them. The

* Betty Friedan, *The Feminine Mystique* (New York: Dell, 1977).

mother of an itinerant musician who lives in a shack in the woods comes back from a brief visit and says, "I could never ask for a sweeter, dearer son. His friends adore him, and he's happy; he loves me and his father. His deepest values are the ones we tried to teach him." The father of the construction worker–home builder confesses, "Dave is a terrific person—he just got turned off by all the academia of mine and his mother's lives. We never did anything physical—I think we practically talked him to death with what he should be reading and studying. He's found his own thing, but I've learned to see that doesn't have to separate us. He respects what we do; all he wants is for us to respect what he does."

Patterns of living—even attitudes—have changed, but what I have found is that sensitivities and feelings are really not so different and that it is possible to build a strong bond of friendship if we are willing to work at it. One mother told me, "Never in my wildest dreams, when Marda was a baby, did it ever occur to me that some day my daughter would be a lesbian and a member of a radical women's group! For three or four years, we hardly saw each other and when we did, we got into terrible fights. I was so upset I went to see a therapist who kept asking me to tell him what I loved about my daughter. I cried a lot, and began to see that nothing had really changed; she was my child; I could be her friend if I wanted to. Most of all, I found out how much she loved me. You wouldn't believe some of the meetings I've gone to with her! I think some of her friends are really crazy. But knowing how much we care about each other makes everything else unimportant."

My daughter's adolescence and early adulthood were very different from my own. My parents were still part of the Victorian tradition, and I was about as good a girl as you could find. As it became clear that my daughter's life was far more experimental and adventurous than mine, I asked her one day, while we were cleaning vegetables at the kitchen sink, how she'd been able to live such a different life than I had expected her to live. "I listened to your unconscious, not your conscious," she said, without a moment's hesitation. She was quite right; I'd been much *too* good, and what I had to face confronted by her greater wisdom was that at least unconsciously I envied her greater freedom, wished I'd had some of it.

I think this is something we need to be aware of if we are extremely uncomfortable with our adult children's way of life. Maybe, deep down, we now feel that we missed some of the experiences they have been able to enjoy. The angrier and more critical we may be, the more this may stem from ambivalent feelings we have never honestly faced. I spoke at a temple luncheon many years ago about the ways in which our then teenagers were living. I mentioned that my mother, with a serious heart condition, had walked up five flights to the apartment of our daughter when she was living with a young man—and that she did it because she loved her granddaughter too much to give in to her discomfort and trepidations about this new life-style. Many in the audience were horrified and disapproving; they made it clear they thought I ought to have dragged my daughter home (even though she was of age and could do as she pleased). One little old grandma, somewhat crippled, who appeared to be about eighty-five, came up to talk to me at the end of the meeting. She whispered in my ear, "All these woman who were virgins when they got married—they can't stand to find out what they missed! I know—I was married for fifty years to a man my parents chose for me when I was sixteen, and I never knew one day's happiness with him."

We were not able to anticipate most of what has happened to our children. We did not foresee the ever-increasing divorce rate, the impossible burdens associated with renting an apartment or buying a house, or the need for graduate education in order to get professional work of any kind. When my parents sent me to college, the tuition was about $200 a semester. A year in college now costs more than what most of us once considered a year's income. And probably the biggest surprise of all is that so many of our children have either wanted to stay at home or want to come back. A friend of mine called me one day and said, "Eda, what did we do wrong? Eileen wants to come home and live with us!"

The fact of grown children not wanting to leave the nest, or flying back, is common today. A play appeared on Broadway in 1984 on this very subject, called *Alone Together,* with Janis Paige and Kevin McCarthy. The audience howled in recognition and identification with the return of three sons just when Mom and Pop thought they could return to an earlier intimacy and passion in being alone again. One comment in the play that brought the greatest laughter was, "Kids when they're little are so cute you could eat them up. And then they grow up and you wish you had!"

I spoke with Ann Landers about whether or not she received much mail about the problem of young adults living with their parents. She told me she received a great deal of mail on this subject, and that much of what was happening was based on the realities of life. Young people with Ph.D.'s often can't find jobs; housing has become a major social problem. But she also said that in many of the letters she received it was quite clear that the relationship between the parents and children had never been very good, and I agreed with her that young people may come home in order to finish unfinished business—not necessarily an unhealthy kind of behavior. For a child who felt rejected or unloved, or was jealous of a sibling, or felt that discipline had been harsh and uncompromising, coming home might be an unconscious way of saying, "I can't go on with growing up until some things get settled between us." The wish may be real, and some parents, if they have matured enough themselves, can meet that challenge and either by themselves, or with family counseling, open up old hurts and develop new and better relationships based on the insights gained. In some cases, neither parents nor children understand this hidden agenda or are not able to deal with it, and all members of the family become frozen in positions that are uncomfortable and eventually destructive.

There are many reasons why a son or daughter will ask to come home. The most obvious is the cost of living alone; the second, the fact of being alone because of being single and/or divorced. There are also more subtle reasons. We didn't really prepare our children for the world in which they grew up; there was no way we could, since we ourselves had no idea how much change, how much stress and turmoil, there would be. For some young people the world they did discover is more than they feel they can cope with. Ann Landers says she often recommends family counseling and advises parents that where healing is needed, it is a good idea to let the child come home while this process is undertaken. Sadie Hofstein, executive director of the Nassau County Mental Health Association, told me that in their work with such family situations, they advise parents to insist that the child take some kind of job, even if far below his or her capabilities, or do steady and meaningful volunteer work. Always it should be clear this is a time for growth and change and that the situation cannot be allowed to become chronic.

When a child comes home, it is important for parents to make it clear this is a temporary arrangement during which every member of the family works together to bring about change, encourage growth. Margo told me, "Nancy came home after breaking up with her boyfriend. She was like a wounded animal, and we left her alone, didn't say anything about the good job she'd left or mention future plans. Then, something very minor happened. We were sitting at dinner and Nancy said, 'We don't have pot roast anymore.' I started to explain that Ben and I rarely if ever ate meat anymore, and then I realized she hadn't wanted anything to be different—just the same as when she was a little girl. I told her we were older and had changed our eating habits, and it was time for her to do some growing and changing, too; she wasn't our little girl anymore. She was shocked and angry, but within two months we'd helped her find an apartment and go back to her old job."

At the end of the play *Alone Together,* the audience applauded loudly when old Dad, encouraged by a son to feel guilty and responsible for the reasons this son remained at home, finally said, "I owe you zilch. It's your package now." Nothing could be more damaging to the maturation process than to allow a grown child to blame us for everything and spend his or her life sucking a thumb in a corner.

There are circumstances in which coming back home can work out very well. Bob and Kate have a big house and they want to stay there. Their daughter Angela is divorced with two school-age children. Kate loved being a mother—she's delighted to have two kids around the house, and Bob has the boys he never had. Angela has a good job and pays her way. She hates cooking but doesn't mind cleaning, so she and her mother share the work according to what they prefer doing. Nobody seems to get in anybody else's way. There are many such situations—two-family houses, for example, where two generations can live in relative harmony.

But there are also many situations in which the tensions are almost unbearable. Joe and Fran had to live with his family while they were negotiating a government mortgage for a house. There was endless paperwork, complications of all kinds. Grandma and Grandpa didn't approve of anything Joe and Fran were doing with their two children. Fran was having a fit because Grandma kept giving the children candy, cake, and soda. The living quarters were cramped; there were constant screaming fights about even the most trivial details of daily living. The relief of all three generations when the house was finally available was very great. For many families, living together, even if unavoidable, can be a seriously destructive experience.

I think we have to be very clear about how we feel. If we enjoy the return of children, then we can live with the inevitable adjustments and problems. But the more we may be happy about the arrangement the more we need to ask ourselves if our welcome is helpful to our child.

Millie told me, "Deborah went to college, wasn't happy there at all, and asked to come back home in the middle of her second year. We told her she could, but only on our terms. If she came home, she would have to be willing to see a therapist to try to find out what was happening to her, and that if she didn't continue college, she'd have to get some kind of a job. She started therapy and worked as a saleslady in a dress shop for about a year. It wasn't easy on any of us, but we felt we were helping her to grow up, not offering her a comfortable nest where she could be a little girl again. It must have worked—she finally met a young man and they were married. She now works part-time and is back at college."

It isn't always that easy. Deborah accepted her parents' terms; some young people can't seem to do it. Sometimes parents have to seek help for themselves in order to make constructive decisions. Maxine, a sixty-seven-year-old widow, became desperate when her daughter, almost forty and an alcoholic, simply refused to leave her apartment. She told me, "It almost killed me, but I was advised, finally, after trying everything else, to change the lock on the door, and pack my daughter's clothes and force her to leave. My brother had to use physical force to get her out. I gave her the names and addresses of people and places ready to help her, and I didn't hear a word for three months of hell. Then she called and she had actually contacted some of the people I had told her about. She was living in a special residence and going to AA [Alcoholics Anonymous] meetings every night. A year later she moved to another city and another protected environment, and she went to work there. Now she has a boyfriend, and we see each other about twice a year. If I hadn't gotten the courage to make her go, I'm sure she'd still be here, drinking herself to death."

There may be real needs and satisfactions in sharing one household. Grandma loves being with the children and daughter wants a career; a widowed mother is delighted to have the company of a grown child; family economics make living together a necessity. What we need to keep in mind is that we are *not* returning to an earlier time; our roles *must* be different. Both parents and children need freedom and autonomy, privacy and responsible cooperation—and to treat *each other* as adults.

The danger of overromanticizing occurs in so many areas. If a widowed mother is going to come to live with her children, they may be thrilled at the outset. Now Mom can go to work knowing someone will be home when the kids come home from school; Grandma loves to cook— what a relief; Mom hates it. The son-in-law is very fond of Grandma and the children are thrilled; they foresee endless games of cards and Monopoly and a much more lax discipline from Grandma about staying up late and watching TV when parents are out.

All this comes to pass; what a wonderful solution! But as Grandma begins to recover from mourning the death of her husband, she may resent being expected to serve as the family domestic. She announces she's taking a part-time job two mornings a week; she joins a bridge club. The children become increasingly difficult to discipline and her son-in-law begins complaining about her combing her hair over the sink and leaving long stands of gray hair for him to clean up.

From the beginning—whether we are involved in a visit or in living together—we need to face the realities we know exist in every relationship. We need to sit down together and make some rules; we need to examine where compromises are necessary; we need to communicate about our feelings. We need to try to anticipate events, but also be ready to be surprised and to deal with the unexpected.

Sometimes we *act* as if we are disturbed about a child's return home or never leaving, but are unconsciously giving a completely different message. A couple came to visit us and spent most of the evening complaining bitterly about the fact that three sons, all grown and working, were living at home and didn't want to leave. Elinor, with a full-time job, was doing all the shopping, cooking, and cleaning. She said she came home tired and resentful, and "the boys just expect me to do everything, even their laundry." When we suggested she could just *stop* doing everything, she sighed and said it was hopeless. After making many suggestions about what they could do, Larry and I began to realize that the truth was they really wanted their sons to stay at home. George was on the road three or four nights a week, and Elinor didn't like being alone; at the same time their marriage seemed to have lost its luster and we began to get the feeling that neither of them wanted to be alone all the time with the other. "I speak to them every week about finding their own apartments, but it goes in one ear and out the other," Elinor said, sighing. But we realized after awhile from her tone of voice that she didn't really mean it.

A father with two daughters still at home said, "We raised them wrong—we made life too easy for them." When I saw him with his daughters, I sensed the most subtle and unconscious seductiveness on his part; they made him feel young and handsome—they adored him. If they couldn't leave home, Daddy was part of the problem.

There is one problem many of us have as parents that started many long years ago when our children reached adolescence. We tended to be so frightened of allowing them to make the necessary mistakes they needed to make in order to grow up that we were far too prone to lecture them at length about our attitudes, all of which they knew perfectly well and had for a long time. Much of their rebellion, their refusal to talk to us, stemmed from the fact that *we* did all the talking, that we never really learned to listen. If we haven't developed this skill, we surely ought to begin, now. It means really hearing what a grown child is saying; it means not interrupting or changing the subject; it means listening to the feelings behind the words. Anxiety is what usually interferes with this process—we want so much to help our children avoid problems, even though we surely ought to know that we grew the most through our mistakes, through painful experiences.

One of the most difficult challenges to any parent, at any time, is standing by while a child is in pain. Sometimes this is exactly what is called for. Jack told me, "My daughter is the light of my life—I adore her. When she married a man I didn't like, I was mortified. She was a college graduate, he was part owner in a trucking business. She was sweet and gentle; he was rough and tough. I figured I'd been right when they began to have marital problems, and I wanted to jump in with both feet, carry Lauri off and bring her home, every time she cried over the phone. My wife told me to mind my own business—Lauri had to grow up and not expect Daddy to get her out of every scrape—that every young couple has adjustments to work out. My wife was right. They *did* work things out and now they've been married seven years and I have two grandchildren and Charlie turned out to be a terrific husband and father."

Allowing pain, allowing suffering, is one of the ways in

which we help our children mature in their own way, in their own time. We don't stand by in the face of any genuine danger or abuse, of course, but as I think back to the early years of my marriage, if my parents had come running every time I cried, every time Larry and I faced a crisis, I could never have grown up, our marriage would never have had a chance to change and mature.

It's exceedingly difficult to watch our grown children hit the same "potholes" we did. Peggy told me, "When we visit Sam and Liz, I see the same things happening to them that happened to Doug and me in the early years. I see my daughter Liz clinging too much, needing constant reassurance that Sam loves her. I see the same impatience in Sam's face as in Doug's, the same restlessness to have some space, some freedom. I want to tell them both what a mistake they are making in acting out roles that might destroy their love for each other, but I try to keep my mouth shut. Doug and I went through hell, but we worked it out. Do they need to go through the same suffering? Or should we try to save them?"

I guess the answer is to wait until asked! A time may come when one or both of them may ask for some advice. And even then, probably the best approach is to suggest some marriage counseling. If we start to tell them everything that happened to us, we sidestep the issue—*them*. And in the long run, too much intimacy at a time of crisis between children and parents and in-laws may create later discomfort.

A question we all ponder is what shall we do when we feel very strongly about something an adult child is doing. One grandparent is deeply disturbed because her daughter-in-law believes in spankings as a form of punishment; another parent worries greatly about a son who smokes a pack of cigarettes every day. Most of us know that criticizing and nagging gets us nowhere—what to do? In the case of the grandmother, I suggested that she say nothing about her daughter-in-law's disciplinary philosophy at the moment, but to try to talk to her daughter-in-law about her childhood, how she was treated, what she remembers, how she felt when she was punished. Rather than being critical, she might try to support Beatrice on the things she's doing right. The more Beatrice can feel approval and acceptance the more open she will be to suggestions later on—maybe a book or two that expresses a wiser point of view. Becoming friends is really the first step to being able to talk. As long as her daughter-in-law feels threatened by disapproval she will surely not be open to changing.

There are, of course, exceptions. Anyone—including a grandparent—who becomes aware that a child is being neglected or abused is required to notify a professional or law-enforcement agency that can help. In one case, Judith went to visit her grandchildren in Vermont and discovered that her son-in-law had deserted his family, that her daughter apparently had had a breakdown and was not taking care of the children. They were seriously malnourished, not dressed properly for the cold, and not being sent to school. Situations like that call for responsible citizenship, whatever one's relationship may be to the children's parents.

Usually, however, the things we differ about are not of that great a magnitude. A friend was going to visit her son and daughter-in-law for two weeks. While she considered these adult children good, kind, loving parents, there were many things about their life-style that drove her crazy. I suggested that she say what was on her mind, give her opinion, in a pleasant tone of voice—and then shut up about it. There is no reason we shouldn't say how we feel, but every reason for not belaboring the point. Our children hear us; we have to respect their way of life. This same friend now tells me, "The system works like a charm: I say what I think without making any demands, and without repeating myself, and every time I visit, it is easier for us to have real discussions of all kinds of issues."

A woman wrote me a letter asking for advice. Her daughter was about to get married and she and her husband felt it would be a disaster—that the man was a charming psychopath who would never settle down and take any serious responsibility for the marriage; they knew he had been married before, had been thrown out by his first wife for "fooling around," and that he was months behind on child support. Nothing they said to their daughter had any effect on her, and the mother wanted to know if I thought she and her husband should refuse to attend the wedding. My answer was that they should attend the wedding, and simply *be there,* be available, if the crash came. There are many times in the course of being parents when all we can do is be present to pick up the pieces. At that point we may be able to be more influential in helping a grown child seek professional help in examining repeated self-destructive behavior.

There is a fact of life that frequently complicates our relationship with our adult children; they will be our *children* no matter how old they are—and no matter how respectfully we may treat them, they still feel infantilized by us, at least to some degree. It is a simple fact of our mutual history—we remember them as our babies, and they remember being our babies. If someone else says, "You better wear a sweater—it's gotten chilly out," they can listen and make a decision without stress. If a mother says the same thing, there is the immediate feeling "She's still treating me like a baby," and listening becomes impossible.

What began when our children became adolescents and first rebelled in order to separate themselves from us and grow up, continues to a lesser extent all through life. Children almost always continue to need to make it clear to their parents that they are adults. We should know—we did it with our parents and may still be doing it in our sixties and seventies! A friend called me one day (she was about forty) to tell me that her mother (sixty-seven) had called her to tell her to be sure to dress warmly, it was cold out. As my friend began to protest being infantilized, her mother laughed and said, "I guess I know what you mean; Grandma [eighty-seven] just called and told me to wear a sweater!"

Sometimes, quite unconsciously, our children encourage us to accept outmoded roles. The greatest service we can do for our children is to not rise to the bait. They may on occasion feel like becoming our babies again; that was comfortable—being dependent—especially if life is hard and challenges are difficult. And it's so easy for us to return to that role, which maybe we miss some of the time. Or an adult child is unsure about something he or she is about to do, and tries every which way to get into a fight with us about it! They really want to test their own thoughts, and they probably think what they are about to do is wrong, so they try to force us into being the heavies—another old pattern of childhood. We can surely discuss the questions they raise, but we have to watch out for becoming the ones who will be blamed for influencing them too much, giving bad advice, overpowering them if we give very strong opinions about how we feel. Better to talk about alternatives, give both sides of an issue, see to it that the child is the one who makes the final decision.

Much the same thing can happen between siblings. Kevin said, "At Thanksgiving dinner Roy starts this big discussion with me about what kind of car to buy. Since I think I know a lot about the subject, I give him my opinion in no uncertain terms. All of a sudden, I realize we're having a fight, like we had when he was fourteen! He trapped me into making a decision for him, so I could be the fall guy if it turned out badly! I suggested he make up his own mind and I turned on the TV so we could watch the football game together."

When feelings of infantilization occur on either side, we need to talk about them. We need to let our children know we admire and respect them but that it is impossible to neutralize the parent-child roles altogether. We need to allow them to tell us when we make them feel infantilized. We better be able to make this an open issue because the day will come, if it hasn't already, when the tables turn, and they make *us* feel incompetent and childish! The closer the relationship is, the more likely there will be some conflict around this issue, but talking about it honestly—even being able to laugh about it—helps a great deal.

Respect for oneself and one's offspring is often the key to good relationships. One woman told me, "My children have drifted away from me. They moved far away, they're not married, there are no grandchildren. I have the feeling I never had any children!" I asked a number of people for their reaction to that statement. Some said she ought to try to re-establish a stronger connection by going to visit her children—let them know she cares about them and would not try to tell them how to live their lives—thus allaying fears that might have been the children's reason for separating themselves. Some said she should have patience and let them do some growing, after which they would seek her out again. *Everyone* agreed on one point: she needed to do more with her own life; that the happier and more fulfilled she could become, the less she would feel so neglected, and the more likely it would be that her children might want to see her.

An even more bitter comment, from a woman who seemed unable to adjust to widowhood or go on with a life of her own, was, "Middle-class liberated children have little respect or tolerance for their parents." It seemed to me she had little or no respect for herself, and some change in her attitudes and behavior would probably have to precede a change in her children.

We need to remember that it is not necessary to agree with our children about everything, and if their opinions are very different from ours it doesn't mean we have failed as parents. As a matter of fact it may mean we've done a good job of teaching them to think for themselves. Life is different for them, circumstances change. Neither do we have to share everything with our children nor encourage them to confide in us about every detail of their lives.

It was quite evident to me that those parents who reported the most positive relationships with adult children were also indicating that they admired and respected their children. Asked what kind of relationships she had with her grown children, one mother responded, "My relationships with my son and daughter are terrific, I think. (Most of the time.) My daughter and I are loyal friends and when the occasions arise, valued companions. I don't often have to snap back into the role of mom. My son and I are also fond friends, but appropriately distanced—as mother and son must be if the son is to be free to focus on his own wife and household. I feel I have both kids' affection and even, startlingly, their admiration at times. As they have mine."

Letting go is another important aspect of good relationships, and it takes many different forms. We need to be prepared *not* to be hurt when our children insist on separating themselves from us. Fran told me, "Our daughter Beth was deserted by her husband and left with two small children. We wanted her to come home for Thanksgiving or Christmas. We felt she would need the comfort of her parents. Instead she said that would be the worst thing she could do. She knew she'd just fall apart. She needed to be alone, work things out, see a therapist. We felt so rejected! Not to be allowed to help—it was a terrible time. Thanksgiving was dreadful, and then I decided I couldn't live through the same thing at Christmas. I invited a whole lot of friends, and it was much better. Parents can suffer from having to let go, no matter how old a child is."

A man who told me he and his wife had an excellent relationship with their grown children added, "We don't depend on them for our satisfactions and fulfillment. We just love them, help them when we can, enjoy being with them." His words and his tone described a genuine letting go, which made a close relationship more possible.

Because of the feelings of infantilization between parent and adult child, we need to accept the fact that our children will choose other older people as their role models and confidantes. I had lunch one day with a charming and talented young woman of about thirty. I'd known her mother first, and thought she was a sensational lady. Chris told me at once that "there are always problems between mothers and daughters" and proceeded to give me quite a different picture of her mother. Her mother and I are very much alike, have the same values, probably react in very similar ways to our children, but Chris seemed to feel free to confide all her problems to me in a way she couldn't with her own mother. It hurts a little at first when we realize that there are other people in our children's lives with whom they can talk far more freely than with us, but I think we ought to see it as a plus; they are exercising their right to grow up and away from parental controls.

I think it helps to establish good relations with adult children if we try to remember some of our own experiences, especially when we were first married and had to relate to in-laws. A young woman who heard I was writing about people my own age, said, "I hope you're not going to blame us for all the problems we have with your generation." She was having a very rough time with her mother-in-law, who was exceedingly critical of how she was raising her child, and who suggested to her husband that he should keep an eye on her because she might be running around with other men. Carol was deeply hurt and very angry. Her mother-in-law called them every single day, asked all kinds of questions about their finances, and managed to fight with her son every time they were together. It seemed clear to me that Carol was describing an extremely neurotic woman who could not let go of her son, and saw his wife as a threat to her power and control over him. Carol wanted to know if she could tell her mother-in-law how she felt, and I told her that if it would make her feel better, to go ahead, but not to expect to accomplish anything—that some situations are just too difficult to change. The important thing was for her and her husband Frank not to allow his mother to come between them—they needed to present a united front and not allow her to "win."

It's very easy to sabotage a new marriage; a young couple is so full of self-doubts, so inexperienced in the art of learning to live together, that any challenge can cause a major problem. At one point in the second or third year of our marriage, Larry's mother suggested that he go to teach at a college some distance from New York, and that I go live with my parents and go to graduate school. When I found out that Larry hadn't told her this was a terrible idea and we would never consider such a separation, I became a screaming maniac; he didn't love me if he couldn't stand up to his mother. I was ready for a divorce if he didn't tell her off. He never did, and I eventually calmed down, but looking back, almost forty years later, I understand the problem was not my mother-in-law but our youth and insecurity. Larry couldn't talk back to his mother, and I was too insecure to treat her suggestion as a silly comment to be ignored.

We have the greater responsibility for not coming between a husband and a wife because presumably we are older and wiser! We need to realize that if we comment to a son that his wife is a lousy housekeeper, we are coming between them; that if we say to a daughter, "It's a damn shame Jed doesn't seem to care about making more money," we may very well be adding fuel to a problem the young couple is already wrestling with.

There are, of course, those occasions when we are convinced—and sometimes rightly—that our son has married a bitch or a daughter has married a bum. *Nothing has ever been gained by expressing such feelings!* If we can stand by with love, we can be there if a disaster occurs; or we may discover, over the years, that we were not seeing the positive qualities our child saw in the choice of a spouse.

I'm sure it will shock no one if I suggest that both we and our children have lived through plenty of crises with each other, as they were growing up. For most of us there is still a lot of "old business" that has never been resolved. A daughter feels we were partial to her brother; a son has never forgiven his father for not letting him go to ballet school; rather than remembering all the times when we were models of constraint, all an adult child can seem to remember about family discipline is the times we were very unfair! We feel some guilts; so do our children. There are unresolved conflicts, hurt feelings. All of these can seriously interfere with a comfortable and loving relationship with adult children.

We are a generation of parents only too happy to be taken on guilt trips! After all, we were the first generation to feel guilty as young parents. We became parents when the trend in psychology was to emphasize environment over all else. If our kids were doing wonderfully we figured it was just dumb luck; if they had problems, it was usually Mom's fault. Sometime during the 1950s I checked through a conference program of the American Psychological Association and found at least twenty meetings about the physical and emotional diseases being laid at mothers' doorsteps—asthma, ulcers, nightmares, delinquency—on and on. The next generation of parents got off much easier; genetics came back into the picture—fathers were thought to have some bearing in childraising! My first book,* published in 1965, contained a chapter entitled "The Guilty Parent and How He Grew." As I met with groups of parents back then, the most common beginning to any discussion was, "I know I must be doing something wrong." Simple answers are always appealing, and the less we knew the more sure we were. With increasing knowledge of genetic factors, personality differences, chemical imbalances that influence behavior, there is at least some less likelihood that younger parents will blame themselves as much as we did, but for us it is a permanent scar on the psyche.

When my husband and I went into therapy, we learned a great many things about our childhood which definitely reflected parental attitudes and behavior. But we never told our parents what we had found out! Our children, far more liberated—and encouraged by our tendency toward "mea culpa"—are not as reticent. Many of us have listened to the mistakes we made as parents. Although our children may have an understanding and forgiving nature, it isn't always easy to listen to our failings! It was also not easy to discover that our children often view signs of their maturation and strength of character and courage as due entirely to good therapists!

There have been many times, as our daughter has explored her own inner life, when the things she told us were painful to hear. Sometimes it seems that when we were trying the hardest we did the dumbest things. But we knew we had done the best we could—and she knew this too— and we tried hard to remember all the things we'd blamed

*Eda LeShan, *How to Survive Parenthood* (New York: Random House, 1965).

our own parents for, also things that had been beyond their control. All we can do is acknowledge that no matter how much you love a child, each generation brings its own inevitable shortcomings, limitations, to the job of being a parent. By talking about all this openly, no old sores are allowed to fester—and one of the happiest outcomes is that both adult children and their parents can work together to undo some old mistakes with the coming of grandchildren. I am so much wiser with my granddaughter than I was with my daughter! As a young mother, I found it very difficult to allow her to have her unhappy feelings; if she was unhappy, it meant I was failing as a mother. Both she and I rejoice together when her daughter, my grandchild, encouraged by both of us, is able to express her feelings, and we are ready to share them with her. When she says, "I feel angry and sad," I can now say, "Oh, I know, it feels terrible." As a young mother, I said really dumb things like, "There's no reason to feel that way."

As parents we all have real regrets, but regret is different from guilt. We surely regret the mistakes we made, but we did the best we could in terms of our own growth. A friend said, "I feel so guilty. I never listened to what my kids really wanted. I was a lousy mother." The truth is that she did dream too much about how her children would be successful—the boy would go to Harvard and be a doctor, the daughter would marry a prince and raise lots of gorgeous grandchildren. It is also true that her children took totally different paths. But what she doesn't include in her self-criticism is that they felt loved enough to challenge her and to rebel and that they are now loving and creative people making the most of their lives.

When our normal human failings may have helped to

create some real problems, we need to remind ourselves that every generation of children has problems growing up, that most of us tried harder than any earlier generation of parents, and that it is now time to make it clear we will not let a child lay his or her problems at our door. We can help them get help, but we are not ashamed—we did the best we could.

Sometimes we feel guilty about the things we cannot do now for our children, thinking that they will be lost without our help. At one point my daughter, having the flu, told me on the phone, "Oh, god, how I wish I had some of your homemade chicken soup!" I was miserable all day because I was too far away to help her. When I called her the same evening and said that next time I visited I would fill her freezer with soup, she replied, "Oh, that's okay, I felt much better this evening and we went out for hot dogs!"

A major problem is the tendency to romanticize all family relationships, as if there really could be times of perfect accord, perfect happiness. True, we come close once in awhile but not often. We plan for weeks about meeting our teenage grandchildren at the airport; it's going to be the best time they've ever had. It turns out Liz is brooding over a lost love and nothing pleases her, and Dick argues politics with Grandpa all day long in a shrill and unpleasant voice. We are planning the biggest and best Thanksgiving reunion of the past ten years—even aunts and uncles and cousins—and we shop and cook and make sleeping arrangements, and cancel every part of our normal lives, and then after three or four hours we think we will scream if one more child spills food on the floor or breaks another cup. Our son-in-law boasts so endlessly about his accomplishments that we have the feeling our oldest son is going to haul off and sock him, and our daughter and our daughter-in-law get into a raging argument about discipline. There is still the good dinner and much merriment—and a great deal of genuine love and affection, but it wasn't perfect, and we feel guilty that we are glad when it is over.

A friend of mine sends out a photocopied Christmas letter each year. One year it included all the terrific accomplishments of her son who was in law school and her daughter the college professor, and her grandson the mathematical genius and her granddaughter, a ballerina at eight. Everything was so wonderful! There was nothing at all in her letter about her back trouble or her lonely widowhood or her fear of retirement. About two weeks after the Christmas holidays, she wrote:

Oh, Eda, what a relief! I believe there is still a mouldering turkey leg stinking up the refrigerator, which I must try to locate, but the peace and quiet are wonderful. There was so much noise, so much energy, so much competing for my approval, I went to bed a basket case every night. Thank god none of them live close enough to visit too often!

I was relieved to discover that at least she wasn't deluding *herself!* Another example of a Christmas letter—this from my friend Helen:

Dennis and his lovely young wife, Annamae, have moved to Denver, where he will be the vice president in a large firm manufacturing software. Margaret has just graduated from a master's program, summa cum laude, and is thinking about going on for her Ph.D. Dan and I went on a terrific safari trip

and brought back glorious pictures of the animals we saw. We
will all be together for Xmas for the first time in many years.

Now, I happen to know that Annamae is black, and this
is the first Christmas together because it's taken that long
for Dan and Helen to accept their son's wife. I also happen
to know that Margaret is thirty-five, and spent several years
in a mental hospital during her late teens. She is still vulnerable and delicate, although a brilliant student. The safari was the reconciliation after a period during which
Helen found out Dan was having an affair.

Does this all sound exaggerated? You *know* it isn't! Everything in the letter is true, everything I know is true.
Every family has joys and terrors, successes and failures,
pain and pleasure. We shouldn't be obliged to tell the
whole truth to friends or relatives; but neither should we
try to fool ourselves. There are wonderful times of loving
and caring, and there are also inevitable stresses and strains.

Somehow holiday family gatherings seem to be a kind of
metaphor for the danger of too many romantic illusions
about family life.

I am not cynical about family life, but I think people of
our generation were sold a bill of goods when we were
young that was romantic nonsense, and we've had to spend
most of our adult lives getting over it. There are, surely,
wonderful moments of closeness with those we love; we
miss them when we don't see them; we rejoice in knowing
there are some very special people in our lives that create a
warm circle of love. *But that's only half the story.* The other
half was the healthy comment of one grandmother who
said, "The *second* happiest day is when the family arrives!"
Little kids wear us out; old emotional business from early

childhood still creates rivalries among our grown children; we never will become fond of some relative, no matter how hard we try. That is just as much a reality as the moment of absolute joy when we first see a newborn grandchild, or when that same child, six or seven years later, spontaneously throws his or her arms about us, and says "I love you!" Or the way a family gathers to comfort each other when some tragedy occurs and we feel enclosed in the warm circle of loving and caring. All true—all mixed—the human condition.

We are sometimes inclined to feel that our children's childhood is now over, and we will all meet as mature adults. We are therefore greatly shocked when we witness an old familiar and very intense rivalry between a son and a daughter at the Christmas brunch; we had also forgotten how noisy and sloppy kids can be, and what ever made us think our grandchildren would be better behaved after the Christmas presents have been opened than our children were? And Grandpa can't stand the racket and retreats to his workshop, avoiding all the tensions—just as he did when he was a young father.

There are ways to alleviate holiday problems beyond readying ourselves for imperfection! In their article in *Modern Maturity* (Dec./Jan. 1984), Caroline Bird and Howard Newberger, Ph.D., made a sound suggestion that it's a good idea not to greet a son at the door with a long list of household chores that you've been saving for him! My mother used to do that, at a country home, and it used to drive her crazy when Larry would head straight for the hammock for a long nap! In general, we will do much better if we don't start off with an agenda, "Why haven't you called me for six weeks? This is the first year the children didn't send me a card for my birthday."

It works both ways. The authors also suggest we say in advance, to a son or daughter, "I know you're eager to call your friends and make dates to see them, but could that wait until after Christmas dinner?"

Often we have an agenda that interferes with good family feelings when we are the guests in our childrens' homes. We need to prepare ourselves ahead of time to adjust to, and accept, their life-style, not to start the holiday with comments like "It looks like you haven't cleaned that stove in years!" Or, "How can you ever find anything in that refrigerator?" (I know about these sins because I committed them!)

On holidays together, we all need to respect each other's autonomy and privacy. One woman said to me, "The secret of a happy Thanksgiving with the children is *overlooking!*"

Now on to a more serious matter: the question of financial aid, one of the most difficult aspects of our relationship to our grown children.

Milton, at sixty-nine, told me, "All right; I can live with the arthritic knee that took me out of the running [marathons] and I'm getting used to being almost bald, and I could make the best of having less energy than I used to, but I did *not* think I would have to send my daughter to graduate school and pay for my grandchildren's nursery school, and find them an apartment and pay the rent because some lousy psychopath ran out on her!" One real estate broker commented to me, "There wouldn't be many young families buying houses or co-ops if it wasn't for Mama and Papa!"

Some of us are too poor to ever consider the issue that young adults must make their own way and not become unrealistically dependent on our largesse; some of us give a little, some a lot. We need to be aware of some hazards if we are helping quite substantially, and that is that we need to do so without any strings attached. If we loan money so a son-in-law can go to law school, and he later finds out he hates it, we are more than likely to feel betrayed. If we help to make a down payment on a house, and then see that no one is mowing the lawn or painting the trim, it makes us mad. If we contribute some money toward the purchase of a car, and then find it filthy inside and dented on the outside, we have some second thoughts about our generosity. I know of no way around this problem except to give nothing unless we can do so without any expectations, without any demands, spoken or unspoken. I think we need to say to ourselves, "I want to do this because it will make me feel good, even if they don't say 'thank you!'"

One thing seems quite clear to me; no matter how needy a child or children may be financially, we do no favor for them, and certainly not for ourselves, if we allow them to remain in any way our *little* children. Just as soon as we find ourselves sacrificing our lives to theirs, we are in big trouble. Paula told me, "My husband and I had saved for years for a trip around the world. When our daughter was divorced we gave up the trip, bought her a car, paid for babysitters and her tuition at a computer school. Eventually it began to poison our relationship; we were resentful. There were other alternatives for her to get help—fighting for alimony, Aid to Dependent Children—we gave up our dream and didn't help her to face reality." Giving more than we can—more than we want to—isn't good for the younger or the older generation.

It is extremely difficult to protect our own needs even in crisis situations. If the young family gets into very serious debt—even goes bankrupt—any financial help we give should be done through a professional counselor—someone in a bank, a lawyer, a financial adviser—with clear expectations that certain rules must be followed. Also, if we are going to be paid back for a loan at an agreed-upon rate per month, it is wise to have all the negotiations handled by a professional outsider such as a bank. The more businesslike and impersonal such arrangements are, the less they can cause complications in the relationship.

There are, of course, emergencies in which we want to help even if it means some personal sacrifice. This is particularly true when a daughter is divorced and has custody of young children. We may want to help in such cases, paying for her to go to school or get training for a job, paying for sitters. However, several people told me that sometimes, if parents respond too quickly and too generously, the divorced father feels free to ignore his financial obligations to his family, and that parents ought not to step in until such issues are settled in the divorce courts. Otherwise it may set up a most unrealistic pattern that cannot be maintained for a long period of time.

One way to be of help without infantilizing our children, or demanding gratitude for everything we do, is a special and different version of the Living Will, which ordinarily is a document stating one's wish not to be kept alive by machines (see pages 347–48). This version refers to giving something to a child before we die.

A young woman who inherited a sizable legacy from her grandmother told me, "Grandma never gave me anything until she was dead! Now there's no way I can thank her." I believe in this kind of Living Will. I've known so many cases where people hold on to everything they've got, spending as little as possible on themselves or their children

or grandchildren, taking what seems to me a strange pleasure in the idea that nobody is going to get what's theirs
until they're dead. I think that's really crazy. If we happen
to have certain assets that we don't need and that our children will inherit when we die, it seems far more sensible to
give them these things right now. Maybe we have some
real estate that we don't want to sell because it will appreciate in value, but we don't need this resource in planning for
our own old age. Maybe we have some valuable antiques
that we can't take with us into a small apartment and
which we can give to our children to keep or sell as they
wish. Maybe we happen to have some good jewelry—more
of it than we will ever need or use again. My attitude
toward giving things while I'm alive is that it means I can
have the pleasure of seeing my daughter enjoy certain
things; if she got them after I died, I'd never see her joy, or
the ways in which these things might make life easier for
her. We must, of course, be careful that we keep what we
need so as never to have to become dependent, but beyond
that, I remind myself I won't be around to see any pleasure
I may bestow on others when my will is read *after* my
death!

If we are lucky enough to have valuable extra resources,
that's nice. But a Living Will may be greatly appreciated
with the giving of an old Persian carpet we don't need
anymore, or a good set of tools that are just sitting in the
garage or basement, or old family picture albums, or some
paintings by a talented relative. Maybe we inherited a
lovely Victorian pin from a grandmother and have cherished it since it was left to us at our mother's death. Our
mother never knew how we loved having it; we can have
the pleasure of seeing a daughter thrilled to have it—before we die.

Another aspect of financial or economic relations may be the situation where a parent and a child work together. A father gets anxious when he sees a son want to assume more and more power in the running of a family business; a daughter feels she's getting less pay and fewer good cases than others of her age and experience in her father's law firm. Sometimes the adult child feels hemmed in; imprisoned without enough challenge because the parent isn't ready to see how mature he is. Sometimes parents find it very hard to see a child doing a better job, improving business, showing greater skills—having had a better education, more up-to-date training. A physician who took his son into his practice commented, "If John tells me about one more new drug or new machine that I don't know about, I'm going to kick him out on his rear!" It isn't easy to see our children exceed us in knowledge and skills, and it isn't easy to be an ambitious, talented young person who feels he or she is being held back because of a power struggle with a parent.

When such conflicts occur, they can sometimes be worked out through candid, open, and honest discussion. When they can't, the younger person needs to look elsewhere, or the parent may decide this is a good time to retire if he or she can do so without regrets. One of the problems in trying to work together is that it may bring about a reversal of roles when the parent, especially, is not ready. A father wants the new sign—WHITMORE AND SON—to mean just that and not that a son is going to take over and become the boss!

One father said, "I resent my children telling me what to do, how to live my life, as much as they resented my doing that to them when they were children. Our generation got a double dose; we were ordered around by our parents, now we get ordered around by our children. It needs some frank conversation to clear the air." A sixty-eight-year-old mother wrote: "My son is overattentive. If anything he's rushing me to make changes in my life that I'm not ready to make. He writes me, 'We want you to move out here because as you get older, you will need our help.'"

Often when it is our lives that are changing, it is the children who need to make an adjustment. Alice told me, "Two years after I was widowed, I met a wonderful man and we were married. I was shocked when my daughter said she preferred not to come for Christmas with her family because 'things would be too strange.' Of course, I understood she was still missing her father, but I had to make it clear to her that she would have to deal with that feeling of strangeness because I was happy; I wanted her family to be part of my life, but not at the expense of my new marriage. Well, it took time—a couple of years—but since her children, especially, are crazy about the new grandpa, she says she's glad I made her face reality."

It is just as hard for our children to see us in new roles as it is for us to adjust to their new life-styles. It is hard for them to realize and accept that we are older; when we retire, they may experience at least unconscious feelings of abandonment. We took care of them for so long—now we seem focused on taking care of ourselves. It frightens them if we get sick. It may anger them if we say we want to have a good time and not have to take care of anybody else, at last. They feel rejected if we decide to move to a warmer climate, hundreds of miles away. If we sense discomfort or anger in response to our plans, we need to talk about it, try to help our children express their real feelings.

Since a great many of us are now dealing with elderly

parents who did not make any plans for their old age, we naturally worry a good deal about how our children will treat us when we are very old. If we have any brains in our heads, we are making plans for a very different outcome in our lives than in our parents', if they are among those who just postponed any thoughts about old age until it happened. But even before we begin to feel really old, the question of the future does come up in conversation; we test our children to see their reactions to our fears, our tentative plans, our wish not to be dependent on them. Selma, aged sixty-four, who looks forty-five, has a full-time job, and travels extensively, told her son, "As soon as I seem to be forgetting everything, and don't seem to know what I'm doing, take me out in the yard and shoot me." Her son took her elbow and said, "Come, Mother!"

When we discussed our fears of the time we might turn into senile vegetables with our daughter, she assured us her plans were all made. She was going to put Larry in a Sunfish with a salami and a canteen of water, push him off shore, and tell him to go to England, and she was going to put me in a room with all the records of the 1940s and 1950s musicals and keep me supplied with large boxes of candy. What a woman! She really knows us—it sounded perfect to both of us!

Sometimes it seems as if our children are ready to think of the abstract idea of our being ancient, but find it very difficult to accept the less dramatic, slower signs of the aging process. Many people described something that I have experienced: that is our children not seeing that we are getting older. A friend told me, "I think my daughter is surprised and disappointed that I get tired after a few hours of playing with my granddaughter. Unconsciously maybe she expected me to have the energy I had when I was playing with her, over thirty years ago." Some of this probably stems from lingering feelings of dependency and conscious or unconscious feelings that any signs of aging force one to become aware that one may lose one's parents.

It may be helpful at some point to bring these feelings out in the open, and let our children know *we* are not afraid to discuss such painful issues.

Most of all, if we are to enjoy an ongoing relationship with our children, and they with us, we need to be clear about our rights.

A woman who is a travel agent told me, "One thing I've learned, and that is we never get free of our obligations to our children and our parents. Almost every cancellation of a trip by people in their sixties and seventies is because of problems with old parents or adult children, not with themselves!"

We are a generation caught in the middle, who tried too hard to please our children and may very well now be trying to meet our elderly parents' needs. "When is our time?" is the refrain I heard over and over again as I talked with my contemporaries about getting older. We have to make it clear to our children that we have certain inalienable rights, that we will not sacrifice our own needs or interests or goals for grown children—that there are some limits to loving! Or should be if we care about ourselves.

~~~~~~

EIGHT

Grandchildren: A Special Kind of Love*

A WOMAN WHO DESCRIBED her relationship with her adult children as quite miserable added, "But of course it's entirely different with my grandchildren—they're great! They make me feel important and needed and wanted and loved."

While this may be an extreme response, I think it is not at all uncommon for grandparents to have a better time with grandchildren than with their own sons and daughters. And there is really a very simple reason; we have no past history with grandchildren! They don't remind us of our mistakes; they don't need to defend themselves against what our children view as infantilization. We are not in charge of discipline—of trying to help them to grow up to be decent, civilized, educated people. We have nothing against these goals, of course, but this time *we are not responsible*. What a relief! We are just for fun! In the speech mentioned earlier, Anne Morrow Lindbergh said, "Grandchildren are fascinating to listen to. You are not responsible

*The title of a book I wrote for children about their grandparents (New York: Macmillan, 1984).

for their upbringing and you are not trying to anticipate their future. They are delightful strangers who can trust you. You are the nonjudgmental adult who lets them be themselves. And who else can show them that life is full of meaning—even after seventy?"

Most of us may have waited longer than previous generations to become grandparents and we tend to have fewer grandchildren, but when they finally arrive the dream and the reality are one: it's wonderful!

It has always seemed to me that grandparents can play a special role which is quite different from that of the other adults in a child's life—parent, teacher, camp counselor, baseball coach, pediatrician, or minister. We are in no way responsible for raising this child, and that leaves us free to offer the most precious gift any child can ever have and needs most desperately—unconditional love. It is a kind of love which says in effect, "I don't care if you're not the smartest girl in arithmetic, or whether you're short or tall, or whether or not you're the boy with the lead in the class play, or just one of eight rabbits—it's just a miracle that you were born for me to love; you are my future, my immortality."

Having just discussed in the last chapter the many ways in which we feel we have failed with our children, or where they didn't live up to our dreams and expectations, it is important not to become trapped into the idea that grandchildren are a second chance! Son Jonathan was terrible at baseball—ah, here's a new opportunity to get his son started early; Lisa should have had dance classes—now we can provide them for her daughter; our children were sloppy, we'll teach our grandchildren to be neat. *Forget it!* This is *not* a chance to be parents over again. Partly because our getting out of the dream business is good for our grandchildren and partly because there are clear and special roles at each stage of life.

There is an old Spanish saying: "If someone boasts a lot about himself it must be because he has no grandmother." Children are buffeted on all sides by adults who must insist they do certain things and not do other things; when we were parents we knew it was our responsibility to teach our children to brush their teeth, not bite or hit other children, do their homework, not steal, get toilet trained, learn not to cheat or tell lies, dress neatly—all the thousands of tasks and limits that help a child become an adult. We've already done all that; now we can leave it to the parents. What we can do is *appreciate,* and with all the dos and don'ts of life, children hunger for the love that is without any claims.

The opposite of the kind of love I mean took place at a YMCA pool where I go to swim. When I came in I saw a tableau that I knew instantly was fraught with stress. A parent and a swimming instructor were standing at the edge of the pool with a little boy of about four, who was clinging to his mother's legs and trying very hard not to cry. The two adults with him were urging him to jump into the deep end of the pool, assuring him he'd done it before, there was nothing to be afraid of. Grandma was sitting in the bleachers, waiting. After about ten minutes of cajoling, bribing, and threatening, the instructor suddenly pushed the child into the water. A wild rage rose in me— something similar had once happened to me with a camp counselor who forced me to dive, so that I was never able to do so, ever again. Instead of minding my own business, I yelled at the instructor, assuring her that she had probably managed to accomplish two things; one, to make the kid hate swimming, and even more important, proved to him that Grandma would only love him if he could perform for her. The swimming instructor was equally furious with me, and said, "He's perfectly capable of doing it, and his grandmother is here from California just for the holidays." Who knows what fears had so frightened this little boy? Not measuring up to expectation—failing at this task which had suddenly taken on such monumental proportions? Who knows—but Grandma had lost an opportunity to give her grandson the gift of unconditional love. She might have said, "It's okay, I don't mind if you don't feel like jumping in today. I'm glad you have fun most of the time, and maybe I'll see you swim when you come to see me next summer." Chances are that with that kind of genuine acceptance the child might have been able to overcome whatever anxiety he was feeling, but that's beside the point. Grandma didn't love him just as he was.

If you have experienced unconditionl grandparent love yourself, you know it was something precious beyond words. I was a lucky child who got it, most of the time. Even when my maternal grandparents (in whose large brownstone house we lived for several years) chastised me, I knew I was totally lovable. My grandfather, especially (I was named after his first wife, who died when my mother was only four) made me feel like some kind of miracle. I saw my paternal grandparents less often, but when we did visit, I always had the feeling that I was something special. If you've known the feeling—and I hope you have—you know what it is you can do for your grandchildren.

Some time ago I read an article written by a grandmother, who was deeply hurt; her young grandson had been very rude and had told her she was old and wrinkled and looked funny. The article was about what rotten manners children have today, how no one teaches them good behavior. Because she was so hurt, she noted every other failing of this grandchild; he didn't say hello to an aunt who came to see him; he was nothing at all like his older sister, who was very polite and affectionate. She later wrote to her grandchild in the form of a story about a rude little boy who hurt his grandma's feelings; she was shocked when there was no apology; when she called, he didn't want to speak to her. This incident had led her to reflect on all the terrible things going on in the world, and to compare it to crime in the streets, undisciplined classrooms, and the general decay of society!

My feeling was that because of some profound sense of insecurity—perhaps unconscious anxieties about getting old—she had overreacted in a ridiculous fashion to normal childish behavior. A five-year-old who knows he is expected to have manners may, feeling ornery one day, refuse to perform. His initial comment may have been simply a naive statement of his observations, without any awareness of how hurt his grandmother would be. If she had laughed and said, "Well, I guess I am getting some new wrinkles all the time, but I can still tell stories and I can still take you to the circus, so I guess I'm not *too* old!" the incident might have passed almost unnoticed. As a matter of fact, she could easily have added, "Sometimes grandmas and grandpas get their feelings hurt when you say such things, but I guess you are too little to know how older people feel." A lesson in sensitivity instead of a war! There is no better way to begin the process of teaching good manners than to exemplify an ability to communicate feelings and to accept the fact that young children sometimes have impulses they can't yet control.

We ought not to get frightened by behavior that seems on the surface to be rude and unkind. Children can be too outspoken sometimes, and it is appropriate to let them know if we feel hurt. But it is equally important to understand that a child's behavior may not be directed at us at all, and is simply an expression of a perfectly normal phase of development. When a two- or three-year-old grandchild responds to our every gesture and entreaty with a loud and resounding No! he is not mad at us, he's just acting like a two-year-old. When a teenager refuses to come to a family gathering, instead of being angry and upset, we need to try to remember some of our and our children's feelings at the age of thirteen and fourteen, when we could just have *died* because grandparents still treated us as children. I clearly recall a time as a teenager when I refused to go to visit those adoring paternal grandparents. I was allowed to stay home and I spent the afternoon drowning in guilt, not understanding at all why I had behaved so terribly. I know now that I was struggling so hard to separate, to become a grown-up, and anything that made me feel like a child, such as a family reunion, was unbearable. Adolescents get over this stage as soon as they feel more confident. The twelve-year-old who never wants to visit you, and the fifteen-year-old who barely says hello and races for his room, is not unloving or intentionally rude or mean—just suffering the terrible anxieties of adolescence, and will return to love you more than ever in a year or two. As a matter of fact, if we can be patient with such occasional shenanigans, we can often find ourselves becoming the adored confidantes of grandchildren who feel more grown up talking to us than to their parents. One daughter who had rebelled with special vigor told her mother, "When Becky gets the way *I* was, I'm going to send her to live with you!"

I don't want to suggest that grandparents should encourage or tolerate behavior which is unacceptable; only that in as many cases as possible they let the parents deal with problems and that when it is really necessary to handle a situation they do so in a way that doesn't diminish a child's self-esteem. One example of this was a grandmother living in Florida, who told me about the problem she and her husband had encountered when their seven- and nine-year-old grandsons had come for a visit. They were noisy and rambunctious, soon tired of "quiet games," and liked best to run up and down the halls of the apartment building. They also made too much noise in the pool. The building was filled with retired older people who became increasingly annoyed. Lillian told me, "All we seemed to be doing was shushing them up, telling them to stop running, be quiet, behave. We knew that when we took them to the airport to go home, they were relieved to be leaving, and certainly didn't want to come back! We felt awful, and then Mike had an idea. He wrote them a letter saying that he and Grandma felt bad about getting angry, because young boys need to run around a lot and make noise. Next time they came to visit, we would take them to a public playground not too far away, and we'd go to swim in the ocean, where they could make as much noise as they wanted. My daughter told me the children loved Mike's letter and asked when they could visit again!" What Grandpa had communicated very effectively was that the children had behaved like children, and that in the future, provisions would be made for that natural condition.

As in all other human relationships, there are complications in being grandparents. Unless there is gross mistreatment of a child, we must not allow ourselves to interfere with parental discipline. Parents are in charge, and we do no service to our grandchildren if we undermine parents' authority. Children need to feel that their parents know what they are doing. Comments such as, "You're too easy on him, he should have been punished," or, "I don't know why you let him buy that junk with his allowance," or, "When did you get to be so strict?" infantilizes the parent and is confusing to the grandchild. If we feel the strong need to make some such comments, we should make them privately, but we should be sure it's important! Being seductive with grandchildren is another extremely unwise procedure: A secret whisper, "I know Mom doesn't think you should buy that game, but I'll give you the money for it," or, "I know you aren't supposed to have sweets before dinner, but I have a candy bar for you," are also not acceptable. We need to respect rules about diet, money, bedtime, amount of TV allowed (even if we know it's too much!). One grandmother admitted to me that she was going crazy watching her eight-year-old granddaughter, Patty, glued to the television set for several hours every day. She commented about it every time she visited, but it was clear nobody was interested in her opinion. When Grandma visited on her granddaughter's ninth birthday, Patty said, "Grandma, we have a special thing at school now. We have to write down all the programs we watch on television, and talk about which ones are good and which ones are no good. Next month we have to not watch television for one week, and then tell what happened." Sometimes outside forces can be far more effective than we can be!

There are special times, and they are fine, if we make it clear that special really means once in awhile. Hot dogs and soda and cotton candy are all right at the circus, and going to bed late on a holiday visit with grandparents is part of the fun of being together, but these need to be clearly defined as not everyday possibilities.

It is easy to be seduced by grandchildren. They may plead in tones of heartbreak that their parents are cruel to make them wait another year for a bicycle or a miniature piano; it is so pleasant to hear their cries of joy and gratitude if we supersede their parents and buy things parents can't afford or don't feel children should have. But this is really a form of sabotage against our children, and we need to control the natural impulse to please the grandchildren. There are plenty of acceptable ways in which we can satisfy our need to be loved in a special way ourselves. In fact, parents seem only too willing to tell us what to buy for birthdays and Christmas—presents they can't afford to buy themselves.

Relationships with grandchildren can easily be contaminated by old business that occurred long before they were born. Maybe both sets of grandparents were against the marriage of their children; maybe they disliked each other, never had anything in common. Maybe one set of grandparents is still full of anger because the other set didn't appreciate their wonderful child; maybe there were differences of race, religion, financial and social background that have made it very difficult for both sets of older parents to feel good about each other. But when grandchildren arrive, there is now a good reason to try to bury old problems—though it doesn't always happen. Rivalries begin over which set of grandparents buys the best presents; one grandma criticizes the other; two grandfathers hardly speak at Thanksgiving dinner—and the children who love them all can't understand what's going on. Old wounds still fester, and we poison the relationship with the grandchildren if we don't make up our minds to start a new chapter and try to at least be civilized to each other.

One thing grandchildren are very aware of is when a grandparent seems to prefer one grandchild over another. The truth is that we sometimes *have* such feelings, and they are better discussed than left to give pain. A grandparent can say, for example, "You must feel bad because I only took Paula on the trip. She's bigger and so it's easier for me. When you get to be her age, I'll be able to take you." Or to admit openly, "Maybe you think I make more of a fuss over Raymond than I do over you. I love you both very much, but he reminds me a lot of my brother who died when I was twelve. Ray looks like him, and it makes me feel good to see his nephew looking the way I remember Uncle Edward." Or, to do what parents need to do too—not to get trapped into a child's statement, "You're not being fair," and to respond quite correctly that fairness has nothing to do with it, that everybody is different and needs different things and each person needs to be loved in his or her special way, that comparisons make no sense at all.

We have an opportunity to teach our grandchildren a great deal about the human condition if we are willing to explain ourselves to them. A mother shouted at her mother, "Stop treating me as if I was five years old!" The granddaughter looked very upset and surprised. Grandma said, "Your mommy is right to get angry at me. The thing is that to a parent a child is always a child, no matter how grown up she may be." Her grandchild responded, "You mean it's like when Mommy wants me to sit on her lap, and I tell her I'm too big?" Grandma was delighted; that was *exactly* her point.

A grandchild may not understand why Grandma can

play for hours one day and be too tired to play on another day. Our grandchildren can learn about getting older from us. Grandma might say, "When people get older they need to rest more often."

Some grandchildren wonder why grandparents might want to move away to a warmer climate; why they retire and want to take long trips. They may view some of our decisions as acts of rejection, and they need help in understanding the different stages of life. We need to tell them how long we have worked; how much we have looked forward to some rest and relaxation; that older people need to make some changes in their lives. Or quite the opposite situation may occur, where grandchildren are aware that some children's grandparents seem to be available most of the time for fun and games, and theirs aren't like that at all. Grandma still goes to her law office, Grandpa still teaches at a college. Some grandparents play golf or tennis; some grandparents like to babysit; some grandparents live nearby—or in the same house. We have an excellent opportunity to talk to our grandchildren about individual differences, and how important it is for each person to find his or her own special way of living.

Caroline told me that her grandson had said, "How come you go to help people in the hospital every week, when your hands hurt you so much, and Grandma Sally stays home all the time and she isn't even sick?" Caroline thinks Grandma Sally is a hypochondriac, a clinging vine, a selfish and self-centered woman, but what she said was, "Every person is different, especially in their feelings. We each grew up with different parents and different things happened to us and we liked different things and so we will always be different."

We can be helpful interpreters of all kinds of differences, not only in personality and behavior but also in beliefs. This is especially true in mixed marriages, where one set of grandparents may celebrate Hanukkah, the other set, Christmas; where one set of grandparents want their grandchildren to say their prayers before bedtime, and the other grandparents never mention anything about religion. We need to remember that children want to love and be loved by all their grandparents, and if we encourage any rivalries, express our misgivings, we deprive the children of the fullest relationships they can have with us.

One of the greatest contributions we can make to a grandchild's life is to be the historians of family life as well as of the world in general. I'm sure the day will come when my granddaughter will think I am some strange idiot from another planet because I think computers are a menace, hate rock and roll music, and would much rather travel by train than plane. I think she'll be surprised to find out that when I was a little girl, it was still a remarkable thing to own a radio; that there was no television when I was a child; that I could ride on a double-decker bus and in a trolley car. Maybe she will even let me introduce her to the kind of music I like and maybe she won't think it's so awful. Most young people are quite fascinated to hear stories about the past. I might take her to Ellis Island, where her great-grandfather arrived in this country from Russia when he was six years old. When she goes to school, it will make history far more like a living experience when Larry and I can tell her "we were there" during World War II, when the first atomic bomb was used; when people sold apples on streetcorners; when Martin Luther King, Jr., led his march on Washington. The best history of all, for most grandchildren, is to hear stories about their parents when they were children. While we musn't undermine parental authority, it's helpful to a child to find out that a father had a hard time with arithmetic, a mother was too shy to go to parties; if *they* could have had problems and still grew up all right, then maybe there is hope for the future! Especially in today's world, where family life is not as stable as it was in our past, children usually love to see family albums, learn about distant relatives and hear stories about them. It is connecting with one's roots, and we are the best source of information for them. We can give them a profound awareness of the natural cycle of life, and how they have become part of a larger circle of ancestors. We can help them to get some perspective on how rapidly the world is changing when we talk about how different life was when we were growing up, or when their great-grandparents were growing up. We can also listen and allow them to educate us about their world. One of the most common occurrences is that children and grandparents, in their communications with each other, are often able to help increase understanding between the grandchildren and their own parents.

One of the most difficult areas is helping our grandchildren deal with our infirmities, illnesses, hospitalization—even the reality of our dying. It is common practice, when children learn about death and worry about dying or their parents' dying, to say, "Oh, most people don't die until they are very old." From a child's point of view, we fit that category better than anyone else they know! I think it's sad if our own fears keep us from being open and candid with children. One grandmother said she was drying the dishes with her grandson when he suddenly said, "Nanny, who will help me dry the dishes when you're dead?" She was startled, but she laughed and said, "Well, I hope I'll be around for quite awhile, and you'll be grown up then, and I hope you will just remember me when you're drying the dishes with your wife or your children!" How different than the response of a grandfather, when asked if he was old enough to die, who answered, "That's a very rude question and don't ever ask me that again." When we give children the feeling that there are some topics we can't bear to talk about, we increase their fears and confusions and lose an opportunity to share with them our philosophy of life, the ways in which we are trying to come to terms with mortality.

If we become seriously ill, it will help greatly if we can understand the normal feelings a grandchild is likely to have. One grandmother, dying of cancer, said, "The worst part of it is that Bruce and Dennis have turned away from me; they don't want to see me, and it's breaking my heart." She saw her grandsons' unwillingness to spend time with her as a loss of love, a rejection. The truth of the matter was that they loved her so much, they couldn't bear to face her dying. They were also angry at her for getting sick; *they* were feeling rejected, unloved—as children naturally (and irrationally!) feel when a parent or grandparent dies. Hopefully parents can and will come into such situations and help, but what this grandmother might have done is ask if the boys would just come to her door; she might have said, "I know you feel very bad—maybe you're even scared to see me. Maybe you feel angry because I got sick. I'm angry too. I just wanted to tell you I love you and you always made me feel happy."

In one case a grandfather who was deteriorating rapidly

after a massive stroke—drooling, paralyzed—asked his nurse to write a letter to his college-age granddaughter. The letter said that he could understand if she was afraid to see him and might even be disgusted by the way he looked, but he wanted her to know that inside his head he was still her Grandpa and remembered everything they had done together. Joyce came home from college, sat next to his bed holding his hand, and they wept together. Young people can be helped to understand that they make death more bearable, that they are our future and their love helps to lessen the loneliness of dying.

A grandmother who has been in a wheelchair for a number of years because of multiple sclerosis told me that she has made it clear to her grandchildren, all in their teens and early twenties, that she understands they must all go on with their lives and she doesn't want to be a burden to them, but if they would take turns, so that one of them would visit each week, that would be a great help to her spirits and make her feel that she was still part of the family. There are six grandchildren, so she sees each one of them once every six weeks, and because she has respected their need to go on with their lives, their visits are affectionate, full of reports of their activities, confidences about their love lives, even requests for advice. She reported to me, "If I had become an old grouch and expected them all to come and see me more often, if I had complained about their lack of attention, I would have lost them all."

I don't believe in sheltering children from the pain and sorrow in life—not even protecting very young children from reality. What a five-year-old can imagine about someone who is sick is far worse than *any* reality, for children commonly believe that whatever has happened is their fault. A seven- or eight-year-old is far more able to express the fear or the sorrow he or she feels if it can be shared directly. One grandmother, recovering from pneumonia after it had seemed she might have died, wrote me, "Alexis came to see me and we cried together for a minute, and then we got to giggling about some crazy things that had happened in the hospital. When you share the pain, then you're free to share the joy of getting better."

Separation and divorce most surely affect our relationships with our grandchildren. The danger is that we may see ourselves as passive bystanders—victims—unable to play any part in these traumatic experiences of our children and sons- and daughters-in-law. As divorce becomes increasingly prevalent, grandparents realize how easily they might lose their rights as important family members, especially when the divorce is a bitter one. Unfortunately when a wife and a husband are deeply hurt by what is happening to them, they are too often inclined to strike out at random targets—most frequently their own children, forcing children to take sides, to relay messages, saying awful things about each other to the children. As if that isn't bad enough, another easy prey for vitriol is the grandparents. The anger one feels for a spouse is very quickly translated into "You wouldn't be such a bastard if your mother hadn't spoiled you rotten!" or, "If your parents weren't so damn stupid, they would have sent you to a shrink."

The best way to punish grandparents for the real or imagined sins of a spouse is to take the children away. This has become so common that forty-nine states have enacted laws outlining grandparents' rights; in the divorce settlement it is then required that provisions be made for grandparents' visitation as well as the noncustodial parent's.

Children can be the losers as well as their grandparents. In one case, a mother, emotionally unstable, afraid she might hurt her children, agreed in the divorce proceedings that she would never see her two children again. Her husband wanted Keith and Judy to forget their mother altogether; he remarried and wanted to bury the past. He had never liked his in-laws—certainly held them responsible for his ex-wife's psychological problems—and he refused to let them have any contact with the children, both of whom had been close to the grandparents when they were very young.

No parent who thinks he can bury the past can ever succeed. These children will live their lives with unfinished business, unanswered questions. In addition to assuming, as they surely will, that their mother left because she didn't love them, they have the added burden of thinking their grandparents didn't love them either. The grandparents took the case to court. They lost on the grounds that being reintroduced to the children in the face of the father's hostility toward them would be more confusing and upsetting. Judges and court psychologists are frequently wrong, and I feel they are wrong if they think you can keep sleeping dogs quiet. One can only hope that when these children are old enough to do so, they will seek out their grandparents. Meanwhile there is serious deprivation on both sides.

In another case, it was the mother who was bitter and filled with anger at her husband who deserted her, and at his parents for having raised such an awful person. Sandra took her daughter and moved three thousand miles away. But Grandma was not so easily disposed of. She simply refused to lose Lori. She wrote letters; she sent birthday presents, valentines, Christmas presents; she called on the phone, she sent money—not only to Lori but to Sandra. She made it clear that she understood her daughter-in-law's anger, that she felt her son had behaved badly, that she wanted to go on being a friend. Lori's mother had a hard time surviving for a few years. Jeanette sent money to help her. She sent money to pay for Lori's nursery school; she lent Sandra some money to pay for a secretarial course. When Lori was eight, Sandra agreed to send Lori back east for a month during the summer. Sandra had gotten the message; there was love and understanding available to her and Lori, and she was getting over her wounds. Jeanette told me, "I knew it was a matter of being patient. We'd once had a good relationship, and I knew that after awhile I could convince Sandra we would pick up the pieces. When Sandy wrote me that she was getting remarried, I flew out for the wedding! Since then, I see Lori at least twice a year. Persistence is what you need."

There are a number of local and national organizations for grandparents,* including support groups for those who have lost touch with their grandchildren. We need to think very carefully about taking action, to be sure we can "do good" for the children, who have already been through a battle. While we are not passive spectators to a divorce, we also need to be careful that we don't become additional adversaries—taking sides, criticizing—fueling the flames of anger, disappointment, heartache. We need to show our grandchildren that while we understand how frightened and angry they may be, we have confidence in their ability to survive and adjust. One grandfather told me, "I did a lot of reading about children and divorce when my son and

---

*See list on pp. 368-70.

daughter-in-law separated. Many of the experts seemed to feel that it took about two years for a child to make an adjustment, assuming the parents were doing their best to help the child. I learned that many children show their distress by doing badly in school and that was what was happening with Justin. So I told him I knew he was having a rough time and if he wanted, I'd meet him after school one day a week and help him with some of his schoolwork. He seemed very glad. I was saying, yes, I know you're having a problem, but no, it doesn't mean you are going to fall apart."

If a daughter-in-law goes off with a lover, or a son-in-law turns out to be a wife beater, we can get as furious as we feel and be relieved by the resulting divorce, but it's another story altogether when there are children. No matter how irresponsible or evil a parent may turn out to be, a child needs and loves both parents, and we do real damage if we try to destroy that love. Even if a parent turns out to be a compulsive gambler who forfeits his children's home, even if a man turns out to be an alcoholic, even if a woman goes to prison for forging checks—*nothing* is served by our telling a grandchild what a rotten mother or father he or she may have. What is far better is to recognize that the child still loves the parent, and that an acceptable explanation for bad behavior is that the parent is a sick person, which also happens to be the truth. Along with the child's parent we have to make it clear that nothing that has happened is the child's fault, since that is the way most children interpret most crises. A friend told me, "I was sitting with my five-year-old granddaughter, helping her make a valentine for her father. I hate the man—he deserted my lovely daughter and wonderful grandchild to run away with a girl ten years younger than he is, and my feelings toward him are murderous. But I showed nothing but approval and understanding of the valentine. I know I must allow her to love him, no matter what he's done."

When a spouse disappears and has no further contact with our adult child and grandchildren, we need to give as much emotional support as we can, offer compassion and comfort, but also be careful we don't cross the line into allowing so much dependency that the newly single family gets the feeling they can't make it on their own. One mother told me, "When I knew that Penny was going to be living alone with my grandson, I marveled at how well she managed, but I worried about what would happen if Penny got sick. I live too far away to help and have a full-time job, so unless it was a real emergency, I wouldn't be of any use. Well, my daughter and my grandson both got a terrible case of the flu at the same time, and I debated about whether or not I should fly there, even though I'd just recovered from the flu myself. I controlled the impulse for twenty-four hours, and by that time Penny had things under control. Several neighbors were bringing in food, her fever was down, a friend sent her cleaning lady over for a couple of hours. She confessed to me that *she* had worried about getting sick too, and felt very good about the fact that she'd been able to survive on her own."

When our children remarry—or when there are several divorces and remarriages—we may find ourselves two of six or eight grandparents! The greater the effort we make to stay close, to be nonjudgmental, the greater the chance that we can have a meaningful ongoing relationship with our grandchildren. It isn't always—or even often—easy to make the necessary adjustments to this new kind of "extended family," but it's necessary if we want to remain part of our grandchildren's lives. A great many grandparents must be working hard at this challenge; a high-school principal told me that each year at graduation they have an increasingly difficult problem. He told me, "Our auditorium was quite adequate in size to allow for parents and grandparents to come to graduation. The problem we now have is how to accommodate three or four *sets* of grandparents, all of whom want to come! It's been 'standing room only' for the past two years!"

We have certainly had to be the most flexible, adjustable grandparents who ever lived! Another fairly recent phenomenon is the grandchild who has, for all intents and purposes, no father at all. This has to do with the fact that so many young women now find themselves still single when the biological clock is running out. At first it may shock us to think of a certain cold-blooded determination to have a child either by choosing a lover for the purpose or through artificial insemination, but if it seems likely that a young woman may never marry, is it fair to also deny her the right to be a mother?

It depends so much on the relevant circumstances. If a daughter seems quite immature, doesn't have a reasonable means of support, and just seems lonely and needs someone to love and to love her back, we ought to make every effort to encourage her to see a therapist before making any decision—to examine her motivation, give herself a chance to mature more fully. If, on the other hand, we are talking about a woman who is an elementary school teacher who happens to be in love with a married man who cannot leave his wife and four children, and is thirty-six years old, that's another matter altogether. What has made it easier for single women to become parents is that so many children whose parents were once married are now being raised by single parents; it's not something that stands out anymore. But of course there are problems which need to be faced, such as babysitters and day care, the financial burden, and the need for male role models. There is a special opportunity for grandpas in such situations to give extra attention and support, and for grandparents in general to accept this road to grandparenthood with good grace even if they have some misgivings. These days unmarried men are also becoming single fathers through adoption. In either case, I think we can point out some of the hazards—the realities of the responsibility—but it seems to me that under most circumstances this is a creative way of fulfilling real needs.

Hopefully, we can allow ourselves the joy of loving a child who may be "different." Many adoptions are of children of another race, or children of mixed races, or handicapped children. If our child has married someone of a different race, we may think at first that we would never get used to white or black grandchildren, depending on which color we are. We need to overcome these prejudices or make up our minds that we are ready to deprive ourselves of the joys of grandparenthood—and how sad that is for both adult and child.

I once asked a friend if she had any moment of hesitation when she first saw her granddaughter who was mulatto with her daughter's red hair and her son-in-law's negroid features. She said, "Honestly—about thirty seconds; all babies are adorable—who can hold out? Now Tracey is seven and has this big Afro frizzy head of bright red hair! It's startling, but she's gorgeous!"

Some of us are never going to have any grandchildren,

or the ones we have live so far away, or are so estranged, it seems as if we don't have any. All is not lost, if we think we'd like to be grandparents. There are lots of ways. A church in Oregon, where many young families live long distances from grandparents and many grandparents are far from their grandchildren, matches up foster grandparents with families. They start the season (among new families) at Thanksgiving, and grandmas and grandpas are invited to have dinner with young families who don't have grandparents available. These relationships can last for many years; the real grandparents and the step-grandparents often end up writing to each other and finally meeting.

Grandparenthood gives us a sense of immortality. One grandmother told me, "I have two grandchildren and one great-grandchild named for me. What a delightful compliment!" A grandfather said, "I have a grandson who has every one of my idiosyncrasies! *That's* immortality!" I know there are times when grandchildren can be just as much of a pain in the neck as their parents ever were; noise and commotion get harder to take. But if we cut ourselves off from children completely, we deprive ourselves of one of the most meaningful parts of life—most of all, the inner child within us that still needs nourishment. The quantity of our relationships is not as important as the quality. Whether we see grandchildren once or twice a year, or live in the same home with them, we need to rethink being close and also allow for freedom, privacy, and individual differences.

In one case Grandma owned her house, and her son and daughter-in-law and three grandchildren came to share it with her when her husband died. It was a big, rambling house, both the adults and the children felt free to be very candid about their needs and feelings, and Grandma loved being part of her grandchildren's lives. One day, the youngest boy came home from kindergarten and told Grandma she had to go to school with him the following morning. Grandma seemed surprised, but Jerry was adamant, and so she went with him the following morning. The teacher looked puzzled at first when Jerry walked in, holding his grandmother by the hand, and then laughed delightedly. "I told the children to bring their *favorite thing* to school today, and while I was expecting stuffed animals, we're delighted to have you," she told Grandma. *That's what it's all about!*

There can be very ambivalent feelings about grandparenthood. Some years ago a young man sent me a touching story about his father's devotion to his grandchild. Despite his father's death when the child was sixteen months old, they had experienced an intense and loving relationship. Some time later he wrote me again: "Ironically enough, I—writer of a story about the beauty of my dad's short time as a grandpa to my son—have seen my wife's parents completely pull away from us and our little ones. I hear more and more of grandparents afraid to acknowledge their grandparenthood because, apparently, they see in it a tacit acknowledgment of unwelcome old age and impending mortality."

On the other hand, another true story: Peter divorced his wife, Mary, when she was four months pregnant, and never again saw her or the child. Neither did his parents. Mary remarried. Her second husband adopted her daughter, who, although she was given the facts of her origin, always thought of John as her "real father" and never

showed any interest in finding out anything about her biological father or his family. When she was twenty-three,
her paternal grandparents searched for and found her.
Mary was furious; they had never shown the slightest interest before—why now? Peter's mother said, "Because now
we are old and this child is our only claim to immortality.
Before we die we need to know we have a grandchild." For
some, grandchildren are seen as a painful reminder of mortality; for others, a joyous gift of immortality.

In many cases grandparenthood gives us a second
chance. One grandfather I know wrote about the fact that
he now sees all the mistakes he made in relating to his own
two children—that he was too distant, too inconsistent
with them. But now it is "his turn" for a love relationship
that has a kind of simple purity about it. He's grown, his
values have changed, he is more open to his deepest feelings
of wanting to love and be loved. He speaks of distance
from his own father, his failures as a husband and a father,
and then in describing the lovely way in which his grandson and granddaughter have reached out to him with unconditional love, he concludes, "The role is so natural, so
easy, so rewarding that it's like tapping a well and having
clear, pure and refreshing water spout forth without further effort."

Personally, I can hardly wait until my granddaughter is
old enough for me to pass along family memories and stories of my childhood. I will hear Larry telling her the stories he made up so long ago for her mother. I want her to
know who we are and what we stand for, and whatever I
give her of myself will be the part of me that will not die.
To some extent, at least, I think we need to be in touch
with childhood, whether our own or other people's chil-

dren, for what are hopes and dreams about if not about the future?

Many senior citizens' centers have discovered that the members who are far away from their families often do poorly, sicken more easily, die at an earlier age. One director, aware of this, invited a nearby elementary school to begin to have joint activities with the senior center. They started a chorus, and some of the children were tutored in subjects they were having trouble with; they played games and went on some trips together. The whole atmosphere lightened, the older people began to feel better, and the children loved it.

A camp for disturbed children hires foster grandparents to be part of their summer program; they have noted a real change for the better in the children. There are children in hospitals who crave love and attention; there are young children in day-care centers and nurseries who find little love in their lives. One woman I know began to teach reading to a young man who had spent his childhood in reform schools, and had been in prison for several years. Nobody had ever faced the reality that part of his problem was that he had never learned to read. He was over six feet tall and black, she was under five feet and white. One evening after they had been working, they decided they were hungry and walked to a small neighborhood supermarket. Bill picked up an apple pie and shouted, "Hey Grandma, they got your favorite thing!" There was a sudden hush as all eyes turned toward her. "Coming, dear," she said. They loved the shock they had provided, and laughed about it many times. Lucky young man; lucky lady.

~~~~~~

Our Aged Parents: Growing Old Together

A FRIEND CALLED AND TOLD me, "After a physical checkup the doctor told my father, 'You'll be ninety on your next birthday? Your life expectancy is ten years.' When I go for a checkup the doctor warns me I could drop dead any day—I'm overweight, I have high blood pressure and diabetes. If my father lives another ten years—and if I don't drop dead before him— I'll be seventy-six. Someone will have to take care of both of us."

One woman told me that she'd walked past two elderly people on the street and one was saying to the other, "But my dear, *my children* are senior citizens!"

A social worker who leads a support group of older people with aged parents told me, "We call the aged parents 'The Indestructibles' in the privacy of our meetings."

Anita told me, "I thought that when my mother died that was the most terrible thing that could happen to me. The fact that my father *hasn't* died is much, much worse. He's ninety-two, and I had to put him in a nursing home when he became incontinent. He looks at me with the saddest eyes—he wants to die at home, and I can't do it. I'm just too old myself and I'm tormented with guilt twenty-four hours a day."

A friend told me, "There is very little I don't know, personally, about the ambivalences involved in having older parents. There are days when I feel overwhelmed with love, days when my guilt at not having my mother live with me disturbs me greatly, and times when I am filled with rage because I thought that in my sixties, like my parents before me, I would be able to feel free of responsibility to others and could do as I pleased."

The old saying that it is strange that two people can raise six children, and six children can't take care of one parent, has some basic flaws. By the time the six children have to take care of one or two parents, *they are old themselves!* By the time we are in our sixties and seventies we can't comfortably or easily manage to take care of anyone for very long; my granddaughter, no matter how much I may love her, leaves me utterly exhausted after a few hours. The older I get the harder it is to take care of myself and Larry; shopping tires me more easily; carrying heavy bags of groceries hurts my arthritic wrists; traveling from one end of New York City to the other to visit my father and to bring him food is more tiring than it was ten years ago. Our parents were in their twenties and thirties when they took care of us; their youth and energy made it possible for them to do so. The terrible thing is that we love our parents but feel too old to take care of them, often don't have the resources we need, and feel a sense of profound anguish at having to watch them change from being strong and well and independent. I watch my father having trouble walking out of a room, holding on to his cane—and inside my head I see a young man running across a tennis court or raking leaves, or running up the steps, taking me to school. My brother recently showed some home movies at a family gathering—my father was in his fifties, much younger than I am now—dancing with my mother, swimming, painting some outdoor furniture. He looked so handsome! So young and happy.

For those lucky few whose parents are not alone, and who have full, healthy, independent lives, there are no serious problems. But most of us, in our sixties and seventies, live with anxiety, love, pain, rage, and frustration.

A friend tells me, "Daddy is ninety-four, in perfect physical shape, except for being a little senile. My husband, Bob, at seventy-one, is having terrible prostate problems. He's in more trouble physically than my father, and yet it is Bob who has to help me take care of my father." What happens to many of us is that we get too old ourselves for some of the burdens we are faced with in relation to aged parents. It is a new emotional and social problem, one for which we were totally unprepared. The entire community was unprepared and so we get too little help from private or governmental resources. Very few of us live in the big old houses of a century ago, which could accommodate an extended family; most of us live in small homes or apartments. The wonders of medicine are keeping people alive longer than ever before, but this longer living involves new kinds of care that most of us simply can't handle. Sam wrote: "Toni's mother was successfully operated on for cancer of the bladder, which was removed. Now Toni has to deal with the aftermath of that operation, and she's in no condition herself to do it."

One of the most serious problems between adult children and aged parents arises from the fact that very often we, the children, find ourselves caught up in a web we could never have anticipated; our parents do the same things to us that they did when we were young, and unless we are very careful, we allow this to happen. Robert tells me, "My father wanted me to become a lawyer and I wanted desperately to please him. At the age of sixty, I would like to give up this profession and do something completely different. Sports have always been my great interest—I think I'd like to become part-owner of a baseball team, and I could afford it, now. My father is eighty-nine, and his continued disapproval stands over me like a dark shadow, or a net that I can't break through. I'm still the little boy who doesn't want to disappoint him."

Janice tells me, "During my childhood and adolescence, I wanted to be an actress. My father, a Victorian, a man who enjoyed the theater but thought it should never be more than a hobby, had other plans for me. I rebelled against what he wanted most—my becoming a public schoolteacher so I could have tenure and a pension—but I didn't follow my own dream. Now that I have the feeling that I might want to explore old interests and longings, I find myself almost back to the time I was a young mother and responsible first of all to my children. But now my father's needs are at the forefront of my mind, not my own. I feel the rage of a child, thwarted once again, and by the same person."

Rhoda told me, "Jay and I have pinched pennies for twenty years so that when we retired we would be able to travel around the world and not settle down until we were good and ready. Now I can't go away because my eighty-seven-year-old mother needs my care. I feel like a little girl again, and Mommy has said, 'No, you cannot go out and play with the other children.'" The feelings are unavoidable, but we *must* find the help we need to deal with the real problems.

I think a little catharsis is called for when we have to deal with serious and complicated problems about which we have such mixed feelings. But, as with all the other problems of aging that I've been discussing, we are not helpless victims, and there are many ways in which we can meet this challenge too. First we need to face our feelings honestly and acknowledge the problems realistically.

Probably one of the most frightening aspects of taking on responsibility for aged parents is that they are a constant reminder of what may happen to us. Dr. Robert Butler writes in the preface of his book: ". . . At best the living old are treated as if they were already half dead. . . . We cannot promise a decent existence for those elderly who are now alive. We cannot house them, . . . or even feed them adequately."* He points out that one serious illness can mean instant poverty—one's life savings wiped out in a single catastrophic illness.

We visit "the best" nursing homes we hear about, and are appalled. We live in terror that a catastrophic illness of a parent could wipe *us* out financially as well, so that we can't plan more efficiently for our own last years. We watch the slow, inevitable deterioration of someone we want to remember as young and vigorous and active—and we know someday our children will see us in this condition.

We tend to blame ourselves if an elderly parent is unhappy or irritable, as if we are entirely responsible, forgetting that there are just as many personality differences

* Butler, *Why Survive?*

among the aged as in any other group of people. Marvin reports that his father refuses to eat anything by himself after an operation—he wants someone to feed him every bite he takes. Marvin adds, "But it's really just an extension of what he's always been like. I can't remember a time when he didn't need constant assurance that we cared about him." Selma, on the other hand, brought me a note from her mother, Ruth, trying to survive in a nursing home after having always been an independent and private person, who wrote, "My children are wonderful. They understand me and I understand them. They give me as much as they can. I would like to see my grandchildren more often, but I understand how busy they are and I know they love me and they know I love them." Selma commented, "That's the kind of person she's always been."

Many times aged parents seem to be looking at us accusingly, as if somehow we are responsible for what is happening to them. If we are going to be as effective as possible in this situation, we simply cannot accept the anger and bitterness which really have to do with the fact of being old, something over which we have no control.

The variation in temperament is also accompanied by great variation in health and energy. One woman wrote me, "I feel very confident about getting older. I have a number of friends over eighty who are still enjoying a professional life—or who have a rich social life and who still travel. I have an aunt who will be one hundred and who thinks as clearly as when she taught school fifty years ago!" A man wrote, "My mother is seventy-nine and she's a wonder. I enjoy her as a traveling companion because she has a delicious sense of humor and a grand curiosity about people and places."

It also makes a great difference if we feel we can have the support system we need. Henrietta said, "My father lived to be ninety-one. I could afford to keep his household staffed with the necessary help and so I enjoyed his company up until the last."

Where relations with aged parents are most satisfying, it is quite clear that an attitude of give-and-take is still operating. Marian wrote:

My stepmother is eighty-four, still lives alone and arranges for the care of her home and property. Our father planned that house to be a retirement home with ease of care as a primary concern. He was a great one to plan ahead. He died when he was eighty-six and up until the last year he kept a garden. Katharine can manage the house well and this summer was the first time she didn't have a garden.

One of us [children] shop for her and will take her to doctor or dentist appointments, if she lets us know. There are organizations that will help and she has arranged with meals on wheels at noon. She is an avid reader and I belong to several book clubs in order to keep her supplied with recent best-sellers. She also enjoys music and a limited amount of television. She works in the yard when the weather is nice and sometimes takes walks. She is a very private person and doesn't talk about personal feelings much at all.

Her retirement income seems to be adequate, but she never talks about it. She often will give each of us $1,000 at Christmas, which indicates to us that she is okay. She appreciates our visits but never makes demands. If there is a man-type chore and my husband comes, she will ask him if he would mind doing a favor for her. She is a very gracious person. I would like to be as gracious when I am her age.

Hilda wrote: "Aged parents and/or other aged dependents continue to be a burden and a bother—but at least they make us feel, to some extent, like the 'younger generation.' They do limit our freedom somewhat, but there are some compensations; they serve to provide a sense of family continuity; they can tell wonderful stories of family history; they can (sometimes) serve as old-age role models.

And Ginny told me, "I have always been close to older people. I lived with my grandmother until I left home at nineteen. Many of our friends were and are ten to fifteen years older. In fact the majority are in their mid-seventies now. I am not put off by age itself, despite its dismal prognosis, but by its more sobering manifestations—dependency, pain, mental deterioration.

"Also, my folks gave a good example of how to treat the aged. They were very good to their respective parents and if their service was laced with healthy exasperation at times, I could see that this was natural and nothing to feel guilty about. Each also provided usable examples of graceful aging when their own turns came, subject to the limitations of their temperaments, of course."

One of the best books I read on aging was published in 1952, but is totally applicable today. In *You and Your Aging Parents,* Edith Stern and Mabel Ross, M.D.,* discuss the fact that the lack of intelligent planning and open communication can lead to misery for both generations. Children (in their sixties and seventies) don't want their lives interfered with, and elderly parents, not happy about losing their independence, don't feel grateful for what is being

*Edith Stern with Mabel Ross, M.D., *You and Your Aging Parents* (New York: A. A. Wyn, Inc., 1952).

done for them. Feelings on both sides are so strong, so laced with guilt and fear and regret, that it seems to be harder to communicate honestly in this relationship than any others we have encountered in the course of our lives.

The authors tell of the aged parent who says, "Let me live with you and I'll never interfere," or the parent who says very openly, "Well, now it's your turn to take care of me."

Panic sets in because we never expected this to happen to us, and we know there is lack of a decent support system for medical care, housing, financial needs. We are often forced to make terrible decisions that tear us apart. Sometimes we find ourselves caught up in an unbearable drama.

Freida wrote:

The day before your inquiry arrived, I brought my eighty-six-year-old mother from her home in Arizona to my home, on an ambulance flight. I had to admit her to a nursing home because she'd had a stroke which had rendered her physically helpless and mentally confused. She had been a wonderful funny, *lively,* independent person—still driving a car! On the flight I was grieving *for* her and *with* her. I now have to fly back to Arizona to drive my car back here to Washington. I am an only child— need I say more?

There is a tendency, I think, when we say the word "ambivalence" to immediately assume we're talking about negative feelings. But most of our pain has to do with love.

I met a woman on a bus who asked me what I was writing about now, and when I told her, she said, "My mother is ninety-four and has been in a nursing home for four years. She had a good life until she was eighty-eight;

now she's blind and senile. I plead with the nurses, 'Stop the machines,' and they say she'll die. I say *who'll* die? Where is there a person? My mother has been dead for four years."

We find ourselves caught up in the insanities of medical practice. Donald told me, "My mother is ninety-three and senile. She was a beautiful, gracious lady, and I see such suffering in her face, now that she's incontinent and help-less. She got pneumonia and we pleaded with the medical staff at the nursing home not to give her antibiotics, but they insisted that they had to. No one can die when they want to anymore. Now she's refusing to eat and they are force-feeding her. We can't bear her agony."

And yet we also know that we don't want to take the matter of life and death into our own hands. Some very old people who seem to have nothing to live for feel differ-ently—they struggle to remain alive, and they have a right to do so. Often it is the children who cannot bear the dete-rioration, and the parent who wants to live, no matter what.

We are not monsters if, under such circumstances, we wish for a parent's death. Nor are we monsters if we in-dulge in a certain amount of gallows humor. One man I know tries to guess what his ninety-one-year-old father will say at his son's funeral—he's sure Dad will outlive him! One friend comments to another, "If you're planning to find an adult community where you can spend your last days, you better find one that will take your father, too." Humor relieves the strain, and catharsis brings us right back to the fact that often our hearts are breaking. I watch my eighty-nine-year-old father struggling courageously to live alone and accept it—the first time he's ever been alone in his entire life—and I feel I cannot bear it. I try to suggest companions, boarders, caretakers, and am turned down each time. The truth is he would probably like to live with me or some other close relative; that's the way life was when he was growing up—families took care of their own. But he never criticizes or asks for more. We talk on the telephone every day; I bring food; I take him out; he visits me in the country. I do as much as I can. His loneliness envelops me so that I can hardly breathe—and since I am working as hard as I ever have, I wonder how I can keep going. Feelings of love are what make it all so damned hard.

We took my father to an outdoor concert near our home in New Jersey. As we sat there, I felt such a longing for my mother—at the same time feeling, how dare she have left my father alone. At the end of the concert, eyes shining, my father said, "Oh, it's so wonderful to get a chance to hear beautiful music, now that I never get out anymore." It nearly broke my heart. He can't walk without help, and going to concerts or plays in the city has become too difficult; in the country we could drive directly to the outdoor tent. His pleasure, his gratitude, made me want to weep.

For most of us, the loving remains so much more painful than the anger! One day I saw my father, hands trembling, taking something out of his wallet. He handed me five of the "LOVE" stamps, a wordless gesture, a simple message. It tore me apart.

Sometimes the other side—the anger—has little to do directly with an aged parent. Often we are caring for aged parents at the same time that many of our friends and relatives who are our contemporaries are dying. A couple in their sixties came to visit my father, then eighty-eight.

They talked animatedly about their son and his new job; they were planning a long vacation in Mexico, now that the husband had retired. It was clear they felt their good years were still ahead of them. A week later the husband died of a heart attack. When my father told me, I could see from the look in his eyes that he was thinking the same thing I was, but what neither of us would say out loud; why the younger man, and not the older one, already widowed, already becoming dependent, already lonely and unable to move about on his own? We see a young man with a wife and two young children die at thirty-five from cancer; we see a young woman's grief at having a stillborn. It doesn't make any sense; it makes us angry. In spite of the evidence of a lifetime, we still look for some logic, some rationality in life and death, and if we happen to have a parent who is senile or wasting away but alive at ninety-six, the injustice can sometimes be unbearable. One woman wrote: "My daughter and son-in-law have a two-year-old who has leukemia, and there is a very small chance that he will survive. He is my first grandchild. My mother is ninety and bedridden in a nursing home. She wants to die, because life is now unbearable for her. If there is a God, this must be some terrible cosmic joke."

The problems of life and death seem to force *us* into an unwelcome godlike role. Dena was raised by her aunt, whom she adored. Aunt Judith was a warm, loving person, devoted to Dena's children and grandchildren; a woman of great dignity—in many ways a very private person, except in her evident love for her family. At eighty-nine she developed congestive heart disease and became an invalid almost overnight. Eventually she became incontinent and senile and had to be placed in a nursing home when she was ninety-one. She told Dena over and over again that she wanted to die, that she could not bear what was happening to her. Dena kept assuring her that she still had much to live for. She went to see her aunt every other day although she lived fifty miles away. With great difficulty Aunt Judith was literally carried to family celebrations—Christmas, a grandniece's wedding, to see a new baby in the family. Dena also took her aunt in a wheelchair to a restaurant for lunch once a week, and spent several terrible times having to clean up her aunt's feces during these trips. One day Dena called me and said her aunt had become so disoriented that she would take off all her clothes and lie on the floor; she was vomiting, defecating, urinating. Dena *said* she wished her aunt would die.

However, as I have listened to more and more people talk about this subject, I have begun to feel that in very subtle, usually unconscious ways the very people who say they wish a parent would die because their lives have become a nightmare are themselves part of the life-support system. In spite of all she was telling me, Dena expected to go on seeing her aunt every other day, to take her out of the hospital, to talk to her about family events. I suddenly realized that it wasn't only the medical profession which was keeping Judith alive, it was Dena—she simply could not let go, and that as long as she went on breathing life into her beloved aunt, she was going to prolong a truly terrible existence. Every time she visited, it was as if an oxygen mask was being placed on Judith's face—the sounds of life and love pulled her back from the death she wanted.

Dena was shocked when I suggested that it was she who was unable to let go and was prolonging the anguish. We talked about her cutting out the torturous luncheon trips, which always ended in one kind of a disaster or other; about her cutting down her visits to once or twice a week at the most, and rather than talking about all the living that was going on in the family, to reminisce about the past, allowing her aunt to move into memory instead of clinging to the present.

As we talked, I suddenly realized that Larry and I had done the same thing with Aunt Lillie. We both cherished her greatly, and when, at the age of ninety-four, she was hospitalized for the last time, and became a wraith—more a corpse than a living person—we went to see her regularly, talked about what we were doing, talked about people she loved, told stories about children in the family, brought her gifts. She would rally from a semicomatose state. She was almost deaf and blind, but she recognized our touch when we held her hands; each time we left, we wept in the corridor for our memories of a dancing, laughing, loving lady. At some point, not really aware of it at the time, we cut down on our visits. We began to say goodbye when we did visit—to ourselves mostly, and what I now realize was that neither Larry nor I had been to see her at all the last two weeks of her life. I now have the strongest feeling that by appearing to desert her, we were actually trying to give her permission to die.

This may sound cruel and unfeeling to some people. But I think we need to examine our feelings when someone we love wants and needs to die, and not blame the medical profession entirely for the ways in which they prolong lives that are no longer really being lived. We add to the prolongation if we cannot let go, whether our feelings stem from love or guilt or a combination of both.

Amy has a ninety-two-year-old father who has Alzheimer's disease and never recognizes her, but she travels by plane every week to visit him in a distant city. She admits he seems more disturbed than pleased by her talking to him endlessly. Marian's brother was dying of cancer, which had spread to his liver, lungs, and stomach. His kidneys were no longer functioning properly, he was yellow and gaunt and in a coma almost all the time. Every day Marian sat beside his bed, talking to him, singing Yiddish songs they had both learned in childhood, telling him jokes, talking about him to other patients, to nurses and visitors. When he was not comatose, Sam stared straight ahead, a look of horror on his face. He was distantly related to us, and one day he whispered to Larry, "Make her leave." Larry stood guard for the rest of that day, urging Marian to rest—telling her she needed to take a nap in the waiting room. Larry and Sam looked at each other, and Sam reached for Larry's hand. Larry said, "Goodbye, Sam," and within an hour Sam died.

This is a very delicate matter. Many people who may be suffering a great deal, or who are no longer able to leave their beds, hang on to life tenaciously. Some who do so eventually change their minds. None of us really want to play God and decide issues of life and death. Fortunately we can't! We don't have any such powers. What we can do is give a person some choice, watch for signs, listen to what a person says. People surely have the right to choose, whatever their circumstances; all we can do is to try to face what *we* are feeling, and to make it clear we are ready to accept the older person's decision. No matter how terrible your condition may be, it is hard to let go if you feel that people are hanging on to you and can't bear to let you go. When we are absolutely certain that someone we care about is desperate to die, we need to let them know. Often it's not even a spoken signal, but just an attitude—body language—that says, "I won't hold you to me, but if you die, I will be able to carry on. I will never forget you."*

We may also hold on too tightly in life as well as in death. Sometimes it is our generation which clings to aged parents. One study found that during the 1970s 1.6 million people over sixty moved, and in the 1980s the number was four times greater. In many cases these were people in their eighties who wanted to move to a warmer climate or to a place where they could live on much less money. Many began choosing adult communities, where they could live among their peers. Often it is the adult children who become very disturbed by having elderly parents move far away. They feel abandoned; they feel the grandchildren are being rejected. It may well be that moving away is seen as the beginning of the final separation which the adult child is not ready to face. If you are fifty-five or sixty you may not be ready to understand why someone who is seventy-five or eighty might prefer to live in a community of older people rather than surrounded by children and people of all ages. Dependency needs never leave us completely and if aged parents want to leave us geographically while they are still well and strong there can be a period of anxiety and stress. In talking with some of those who moved to a warmer climate, they told me that a typical response of their children was, "Don't you care about your grandchildren? They will become strangers!" It's a painful argument, and may well interfere with plans that are important to the aged parent.

*There is a magnificent book, *Last Wish,* in which Betty Rollin tells how she helped her mother to die (New York: Linden Press, 1985).

Ambivalent feelings can sometimes lead to behavior that cannot be tolerated. There is a big difference between being able to understand and accept our hostile feelings— our daily frustrations—and acting upon them. In fact it seems to me that those of us who can talk about our negative feelings are less likely to ever do anything harmful to a parent. The seriousness of that problem is painfully described in a Public Affairs Pamphlet by Harry Milt entitled *Family Neglect and Abuse of the Aged: A Growing Concern.* * He reports that child abuse and wife beating are not the only kinds of family violence—there is also "elder abuse." He describes terrible mistreatment of aged parents by family members, sometimes deliberate, sometimes created by uncontrollable anguish, almost always related to the lack of necessary help from community agencies. Sometimes it may stem from abuse suffered at the hands of a now elderly parent when one was a child. The author discusses the necessary kinds of preventive measures and protection for the aged parent, and if there are some among us who find ourselves going beyond an occasional private expression of verbal hostility, it may be important to get this pamphlet as a beginning to seeking other kinds of direct intervention and help. The pamphlet lists more than ten useful national resources.

Ambivalent feelings need to be controlled, but they are inevitable; there are just too many experiences that cause mixed feelings. The older our parents become, the more dependency needs they develop. The old parent feels this new helplessness as a terrible reversal of roles, and this is reinforced by the children feeling the same way, creating

---

*Public Affairs Pamphlet #603, 381 Park Avenue South, New York, NY 10016, 50¢.

anxiety and anger for both. Some older people fight the dependency unsuccessfully through anger, irritability, rigidity. Others, feeling hopeless, give in and give up; they begin to use illness and helplessness as a way of punishing others, justifying failure.

Watching the deterioration that comes inevitably with advanced age, we shrink, we cringe, faced with the total reversal of roles and our sometimes unconscious terror that we stand next in line.

When I was about nine years old, my father began teaching me to play Ping-Pong. I remember having such a terrific time playing with him all the years I was growing up, and later as a young adult. We have a Ping-Pong table at our house in New Jersey, and my father, at eighty-eight, tried to play, but he couldn't. I wanted to die, watching his embarrassment, feeling my own. We both tried so hard to treat it with humor, but we didn't succeed. It was so poignantly clear that this father role was over for him—and I wondered how soon it would be when my daughter would discover mother roles I could no longer play.

There is nothing abnormal about not wanting to be witness to such changes, to be filled with both pity and hate, to wish that one would not have to endure the deterioration.

Dorothy told me, "When I was a young child I used to have nightmares that my mother wouldn't recognize me. I learned that wasn't too uncommon to children, but it is happening to me now, as a middle-aged adult. My mother has Alzheimer's disease, and she hasn't recognized me for five years. It's the same nightmare."

In a lovely and touching book of personal reflections, *Raisins and Almonds,* * Fredelle Maynard writes:

*Fredelle Maynard, *Raisins and Almonds* (Markham, Ontario, Canada: Paperjacks, 1980, 6th printing), pp. 173–179.

There is a special sadness that comes with reversal of roles in the life between parent and child—when the child literally becomes father of the man. I grew accustomed to that sorrow. Still I cannot think without pain of the day I bathed my father. It was a logical task to assume; my mother had trouble with her shoulder. I was younger and stronger . . . I took his arm and persuaded him to the tub . . . he did not speak as I fumbled with buttons and zipper, easing him out of his clothes . . . His skin was whiter than I would have believed possible . . . his sex hung enormous . . . My father met my eyes. He began to stutter . . . I saw that he was crying, but then the cry became a laugh, a strange hysterical mirth . . . shrill despair. . . . Drifting away he was, lost and confused and wandering, but that brief indignity had summoned him back to protest . . .

We found a nursing home. My father wore his best suit for the journey (by ambulance . . .) . . . he said not a word . . . a nurse flicked a cold eye over his possessions. "You can take back the pajama bottoms," she said.

The family was told to take home his coat—he'd never need it again. They were told supper was served at four, so patients were ready for bed by seven. It was a slow, torturous deterioration, surrounded by patients who were more senile, who emptied their bowels freely.

Ms. Maynard goes on:

The last time I saw my father he lay high on pillows under a white sheet . . . His mouth hung partly open, revealing the smooth gums . . . "Papa," I whispered, . . . "It's me . . . Fredelle." . . . Intelligence and recollection gradually suffused his face. . . . "Fraidele," he repeated wonderingly, "Dear child."

[Some time later] I worried about not being able to cry at the funeral. How could I explain that his passing was a relief, that I had been waiting for death to give me back my father?

285

In a poignant and touching article, "When Age Does not Come Gently," Joan Gage describes the slow, inexorable deterioration of her father from a proud and competent man to a feeble and helpless invalid. She writes:

While I was growing up in Minnesota my father went off every day to his office wearing a dark suit with a white shirt and a fresh white handkerchief protruding from his breast pocket. . . . By nature my father was a solitary, taciturn man, but the Depression forced him into taking a salesman's job that required him to court and entertain people all day long. . . . After my father collected his gold watch and retired . . . he had difficulty adjusting to his idleness. . . . My father withdrew slowly and became a general nuisance around the house, fussing about little things; what time the postman would arrive, how my mother folded his newspaper. . . .*

The author goes on to tell of the fiftieth wedding anniversary of her parents and how her father, now suffering from Parkinson's disease, fell down while pictures were being taken at the party. When his wife had a stroke and was hospitalized, he began to forget where she was and would wander around the neighborhood looking for her. When he came to stay with Ms. Gage he became very disoriented, and every night would pack his bag and announce he was leaving. He began to hallucinate. When he returned home, his wife still away, he became belligerent and frightened away nurses hired to care for him. Eventually, in a nursing home, he wanted his daughter to bathe and feed him and tell him bedtime stories. Six months

*The New York Times (Jan. 10, 1985).

later, having fallen and cut his head, she found him in a hospital bed, naked, restrained by a cloth harness. His false teeth had been taken away. Finally: "He sits in his room and is fed and changed. He often disturbs the others by shouting, 'Help!, Help!' until someone comes and asks him what he wants and he replies 'Nothing.'"

In this instance much of the rapid deterioration seems related to being separated from his wife. It is surely one of the sad and poignant aspects of our problems that we are almost always dealing with a parent who is separated from a spouse by illness or widowhood.

When I got onto a bus with two heavy bags of groceries one day, an elderly woman asked me why I was traveling with all that food. When I told her I was going to visit my eighty-nine-year-old father, she asked me, "Does your father live *alone?*" When I said he did, she sighed deeply and said, "Oh, how terrible for him!"

One day in October I called for my father to take him for a ride in the country to see the fall colors. As we were getting into the car, he said, "Lil just called as I was leaving. She sounded so sad and lonely. It felt so good to tell her my daughter was coming to take me out!" Lil is a widowed friend, also living alone, mostly abandoned by her son. My father seemed to be in a mood to talk, to tell me about his concerns about the future and what he ought to be thinking about doing; he said, "Now that I'm alone, I'm thinking more about it."

As we came into the countryside and we both oh-ed and ah-ed over the glories of nature, he suddenly said, "I finally figured it out—Browning's poem is not about old age at all! 'Grow old along *with me, the best is yet to be.*' It's not the getting old that's important—the important words are 'with me'! It's about being with someone—then getting older doesn't matter." Although it was his second wife who had recently died, I knew he was thinking about my mother, to whom he'd been married for fifty-two years. I had thought of going to a restaurant in Connecticut, but when we passed a sign to Brewster, New York, he said, "I'd rather go there." He and my mother had had a home there for many years, and as we drove on, and he admired the breathtaking colors around us he kept saying, "Just like Brewster—that was a marvelous time! What a happy time of our lives!"

My father seemed so happy to be with me. We got lost, drove through the main streets of a town, then on a winding road with some old colonial houses like the one he and my mother had bought, and since it was getting late we stopped at a restaurant before getting to our destination. It was called Nobody's Inn, and he loved the name and was so enthusiastic about their homemade clam soup and chef's salad, we might have been eating at a gourmet restaurant rather than what was really a cross between a bar and a coffee shop.

On the way home he kept talking about what a wonderful day it had been, how his soul had been refreshed. He was so grateful to me, it had been such a perfect day.

When we got to his apartment, I helped him upstairs. The apartment was dark and silent. I'd noticed him looking at his watch a few times, and when I asked him if there was some reason why he had to be back at a certain time, he said he wondered whether Millie had left yet. Millie is the cleaning woman who is much more than that—a young woman who loves him and is very devoted to him. As I left him (I was parked illegally downstairs) I knew why he'd wanted to get home before Millie left, so he wouldn't come into an empty apartment. He tried hard not to show the feeling of letdown—smiled, kissed me, kept thanking me for a wonderful day. I wept in the car for his loneliness. I too suddenly understood "Grow old along *with me.*"

It is very hard to remember that however old someone may be, he or she has rights, must be allowed to make personal decisions. One old man, forced to make decisions he didn't like, made himself a sandwich sign, which he then wore, walking up and down the street in front of his daughter's house. The sign said, "My daughter is cruel and inhuman to her father." When I apparently became too bossy and manipulative with my father (trying to convince him to have someone live with him) he handed me an article I'd written for *Woman's Day* magazine,* when he was married to his second wife and going to work every day. The article was about allowing aged parents to make their own decisions—that "too much loving protection can be deadly!"

In the article I told the story of an elderly man found wandering the streets of Paris. He was carrying a suitcase but couldn't remember the address of the hotel to which he was on his way. My friend, who found him, looked in his pocket and found the name and address of a son in Oklahoma, whom he called. The son said he'd made a reservation for his father at one of the best hotels and had sent him off by ship. He'd had misgivings, but this was what his father wanted to do. He told my friend, "My father was a

*Eda LeShan, "When Parents Start Showing Their Age," *Woman's Day* (Oct. 18, 1977).

powerful, active man all his life, I didn't want to shame him now that he is sometimes confused and disoriented. He wants to live out his life in his favorite city."

My friend kept in touch with the old man, saw to it he received the money his son cabled to him. The old man died a year later while sitting on a bench in the Bois de Boulogne, feeding the ducks. Just the way he would have wished to die.

We need to be so careful about coming to wrong conclusions too easily—expecting stereotypical behavior and then misreading it.

Dr. Robert Butler* gives the example of the man of seventy, living alone, who suddenly became confused and disoriented. The neighbors pleaded with the man's doctor to make a house call, and told him the man belonged in a nursing home. Finally, they got a doctor who would come to the house. The man had a viral infection, which was causing his mental symptoms, and after being given antibiotics he recovered and continued to be able to function on his own.

When we are forced into having to make plans for aged parents, we need to do everything we can to continue to allow as much autonomy as possible. A woman who hated having to talk to her widowed father about moving into a home for the aged was both surprised and relieved to find that he was making plans, within the limited scope of possibilities. He told her, "I know I can't go on taking care of myself. I see the handwriting on the wall. One of the things I'm doing is taking the boxes of photographs I've had stored in the closet and putting them in albums. I can take

*Butler, *Why Survive?*

them with me wherever I have to go. I'm also reading all my old letters and throwing away a lot of them. The rest I'll want with me. I never played cards in my life, but now I'm taking bridge lessons. I also bought myself some water-colors, and I'm painting, for the first time in my life. I need new diversions so I won't feel as if it's the end of everything when I have to move."

It is extraordinarily difficult to find a balance between respecting whatever autonomy an elderly person still needs and also supplying necessary help and guidance. Unfortunately what seems to happen most frequently is that we find ourselves caught in a crisis situation in which decisions have to be made too rapidly. A parent who has been managing very well suddenly falls and breaks a hip and will need nursing care for many months; where do we turn, how do we share the decision making with the parent? What do we do when we are absolutely certain a parent needs custodial care, and we see a look of terror and despair in the eyes of this person whom we love?

These are terrible dilemmas. But there are two factors that I think can make a difference. The first is to begin to prepare ourselves ahead of time, if at all possible, not only for an aged parent but for ourselves. To talk to geriatrics specialists, visit social agencies, explore all the possible resources, visit adult homes, nursing homes, senior citizens' day centers. Every state has a Bureau or a Department on Aging; there are excellent reference books, private and public information centers. Fortunately the possible choices have increased tremendously in recent years. Hospitals that now provide home care on a daily basis; foster placement for the aged; shared housing with matching of clients supervised by a social agency; day centers, meals on wheels; a great variety of home-care services, some very expensive, some run by religious and charitable agencies that are less costly. We need to get information about just what is available through Social Security, insurance policies, Medicare, pensions, and other possible sources. We need to seek legal aid, learn more about taxes, savings, investments. We need to search for recreation resources, doctors who will make home visits, geriatric clinics, agencies that arrange for volunteer home visitors. By having a good file of information, we can make better choices and assure an aged parent that if one solution doesn't work out, another can be tried.

There is no question that much of our frustration stems from painful reality problems. Robert Butler* points out that because of the rapid rise in health-care costs, old people are now forced to pay more for medical care than before Medicare! But even beyond financial problems, it is almost impossible to get counseling or psychotherapy for older people—a resource that might be helpful for both old parents and their children. Few people are interested in working with the aged.

William Schofield† has described the "Y.A.V.I.S. syndrome"—the tendency of psychotherapists to treat young, attractive, verbal, intelligent, and successful (which means well-paying) clients.

It is a struggle to find emotional support as well as information, but even more important than information is our attitude—all the different kinds of hidden agenda that may unwittingly enter into our decision making, whether

---

*Butler, *Why Survive?*
†William Schofield, *Psychotherapy: Purchase of Friendship* (Englewood Cliffs, NJ: Prentice Hall, 1974).

shared with a parent or not. A woman of eighty-five told me that her daughter came to visit her in the home for the aged. That day there was a dance and Marsha was dancing with a man of seventy-seven. Her daughter said, "Ma, you're making an ass of yourself—you're too old to carry on like that." Marsha was crushed, ashamed, suddenly felt all of her eighty-five years. What was going on? It seemed to me that her daughter had some stereotypical notion of how an old woman is supposed to act and somehow felt threatened by seeing her mother having such a good time.

The children of the aged are often fearful of a parent developing a new love relationship. Unfortunately it often has to do with money. Betty and Joe, in their seventies, both widowed, each living alone in Florida, met and fell in love. Joe told me, "We thought our children would be happy for us. Instead they acted embarrassed, and started asking questions about whether or not we were going to get married and change our wills! Each set of children were afraid the others would benefit and they would lose! It was so disheartening, I cannot tell you. Fortunately Betty has a son who was happy for us and he told the others what we were too angry and hurt to say."

There is every reason why most of us can become very anxious about possible financial burdens. The reality is that even the most awful nursing homes cost a fortune, that our current government policy is to provide less and less aid to the elderly, that one long illness can wipe out a whole family's assets. In New York City alone, there are twenty thousand elderly people on a waiting list for subsidized housing. What does a family do when society refuses to meet the genuine needs of older people? Ogden Nash once wrote a poem, the title of which was "Father, Dear Father, Go Jump in the Lake; Or You're Costlier than You Think."

Deep inside each of us there is a little child who counted on his or her parents to take care of all our financial needs; some of us still long for that dependency; some of us have worked terribly hard to support our own families and resent new worries, new burdens. It is also human to look forward to some financial relief when a parent dies; some of us hope a parent who is terminally ill will die before all his or her resources are gone.

It seems to me there is far more damage done to one's relationship if the subject of finances is avoided by both parent and child trying to ignore their common anxieties. Jed was supporting two college-age daughters and was struggling to carry the burden of sick wife and an apartment in New York City, where rents are now monumental. His mother's car finally broke down for the last time; he had no choice but to buy her a new one. It meant going further into debt. He was filled with rage and resentment—exhausted, overworked, hopeless. His mother said, "If there is any way you can figure out what I could do, where I could go, to live without a car, I'll do it. I cannot bear your suffering." Jed wept and hugged her; he felt so loved. "You always knew when I was in trouble," he told her. "We'll get through this."

Children of the aged often have trouble seeing their parents as sexual beings. Children have that problem from the time they are old enough to know about sex, but one would hope they might have gotten over this by the time they are in their sixties or seventies! There have been many studies of sexuality and aging,* and there is no question that

*One well worth reading is *Sexuality and Aging,* edited by Kathy Carroll, Ebenezer Center on Aging, 2722 Park Avenue, Minneapolis, MN 53407, 1978. They also publish a useful pamphlet on health-care costs of the aged.

many old people can and wish to remain sexually active in some fashion all their lives. Too often they, and we their children, act as if there were something slightly obscene about this; they sense our disapproval and feel confirmed in their own doubts. In truth, what better time of life to celebrate life in all its sensual pleasures?

Ida and Sam, both in their late eighties, both in a nursing home that did not allow unmarried people of the opposite sex to visit unless they left the door open, found a solution; they would stop the elevator between floors so they could kiss! Ida said, "People can try to make love a dirty thing. How could it be bad to want to be hugged and told you're beautiful?"

Attitudes influence the style in which we try to help a parent make necessary decisions. Arthur told me, "When my dad died, my sister and I decided our mother shouldn't stay in her apartment, but should move to a warm climate, and be with other people her age in a safer neighborhood. She was too grief-stricken to fight us. We had no business making any decisions for her. All we should have done was help her think about her options when she was ready. Instead we had to move her back to her old neighborhood!"

There was no subject I found more fraught with anxiety and guilt than placing an aged parent in a nursing home. The most common response was "I felt like a murderer!" If we have already had to make this decision, there are ways in which we can make life in a nursing home more palatable. We can try to see to it that our parent is treated with dignity. Larry and I once took an elderly relative to a nursing home where, at ninety-four, she was greeted by her first name; we raised hell about it. We can insist that a parent be allowed to have his or her most precious possessions in the room. We can provide a radio with earphones, so listening won't disturb others. When we visit we might bring along a tape recorder and encourage a parent to tell his life story, be a historian.

A young social worker who runs a senior citizens' center has set up a weekly meeting called "Down Memory Lane." She brings in a tape recorder and the members are encouraged to tell stories about themselves—to recall childhood adventures, to tell stories their parents had told them, to describe where families came from, what they did when they came to the United States, who the interesting or unusual characters were in their past, what life was like when they were young. The social worker was surprised to get an avalanche of requests from the children of her clients, who wanted copies of the tapes for themselves and their children. "People are now so interested in their roots," she told me, "that quite inadvertently in setting up a program for the benefit of our elderly, we set in motion something with great appeal for their children and grandchildren. We now sell the tapes for three dollars each, and use the money for going on trips! It's ironic that the age group which is so often categorized as never remembering anything now calls itself The Memory Bank Club."

Instead of sitting in a room trying to make conversation when we visit, we can join in whatever activity is going on at the time, going with a parent to an art class or a chorus rehearsal or an exercise class. We need to touch and hold and hug, we need to talk about love and memories. We need to celebrate whatever ways there may be in which the aged parent shows a need to go on being active. One woman reported that when she took her father to the home for the aged, he looked at all the listless, staring faces of people sitting around the lounge, and commented, "I'm going to have to turn this waiting room into a living room!" His daughter thought that was great, and worked with him, the staff, the residents, to do this. She found out about bus trips, about special prices for concerts, about bringing people into the home to lecture or entertain.

A friend of mine told me that her ninety-two-year-old father, now in a wheelchair and living in a nursing home, told her that he had always wanted to travel more and deeply regretted not having seen more of the world. She began collecting travel folders for him and books about different countries, and he was delighted. He wrote away for more folders and maps, and spends most of his time planning trips and imagining his adventures.

For those of us now facing the possibility that sometime soon *we* may need such resources, now is the time to begin our investigations—not only for our parents, but for ourselves as well! When we think about what we might need, we may do a better job selecting care for someone else! For example, *I* would be outraged by any social worker or nurse calling me "Eda" until *I* told them it was all right; I would immediately dismiss any institution that would infantilize me in any way.

Sometimes it helps to know the worst; May Sarton's *As We Are Now* * is the most harrowing story I have ever read about a nursing home; it is written as a novel but is based on a true story. If we ever want to fully understand the ways in which the elderly can be mentally as well as physically tortured, we need to read this book. By its horror, we learn what must never be allowed to happen.

*May Sarton, *As We Are Now* (New York: W. W. Norton & Co., 1973).

For constructive help—and there are many sources of information in any library—I recommend a Public Affairs Pamphlet by Irving R. Dickman that provides valuable information for decision making.*

What happens to many people after investigating available institutions is that they then figure out some alternative. In his book *Why Survive?*, Dr. Robert Butler has a chapter on nursing homes entitled "Houses of Death Are a Lively Business."† Seventy-nine percent are profit-making; fourteen percent are nonprofit, religious, and fraternal; seven percent are government-sponsored. Edith M. Stern, in her article "Buried Alive"‡ wrote: "Unlike some primitive tribes, we do not kill our aged and infirm. We bury them alive in institutions. To save our face, we call the institutions homes—a travesty on the word . . ." About eighty percent of the aged are cared for in the homes of their children, and to some degree at least this is because of the poor-to-terrible quality of many institutions and the high cost of these "services." One of the most serious problems we must fight to change is that while there may be Medicare or Medicaid funds available for institutionalization, no such funds will be provided for care in the home. There are some pioneers, such as Richard Brickner, M.D., of St. Vincent's Hospital in New York, who are proving that in the long run preventive health care in the home and medical supervision of the ill in their own homes is far less costly and much more humane. We all need to support

---

*Public Affairs Pamphlet #566, 381 Park Avenue South, New York, NY 10016, 50¢.
†Butler, *Why Survive?*, Chapter 9.
‡*Woman's Home Companion* (June 1947).

such projects and let the federal and state governments know how we feel.

While those of us in our sixties and seventies almost universally say something like, "I would rather die than live with my children," our parents more often see that as the least painful solution. It can work out very well for some families; for others it can be disastrous. Edward told me, "When my father died, I felt so terrible for my mother, that I moved her into my house without really consulting my wife and my children. Her presence was more of a burden to them than to me, and they bitterly resented my unilateral decision. They took it out on my mother, who was still grieving for my father. It was a disaster—it ended up with everyone in a rage. If I'd discussed it carefully with my family, it would have been a different story."

Sometimes the problems seem insurmountable. In *You and Your Aging Parents,* Edith Stern and Mabel Ross, M.D., discuss many of the imponderables. The parent who won't budge from a big, expensive house; the parent who absolutely refuses care by anyone but his or her children; the parent who insists on staying in an apartment in a dangerous neighborhood; the parent who says, "Kill me before you put me in a nursing home."

Sometimes the problem seems just as great for the aged parent. An independent woman, with a full and active life, realizes she has hurt her daughter deeply by refusing her offer to share her home. An aged father, living in one room, who loves his privacy, is perfectly willing to live at a poverty level just so he can do as he pleases; his son tells him he must come to his house—he's ashamed to have people think he'd leave his father in such squalor. His father, who always hated being ordered around, loves doing as he pleases—leading "my bachelor life again!" Sometimes we tend to jump too quickly to the conclusion that a parent can't live alone.

When my father's second wife died, I thought it would be a great idea if a student from a nearby university could come to live with him, free room and board in return for shopping and cooking and doing odd chores for my father. My father made short shrift of that, and kicked him out! When I went on a vacation, I hired a woman I knew he liked to drop in on him a few times. He practically threw her out! I'm having a tough time with it, but I am learning to let him make his own decisions.

Sometimes situations that seem impossible to us can be worked out. An aged and handicapped woman was living alone in a three-story house after her husband died. Her children assumed that she could not possibly care for herself and would have to sell the house. Instead she rented the two top floors to some married college students, and with the money they paid her she was able to hire a housekeeper. As it turned out, one of the young renters was pregnant and the old lady ended up earning more money as a babysitter!

Whatever the circumstances, here—as in all other situations involving close relationships—talking, communicating honestly and openly with each other are essential. If Grandma or Grandpa is going to live with us, a great many issues need to be discussed ahead of time. The older parent is usually afraid of being infantilized, of not being allowed to do anything. The wife may feel she will lose control over her own home; the children may feel their freedom will be curtailed; the husband may wonder if he and his wife will have any privacy. Sometimes a pattern is set in which the parent is a guest and his or her children are host and hostess, creating an unnatural atmosphere. The attitude "There's nothing to worry about—we always got along well, didn't we?" is likely to be a kiss of death. Arrangements need to be made for seeing to it that everyone has his or her own "space," that differences in temperament are taken into account. It may be that Grandma is accustomed to a big dinner on Sunday at noon, and her family likes to spend Sunday informally, each person doing what he or she pleases. A wife may insist on everything being in perfect order—including Grandpa's room—when he enjoys his own sloppy comfort. How are finances to be handled? What plans can be made if a parent becomes ill? What new rules are needed to provide each family member with necessary tasks as well as privileges? Is the aged parent willing to allow her children to raise their children without interference? Does the aged parent want to participate in household chores and if so, which ones might be genuinely helpful? Would she enjoy babysitting when the children come home from school? Will anybody mind if Grandpa brings his dog and his fish tank?

Sometimes I think we are too afraid of broaching subjects that need to be talked about. We are desperate to express our discomforts but terrified of hurting a parent's feelings and starting a new crisis. The truth is that if we bring up a subject in a suitable and sensible way, without anger, the results may be far more successful than we ever dreamed possible.

Sadie told me this story: "Every time my mother went to stay with my sister [in another country] she drove Cecily crazy, nagging her from one end of the day to the other. Nothing was ever quite right or on time or clean enough—

she nagged and nagged until at the end of a torturous two-week visit, Cecily took Mom to the train station and very calmly and quietly told her, 'Mother, you are going to have to make a choice. If you can't stop nagging me all day, every day, I simply can't invite you to visit us anymore. If you can stop nagging me, we can have a very good time together and it will be a pleasure to see you.' Our mother got a little tearful and quiet and looked very thoughtful when she said goodbye and got on the train. A few hours later she called Cecily on the phone and said, 'I'm sorry. I guess it's because I miss Daddy and feel frightened sometimes.' Cecily was understanding and comforting and they had a fine time on the next visit."

Another issue in decision making about many aspects of an aged parent's life has to do with the relationship among siblings. In the best of all possible worlds brothers and sisters are all crazy about the parent or parents, and want to share equally in helping. Sometimes this may mean wanting a parent to live in one household for six months and then in another. Or, where all feel a sense of obligation, they may decide on their own that a parent should be moved from home to home every two or three months. (Unfortunately this sharing usually leaves the parent feeling he or she has no real home and is forever an itinerant wanderer.)

What I found was that daughters seem to be taking far more responsibility for aged parents than sons. The only time this seemed to be less true was when the son's wife was willing to be helpful. To some degree this pattern is probably the result of having been taught in childhood that nurturance is the role of women. Sometimes it seemed to be that the daughters-in-law were reluctant to make any sacrifices—saw the elderly in-law as some kind of rival—and made it very difficult for a son to be responsible. The husbands of daughters seemed almost universally more accepting of their wives' feelings of responsibility.

Old rivalries, old hurts, play some part in what happens. Sometimes a daughter who has actually felt rejected by a parent will now compete with siblings to be "the good one" at last. Siblings who have spent a lifetime competing with each other or disliking each other find themselves caught in all kinds of complicated emotional and financial negotiations.

Sometimes martyrdom interferes with a fair distribution of responsibility. We need to ask ourselves if we have really allowed others to participate. Do we take over too quickly? Do we infantilize younger brothers and sisters by demanding too little, or are we showing off how strong we have become to older siblings? The martyr's line is, "What can I do? *Somebody* has to take over." This is often a person who craves more appreciation from a parent than was forthcoming in childhood, and now it seems the moment has come to be the most appreciated.

What is needed is family meetings where all kinds of feelings can be expressed and brothers and sisters can face all the issues before them together. Often this is difficult because families live far apart, but a gathering can be arranged around some family brithday or holiday when the clan gathers and can plan for a meeting time. Unless a parent is senile or too ill, he or she should of course be part of any family counsel. Sometimes, however, old people have far more trouble expressing real feelings and cannot tolerate as much honesty as their children can, especially when they may feel attacked and outnumbered. Under such circumstances it may be wise to hold a family counsel for everyone and then have the younger generation meet again for further discussion.

Whether a parent lives in a child's home or alone or in an institution, there is one strange irony that really bothers me: the gradual disappearance of a sense of connection to whatever friends and relations are still alive. It is understandable that contemporaries may be too old to visit, but my father has friends of the past seventy years who were very devoted and who never call up anymore. My father has begun to reach out himself and call people he cares about, but what really infuriates me is that I know that when he dies, probably several hundred people will come to the funeral—mostly nieces, nephews, grandnieces and grandnephews, my friends and coworkers, many of whom have known my father for fifty years or more, in-laws who never come to see him, people from his former law office, people who remember my mother, and so on. What I am thinking of doing is writing a letter to all these people saying, "I know you will come to my father's funeral, but he won't be there to enjoy your company. *Visit now,* and forget about the funeral!" The only thing that stops me is that I tried this once before with a relative I loved greatly and who was deserted by all the people she had loved and been so good to. I even offered to *pay* anyone who would visit her. I sent the letter to thirty people. One aunt responded.

One of the tasks that can make our relationships to an elderly parent far more comfortable is when we and they try to make peace with each other. Old wounds, old hurts, need to be aired, if both are willing. One eighty-one-year-old woman said that she and her sister, eighty-five, had been rivals since early childhood. When she found out her sister was ill, Alice went to see her and said, "Now Rachel, let's talk. Mama said you were beautiful, Papa said I was the smart one. I was jealous of your boyfriends; you were jealous of my success at my job. Now we are two old crones—let's forgive and forget!" They had a wonderful time together!

There are so many things that can still be shared. When PBS aired a whole evening's concert of Rodgers and Hammerstein's musicals, my father was listening in his home and I was in bed with a cold in mine. We called each other three or four times during the fund-raising intermissions to reminisce about when we had seen the musical, or how many musicals we had seen together with my mother and the rest of the family. When the program was over my father called and said, "I can't remember having so many lumps in my throat!"

In every one of the ages and stages of the human experience, there is the opportunity to learn and to grow. Also, as in every other phase of our lives, we may need support and help from others. In many parts of the country support groups are springing up that can help adult children deal with their problems. Often these groups are sponsored by mental health clinics, hospitals, churches, and other community agencies.

Two years ago Nan had to put her mother in a nursing home because she needed special care around the clock. She told me she feels just as guilty now as she did in the beginning. Before that, Nan had tried to do the job herself. She had become a prisoner in her own home. With all her anxieties and guilt, she found out about an organization designed to support Care Givers of Elderly Relatives, to deal with the often desperate problems of aging relatives. Professionals in the area of geriatrics realize that adult children don't usually want to abandon their parents—that they are torn apart by the complex problems they must deal with. In fact family members provide more than 80 percent of all assistance to aged relatives. Most support groups cost little or nothing, some have membership dues. Sometimes the groups are started by social workers or psychologists, but most often professionals serve as consultants to groups started by concerned adult children.*

Whether we are in groups or on our own, life with aged parents teaches us so much about what it means to be human; our aged parents are, in some ways at least, our guides into our own aging.

The psychologist Abe Maslow once told me, "You learn more from the death of a parent than what is written in all the psychology books." What I have discovered is that we can learn as much or more from facing life with an aged parent.

In a poignant and touching article in the "Hers" column, Phyllis Rose tells of her relationship with her mother—what she feels, what she is learning about her own life. In sharing memories with her mother, she realizes that not having anyone to reminisce with is a special form of loneliness. When her mother dies, with whom can she share their special memories?

*Information about support groups can be obtained from the National Self-help Clearing House in New York City or the Self-help Center in Evanston, Illinois. For materials to aid individuals in starting groups, one can write to Children of Aging Parents, 2761 Trenton Road, Levittown, PA 19056, or the National Support Center for Families of the Aging, P.O. Box 245, Swarthmore, PA 19081.

She tells the story of a mother bird who questioned her three babies, "Will you care for me in my old age as I have cared for you?" The first two say "yes" and she calls them liars. The third says, "I can't promise that. I can only promise to care for my own children as you have cared for me." Ms. Rose writes, "It's a truthful response. . . . But when I imagine my son saying the same thing to me . . . I don't seem to find much comfort in it."* We learn about vulnerability and pain; we learn we will become our parents. We are given an opportunity to learn about surmounting loneliness and pain; we learn about dying.

My father forgets the cooked chicken and fruits and vegetables I put in his refrigerator, but he can recall the names of his elementary-school teachers, the number of the apartment he lived in when he arrived from Russia at the age of six. He is looking through all the memorabilia of a lifetime, and while I imagine it must hurt terribly, he now gives me some of the letters he wrote to my mother during their yearlong courtship, and the letter he wrote to her on their wedding day.

With one batch of photographs, souvenirs and letters, he enclosed a letter to me, making it clear he was making me the keeper of the flame: "The time has come to adjourn, the presiding officer stops the clocks . . . It is wonderful to have one's children become witnesses to the beauties of the past . . ." The letter starts, "Dear Edakins," the special name he called me when he wrote me letters as a child, telling me stories about Tom Thumb. He has also been returning to me letters I wrote my parents, renewing my awareness of my own past with him and my mother. He's

The New York Times (May 3, 1984).

done the same with my brother. When we are together now, it is as if most of the present has become far less important than the memories of a happy, creative love-filled life. I hear stories I never heard before. One day he began to reminisce about walking across an open field—farmland in Brooklyn!—with his mother and brother when a large dog suddenly attacked his brother, and he was terrified; how his mother tore the dog away, suddenly wildly strong, even though she was a small woman. I was so surprised, because my brother had been bitten by a dog at one time, and my father never mentioned his own story. As a young father he had probably forgotten all about his own experience; now his childhood is returning fresh and new. He is exploring the meaning of his life, and while he is forgetful and sometimes inarticulate about the events of the day, he is crystal clear about the past.

His clothes are getting worn; he needs to give me clothes to take to the cleaners, buttons to be sewed on, but he doesn't bother. I see his face light up at the sight of his great-granddaughter; I marvel at his huge appetite (and perfect digestive system) as he gleefully puts away a breakfast of three eggs, three pancakes, and bacon. I see his face becoming thinner; I remember he was a handsome young man—a full shock of black hair, warm, kind brown eyes. I see him stumble getting out of a car; I see his loneliness for my mother—I see that almost all his contemporaries are gone. I remember fascinating dinner parties when I was a child—my parents both did interesting work, made truly responsible community contributions—he and my mother were respected by leaders in fields of social work, law, education. When I wrote to Larry during World War II, before we were married, about some of the people who visited my home, he wrote back, "When I get to New York, I expect to find Madame Chiang Kai-shek and Winston Churchill holding a conversation in the hall."

How *dare* this man get old! Where is my father? My Rock of Gibraltar? How could someone who got all A's in mathematics and worked as an accountant sometimes be confused about financial matters? How could a lawyer, a union-management mediator respected by both sides, a philosopher, a teacher, a man who taught me to be a liberal, a humanist, a social democrat—how could he have become so conservative?

Mostly I experience worry and guilt about his welfare. And frustration, as I try to figure out some plan that takes into account my work schedule, the distance between our apartments, his safety. My brother helps when he can, but he has other burdens and a job that makes his time much more inflexible than mine.

On one particular day I was in a swivet. I'd spent many hours for several days on the phone trying to get advice and information about hiring some companion-homemakers. I was terrified by the expense involved. I was exhausted by an excruciating pain in my wrist for the past month which was still undiagnosed despite many doctors' examinations.

When I walked into my father's apartment, he was sitting at the dining room table, with a small jewelry box in front of him and a letter—both for me. The letter reads:

In one of your recent letters you thanked me for helping you to come to terms with your mortality. There was no particular chain of thoughts, but I took out the medal that I received at the Baron de Hirsch School in the Educational Alliance—a short two years after we landed in New York.

It was a school for "greenhorns," immigrant children, where we could learn English before going to the public schools. I was eight years old, when they gave me a medal of merit, and I suddenly recalled how my mother was so proud—not knowing what "merit" meant, but a medal was always a great honor, and I was an open-eyed green-horn, a scared newcomer to America, and I remember Miss Jacobs my first teacher in America presenting me with something that I knew was very precious. To my mother it was the highest praise and she showed it to everybody.

It suddenly dawned on me that I wanted you to have it—for the merit of a life for all of me and all of eternity in my concept of mortality, the precious love of a mother for her bewildered child.

To be involved (as my mother and I were then) is a "Peak Experience" in the words of your friend Abe Mas-low, is being fully human. What more can one see in fur-ther peaks of life's dreams except to know that all around are heartbeats of love—that give meaning to life.

Much, much love,
Dad

In the jewel box was a small deeply tarnished silver medal given to my father in 1904, beautiful, delicately de-signed with one part on top saying "Merit," joined by two chains to a slightly larger round medal with the name of the school on it.

As I write about it, I weep. Visions of my father, the little "greenhorn," fill my mind. The stories he told me of his childhood—life in a small Russian village, his mother and brother making the pilgrimage to America to join the rest of their family, the first sight of the Statue of Liberty, his father and brothers rowing out to meet the ship as it neared Ellis Island.

Floods of memories—his, mine, our family. Frightening illnesses; vacations in Maine; the time I heard my father crying because of money worries during the Depression. His silences, his pain when my brother had polio. I remember him holding my head when I had trouble breathing, giving me medicine, all night long, night after night when I had whooping cough. Or the time I had rheumatic fever and had to stay in bed for almost a year—the poetry he read to me—the newspaper he helped me start called *The Bed Post*. I was the editor and collected articles from each member of the family, wrote my own column, put it all together, and we read it aloud on Saturday mornings.

My father was a man who gave me such a profound moral sense of what an ethical life must mean that it was really more than I could cope with as a child. But as an adult, how I appreciate my sense of outrage at injustice, my idealism, my unquenchable desire to fight for human rights and dignity.

He *always* wrote beautiful letters—and there I was, being given one of his most treasured possessions—kept in a box, pinned to a small faded satin cushion, for more than *eighty* years! A child's wonder at being accepted, honored—a citizen in a new land of hope.

And in that moment, feeling the pain at his living long enough to be a very old man and also the love, the memories, the pride, the sense that my childhood would die when he died. Stubborn and intractable one minute, tender and loving the next. Confused at one moment, forgetful, and then playing the meanest and best games of chess with Larry the next. A life full of hazards and inconveniences and frustrations and shock at watching the aging—and then, suddenly, overwhelming love and pain at the inevitable separation to come.

I answered his letter and thanked him for the gift of his merit badge:

Dear Dad,

Oh, how in the world to tell you what I feel? So much of life for you and me is now necessarily filled with frustration and worries and readjustments, and then suddenly you put the whole thing in perspective by giving me that treasured medal of merit! Something so deep and so precious a memory, that you kept it through so many moves, high school, college, work, marriage, parenthood—a treasure never lost, a memory full of wonder—the symbol of acceptance in a strange new land.

I had myself a good cry and allowed myself to be flooded by memories of your childhood and mine. Your medal of merit is a tangible gift, but I have plenty of other gifts that have sustained me through my lifetime—a profound sense of ethics, moral outrage at injustice, idealism,—and most of all so many memories—thousands upon thousands of memories of our good life, and the ways in which my childhood (and yours) prepared me for the rich, creative life I've had, including so much love. I don't want to get old any more than *you* are crazy about it, but in your eighty-eight and in my sixty-two years we have both been graced with fullness of adventure in loving and living shared by very few people.

I cannot tell you how touched I am—I understand the message of how it all was for you and what you made of your life, and someday I'll share the story and the medal with Wendy, and someday she will share the story and the message with her daughter, and that scared, proud "green-horn" and his adoring mother will live forever.

Much, much love,

Eda

TEN

~~~~~~

Widowhood:
Loss, Grief, and
Letting Go IN A BOOK ON AGING, A

discussion of widowhood is as important as a discussion of marriage. It is a fact of life for many, and a terror for many more.

Years ago, on a business trip to Chicago, I was able to see a friend I'd known twenty years earlier. We had kept in touch by mail but hadn't seen each other. She had been widowed four or five years before our reunion. When she opened the door to her apartment, I hugged her. She held tight for a minute and then she said, "You have no idea what human contact, *touching,* means to me now. I hunger for it every day, and the only people who hug me are my grandchildren."

I was startled and shaken. It was a moment of sudden clarity about what widowhood must mean to people who have been happily married. I tried to imagine what it would be like to have to live without being held and hugged and touched. It felt like some dark, barren, empty place.

Sometime later, another recently widowed friend, fifty-four years old and very attractive, told me, "Eda, you can't imagine what it's like. The men—the creeps—are coming out of the walls! Some are the husbands of my best friends who say they just want to comfort me. Others seem to get aroused by the idea of having sex relations with a woman who is grieving! It's ghoulish. But the worst of all is that while I miss sex terribly, I can't even respond to the few men who really appeal to me. I'm shy! I haven't been with anyone but Manny for more than thirty years! I'm ashamed to let anyone see my body—which is pretty good, but not like when I was twenty!"

Another woman I know, widowed at only forty-two, expressed her feelings of devastation in a way that is common to many grieving men and women—she went to bed with anyone who asked her. It's a kind of manic search for reconnecting, feeling close. People react in very individual ways to trauma, depending on their particular life histories and personalities.

Widowhood, of course, is only one of the many kinds of losses we face in life and there are similarities in the process of mourning, whether it be a divorce or the death of a child or a friend. One of the most poignant responses to my questions about aging was part of a letter I received from my Aunt Edith, who said in part, "As long as I can remember, my arms have reached out for relationships with family and friends that were meaningful, but now I can't extend my arms as far and there are fewer loved ones to embrace."

The experience of loss in the later years of our lives was poignantly expressed by Laura Hobson, who said that when her mother died, her father commented: "Life reserves the hardest lessons for when we are too old to learn them."* A loss is terrible enough when we still have youth

*Laura Hobson, *Laura Z: A Life* (New York: Arbor House, 1983).

and resilience, and only more traumatic when we feel so much more vulnerable and afraid of the future. May Sarton describes the death of people we love as being like "an earthquake that buries a little more of the past forever."* One widow told me, "I still miss romance and being praised." How much we need to feel connected to others! My most painful losses, thus far, have been my mother, two aunts whom I adored, and five friends whose deaths devastated me. I have talked or corresponded with a great many articulate people who have helped me as much as they could to understand their feelings, and while I have not experienced widowhood, I have surely felt grief, and think I understand some of its universal dimensions.

A special concern of the widowed with whom I spoke was the terrible fear of not being able to take care of themselves; many said, "I worry about who will take care of me if I get sick; we counted on each other to share the problems of getting old."

Many widowed people seem to fear a loss of their identity; they feel that their spouse was the only person who really knew them; that things that were shared were private—even one's children and friends couldn't know the identity one had with the most special person in one's life. One woman said, "I realized that nobody will ever know the pet names Robert called me; they were so dear to me, but private."

I found that those who suffered the most and the longest tended to be people who had never been alone in all their lives. They had gone from their parents' home right into marriage, and the relationship had been one in which the

*Sarton, *The House by the Sea.*

couple was inseparable. They had to start from scratch learning something I could wish they had learned long ago, before becoming alone was such a sudden reality—that all our lives we have an inner companion that needs to be cultivated and cherished and is always available to us. A widowed friend visited me in the country some time ago; we spent some time together talking, picnicking, swimming, but I had told her in advance I would need some time alone. I went off by myself to read; she gardened while I worked, she sunbathed while I cooked. I noticed her watching me quite intensely and I finally asked her what she was thinking. She said, "We've been here by ourselves for five days, and you seem so self-sufficient. I wish that David and I had had some of the separations you and Larry have had—his traveling so much, you staying alone in the country. Being alone is nothing strange for you. You seem to enjoy solitude."

She was right—up to a point. I have learned to enjoy my inner companion; I am not lonely when I am alone. But there was still a great difference; Larry called me from California every few days, and I knew we would be together again. But it is true, I think, that where there has been great dependence, the shock, the suffering, the sense that *everything* has changed, is greater than for those who have already brought into a marriage relationship more space, more freedom, more opportunities for discovering the profound satisfactions of solitude. If one hasn't yet experienced being alone, it is one of the kinds of new learnings that must take place if life is to have meaning after the loss of a husband or wife. One man wrote: "Beth and I were almost never apart. Her death has accentuated my feelings about getting old, and I feel it now has accelerated the aging process."

A widow wrote: "I have enough of everything except companionship and it is unbearably lonely. So much so that I wish life to be over." When people we love die we have two choices; we can allow the loss to destroy us—we can lose totally the past that we shared with the person who has died, or we can use that past to strengthen us, make us more human than ever before. It is one of the greatest challenges a human being can face, and the capacity to do so depends on a number of things—but most of all, it seems to me, on this issue: can the widowed person face the natural, normal ambiguities in the relationship he or she has lost?

One widow wrote: "If Lou had lived this would have been the most perfect time of our lives. We would have had plenty of money to do anything we wanted, I would have helped Lou to finish his book. When we got old, we would have each other." I knew this woman well, and I knew that it was more than likely that some of the very severe stresses and strains in this marriage may possibly have speeded her husband's heart attack. The more she romanticized their relationship, denied the problems in their lives, the harder it would be for her to find any way to go on with her life; she would be using all her psychic energy in defense of a myth.

Larry and I visited an acquaintance some time after his wife had died. We had heard he was inconsolable. His wife had died fourteen months earlier, but when we walked into his house, we saw that her knitting was still on the coffee table, her glasses and an open book were on the bedside table. Her clothes were still in the closet. He had remained in a deep depression, saw no one but his daughter and son-in-law and grandchildren, had given up gardening. He spent most of his time sitting in a chair and staring into space. Whenever his daughter appeared with his groceries, he would sit and cry the whole time she was with him. It sounds very sad, doesn't it—such a close relationship, such a lost soul. Not at all; he and his wife rarely had a good word to say about each other, their marriage was a mutually agreed upon battle of wits. It may be that in the beginning they may have cared about each other, but in the last twenty years of their life together, they had spent most of their time fighting. Endless mourning becomes a way of denying ambivalent feelings.

The work of grief and mourning are surely necessary. We know, for example, that it is unwise to make any major life decisions during this period. One widow called it her "crazy time," when judgment is suspended. Allowing waves of grief to sweep over one, giving in to the agony, is the first step toward recovery. People who seem stoic, who don't weep, who try to go on with their lives too quickly— who fly into a kind of pseudo independence because they are so terrified of their dependency needs—pay a heavy price later on; when our human needs go unmet they don't go away—they cripple us sooner or later. One needs to give in to mourning.

The "end" of mourning doesn't mean the end of grief, or of forgetting. The nineteenth-century poet Phillip Brooks wrote a condolence letter to a friend in which he said, "People bring us well-meant but miserable consolations when they tell us what time will do to help our grief. We do not want to lose our grief, because our grief is bound up with our love and we could not cease to mourn without being robbed of our affections."

Also in a letter, Marcel Proust wrote: ". . . there is no

more ridiculous custom than the one that makes you express sympathy once and for all on a given day to a person whose sorrow will endure as long as his life. Such grief, felt in such a way, is always 'present,' it is never too late to talk about it, never repetitious to mention it again."

All quite true; anyone who suggests in any way that one should try to forget and get on with living is interfering with the healing process.

I asked a widowed friend to read this section of this book, since I was not writing out of personal experience. Her response startled me. She said, "All you wrote has to do with the suffering and the loneliness. Some widowed people are strong and adventurous. They do great and important things with their lives. Some are refreshed by experiences they never had before. We can make new friends, have lovers, even marry again!" How right she was. In the face of grief and mourning, we can forget to look beyond. But it is also true that the very facing of pain can help to bring about that later strength.

Larry, having worked for many years with grieving families, was very helpful to me when my mother died. He told me I would never get over her death, but as time passed, the waves of pain would come less frequently and with less intensity. That's exactly what happened. When the pain comes, it is still powerful; memories become more important, more meaningful as time passes, but these now enhance my life.

How can one know when it is time to turn one's grief into actions that keep memories alive but allow us to become whole again? From my own experience, and from the reports of many others, it seems that three to six months is usually the period of most intense shock, grief,

and immobilization. When a person doesn't begin to recover and move back into life for a year or more, it is
almost always (unless one has been unusually dependent all
of one's life) related to an inability to accept the bad memories as well as the good ones. When I spoke at my mother's
funeral, I spoke not only of her talents and her love, but
also of the stresses in her life that had made her the complicated person she was. In the months that followed, I
was able to remember the times when we were close as
well as the times when I was furious with her. *I kept her
whole*—and she remains so now. Because I can remember
her shortcomings, I am free, open to the equally strong
feelings of love. I see a woman on a bus whose eyes are
like hers, or I see a woman walking down the street in a
coat like the one she had, and for a moment I am once
again overwhelmed by grief, even thirteen years after her
death.

Remembering a real person is the way we begin to recover. There is no way we can recover completely from the
death of the people we love, and we find our own unique
ways of dealing with the never-ending sense of loss. Recently my Aunt Edith sent me the first draft of an article
she was writing about my mother and my aunt, her two
sisters who died some years ago. The relationship between
the three sisters was unusually close, and Edith was trying
to recapture them on paper. She writes of special memories,
of the shock their deaths brought, and of her permanent
sense of loneliness, despite leading a full and useful life.
Whether or not she ever sells the article, it seemed to me a
touching and creative way to deal with her mourning.

Another aspect of recovery is that we need to take action
of some kind that translates our grief into living memories.

A beautiful example of using grief creatively and humanly is *In the Midst of Winter,* * edited by Mary Jane Moffat. The title comes from Albert Camus (in *Actuelles*): "In the midst of winter, I finally learned that there was in me an invincible summer." Mrs. Moffat explains in the introduction of the book that this collection of literature having to do with death grew out of her own need for solace when a long and happy marriage ended in the sudden death of her husband. As she went through the letters of condolence, she found a letter that included Camus's inspiring statement, which she said were the first words of solace she'd been able to comprehend. She writes that when she emerged from the first weeks of dazed disbelief, she felt the need for some kind of emotional inspiration, and as she began searching through poetry, fiction, and nonfiction for solace, she began to think about sharing her exploration with others who might also need such comfort. The creation of an important, compassionate book that grew out of her personal grief has given her husband's death special meaning.

Giving money to a good cause that was important to a loved one is one way of turning sorrow into action; even better, doing something, working at something, that had meaning for this person will help one to begin the healing process. One widow told me, "Everybody told me to get rid of Jim's clothes and for a long time I couldn't do it. Then my daughter brought a young man home who was a senior at her college and had just gotten a wonderful job for after graduation, but he had no money at all to buy the kind of clothes he needed. He was about the same size as my hus-

* Mary Jane Moffat, ed. *In the Midst of Winter* (New York: Vintage Books, 1982).

band and we completely outfitted him—suits, sweaters—even shoes. Much to my surprise, I felt closer to my husband, knowing some part of him was helping someone else."

We need to find ways to express in some real way what was best in the person we have lost; what he or she would want most to be remembered for. And probably, what helps most of all, is to incorporate into ourselves the qualities that characterize the person who died—not trying to become that person, but using what we can in our daily lives. For example, a widower who had depended on his wife almost completely told me, "Molly did everything, she ran the house, she took care of the finances, she took care of the children most of the time. She was the strong one; I needed her to take care of me. I thought I would be unable to survive without her. Then, one day, about four months after she died, I started cleaning the house and the garage; I oiled the lawn mower; I washed the car; I called the kids—one at college, one married—to tell them I missed them and hoped they'd come to see me. At the end of the day, I was shocked to realize I was *whistling!* At first I felt ashamed—and then I realized I was doing the things Molly might have been doing, and she felt very close to me."

We may begin to move beyond the intense period of mourning not only through active remembrance, but also through recognizing the possibility for a new autonomy—something we have no reason to feel guilty about. Marriage always involves some compromise, and there may be many things one never did because a spouse wouldn't have enjoyed it. One man had never flown in a plane because his wife was deathly afraid of flying. Two months after his wife's death he flew from New York to Florida to see his brother. On the flight home, the plane reached Manhattan just at dusk, as the lights were coming on. "It's a fairyland!" he exclaimed in great awe and excitement. He was my father, and I knew that this was a turning point; he was ready for new adventures on his own.

One of the factors that brings the bereaved back into life is all the practical realities that must be faced: dealing with a will; trying to decide whether to sell a house or stay put; figuring out one's financial status; getting back to work; or continuing whatever activities had been part of one's retirement. During the intense period of mourning, one should not make any important decisions, no matter how much pressure may be brought to bear by others. Time is needed for quiet reflection, alone. A time for reassessment of one's life, one's needs. In what ways should one seek meaningful changes? In what ways does one need to hold on to the life one has led?

One widow sold her house within a few months after her husband's death. Then she bought an apartment, and instead of giving herself a chance to rebuild her life, make new friends, and experiment with new activities, she abruptly sold her apartment, moved across the country, and took an apartment near her married daughter. She later said these decisions had been the worst ones she had ever made—she ended up feeling that no place was home, that she was a wanderer trying to tie her life to one or the other of her three children, all living in different cities where she knew no one.

A widower, on the other hand, told me that when his wife died he simply could not bear the thought of selling his home, even though it had been far too big even before his wife had died. Here was all the memorabilia of their life together, raising the children, and it seemed to him that he would be destroying all his memories—somehow hurting his wife—if he were to move. He said, "I kept up the struggle for three years. I rented a couple of rooms out, but I couldn't stand the noise and having strangers around. The heating bills got worse and worse. I realized I was getting too old to take care of the yard and I couldn't afford getting any help. Finally it got so bad, I knew I would have to sell the house. I bought a small apartment in one of these adult communities, and I love it. I have people to talk to, I play a little golf, everything is taken care of by other people, and I have enough money from the sale of the house not to have to worry anymore. I took all the furniture my wife loved the most, I have my paintings and my picture albums—I have the best of the past and my own future."

Money and worries about independence are very real. One widow told me that when her husband died she "started to think about my old age, and I've become a real miser. I hold on to my money so I can *buy* the help and comfort I'll need someday." In all my conversations with older people in general and the widowed in particular, I never heard anyone say they would willingly allow children to take care of them. Independence was most important, which represents a tremendous change in social attitudes. Where it was once inconceivable to think that children would not take care of their elderly relatives, it is now exactly the opposite—we dread it. And this is not always an accurate reflection of how our children feel. It is that the idea of independence has become a matter of personal pride and status; we see dependence as a loss of our self-esteem, even of our identity. A widow told me, "Becoming a widow has accentuated what most of us already feel—that old people are not respected, that we are considered throwaway people. Nobody will care about us if we don't take care of ourselves."

Autonomy and total independence aren't always possible and we may need to learn ways to accept dependency with some grace, and without giving up our own needs and rights. A widow told me, "I had no choice; after Will's long illness, I was really poverty-stricken, and when my son and daughter-in-law said I could live with them, I said yes, even though I dreaded it. We sat down and had a long conference—about how we could do this and make it work. At first they were suggesting that I share my grandson's room. I told them that was out of the question—he'd end up hating me, and that was no way for a seventy-year-old woman to live. They had an unfinished basement with a toilet and a sink. My son and I agreed we would share the cost of making it over into a place for me. When I said I knew this was my daughter-in-law's home and I would only do something if she asked me, she was so relieved! As soon as I moved in, I located the nearest senior citizen center, and thankfully they had a bus service, so I spend three days a week there. When my family go out, I don't assume they want me along unless they ask me. I pay a small rent, which makes me feel better; my son says they are saving the money for my grandson's college education, which makes me feel really good."

It seems to me we needn't feel quite so fearful of being dependent in some way, if we participate in the planning, if we try to anticipate the problems, and if we find ways to live in dignity. That means being resourceful, looking for activities that we can do on our own. One widow told me that she thought she would become a "nonperson" in her daughter-in-law's house. She asked her daughter-in-law to make a list of things she could do that would be really helpful and noninterfering. She said, "I don't feel at all the way I expected. I have definite jobs to do and I know I'm making life easier for my daughter-in-law."

For those widowed who continue to live alone, fear of illness is a constant background theme. If we have plenty of money, we can hire caretakers. Few reach old age in that state. One woman told me that she had a favorite niece with whom she'd always had a good relationship. In her seventies she talked to this young woman about what might happen if she became helpless or ill, and said she would like to pay some minimal amount to the niece for doing whatever might be necessary and would leave her some money in her will. It was an arrangement both affectional and financial. She said, "My children would feel a duty to me, and frankly, I couldn't bear to be dependent on them—the relationship is just too close. With my niece, I would still feel as if I were in charge of myself."

Widowhood may require accommodations, changes in our goals. One widow told me, "I have always saved money. I wanted to be independent and to be able to help others. In a very small way, I was able to do that while my husband was alive. I worked from the time I was fourteen, and reading was always my passion. Someday, I thought, I shall have time to read and read, and my husband and I would have enough money to go to England and Paris. By the time he died, I knew I'd never have enough money to travel. But as long as my eyesight holds up, I can read and read."

The period of recovering from intense and constant

mourning is a time of letting go—of saying goodbye—of taking hold of one's own life and making new choices. Helen is an excellent example of this process. When Herbert died, she was devastated, in a state of shock. For several months thereafter she went through the motions of living, but cried almost constantly. Then she began to have feelings of terror; she was aware that she was alone in the world for the first time in forty-seven years. She became extremely dependent on her only daughter, who had a job and a family of her own and couldn't be as available as Helen wanted her to be. I met her seven months after Herbert's death; having observed the intensity of her suffering, I was astounded and delighted when, very calmly, she said, "Oh, I'm working. I have a volunteer job at a physical rehabilitation center. I work three full days a week. It's wonderful to have to think about other people's problems."

The death of a child is probably the most excruciating of all grief experiences, and one sees so clearly the difference between those parents who use such a terrible tragedy for life and those who are destroyed by it. Even within one family there can be startling differences. When a child died of leukemia in one family, the mother retreated from the world, neglected her older child, rejected her husband, and remained in a deep depression for many years, unable to handle her guilt, her anger, her ambivalence. The father spends almost every Saturday afternoon in the children's ward of a hospital, where he helps both parents and children to deal with terminal illnesses. She sacrificed her humanity in her suffering; he uses his suffering in a way that shows just how much pain a human being can surmount, how much suffering human beings can endure.

A few years ago I met a couple whose twenty-one-year-old daughter had been killed one day after her college graduation in a car accident involving a drunken driver. She was their only child, and they adored her. The wife gained one hundred pounds in the next year, and her husband retreated into silence. They never shared their grief with each other, but suffered in isolation and loneliness, unable to bridge their grief to reach each other. Eventually the marriage collapsed altogether. Another family, dealing with a similar tragedy, started what has become a national movement against drunk driving, with new legislation resulting in a marked decrease in accidents. A true memorial to their child, and a positive and creative way of healing their own terrible wounds.

Many years ago, a dear friend of mine died. He had two daughters, eight and ten, and they and their mother came to visit me shortly after Bob's death. After many discussions with the children I realized how important it is to help young children deal with their grief. I decided to write a book for children about the death of a parent;* I dedicated the book to Bob and his daughters. It helped me to let go, and move on.

Some time after my mother's death, my father gave me a letter she had written to him about how she felt on my first day at kindergarten. I had never been separated from her in this way. Although she worked, I was always at home—now *I* was moving out into a larger world, by myself. I remember that day very clearly myself; I was miserable! I felt deserted; I cried most of the first day; I didn't feel at all sure I'd ever be taken home. I remember being in what

---

*Eda LeShan, *Learning to Say Goodbye: When a Parent Dies* (New York: Macmillan, 1976; New York: Avon, 1978).

seemed a cavernous, enormous room, far away from everyone else. In truth it was a small room, but what I felt
changed the reality.

We all experience saying goodbye, letting go, in a thousand ways in the course of our lives: to people, to places, to
stages in our lives. The more meaningful an experience or a
relationship has been, the greater the pain—but how awful
it would be if it never mattered. A young man who had
had a miserable childhood and had spent several years in
prison was watching television with me the day the hos-
tages came home from Iran. As families ran toward each
other, his eyes filled with tears. He said, "I wish I knew
how they were feeling." It was one of the saddest comments I'd ever heard.

Letting go and saying goodbye mean the beginning of a
reassessment of one's life—it's a treasure hunt for inner
strengths and talents and interests that may never have
been fully tested, and which could bring new meaning to
life. Of all the things people told me about that were bene-
ficial in the process of recovery, one thing stood out above
all others: they felt better when they were being *useful to
other people.* Many said that this was the first step to becoming ready for remarriage. One example was the woman
who told me, "I couldn't imagine anyone ever loving me
again. And then I went to work as an aide in a nursing
home. I began to feel loved—I began to feel worthwhile.
The more the work brought back my confidence, the more
I seemed to be ready for what happened; at seventy-three I
met a seventy-two-year-old widower and now we've been
married for four years!"

Each person must find his or her unique and individual
way of accepting what has happened. One widower says:

"As a widower I am acutely aware of loneliness. But—and this is a big but—I would rather grow old alone than have a live-in relationship just to have another body around. I hope no one ever thinks of me in those terms either. I want someone to share my hopes, fears, ironies and humor as I share hers."

A widow said, "I was widowed at fifty-nine. Now I'm eighty-three. It took me about twenty years to become a whole self again. I'm now on the board of a college and I travel extensively. I'm lucky to be very healthy, but I wish I hadn't let my loneliness go on so long."

Another widow wrote: "I turned to nature when my husband died. I garden, I explore the woods, I feed the birds and the ducks. But there will always be the moments when I wish I could turn to my life's companion to giggle over something, or exalt over a sunset or a brilliant maple tree in the fall!"

It is natural to need time for healing. A widow told me, "It's three years, and I still find myself running to the phone to call my husband at the office when something exciting happens. Or when something goes wrong with the refrigerator, I feel so alone because he's not there to fix it. Silly things. We had separate lives, but we always came together at the end of the day and that's the loneliest time of all. I try to make dates with friends for dinner and a movie, or theater, or the ballet, so I won't be home at the end of the day." We need to be gentle with ourselves, and accept our pain; we need to be proud of our courage; we need to give ourselves the love we miss.

In a 1983 speech, Anne Morrow Lindbergh said, "Everyone has her own list of treasures still intact. Those who have husbands are lucky. To share one's life and memories, walks and laughter with another person is a treasure. When I see an older couple walking hand in hand, I look the other way, partly because I don't want to intrude on something very precious I no longer have. I am a widow and I live alone.

"But one *learns* to walk alone, and that is one of the opportunities in age, a last chance to learn to be truly independent and free to choose one's life and interests and friends, enjoying them but not leaning on anyone. A state we dreamed of in adolescence and never quite found."

Perhaps the hardest task we face is to allow ourselves to experience pleasure and fulfillment again. What we have to remember is that nothing could be a better memorial—a testament of love—than the courage to be happy again.

Growing Toward the Light: Dying and Death

ONE OF THE GREATEST joys of my middle years was the discovery of the poet May Sarton. I just happened upon one of her books of fiction in a Cape Cod library, and within a week I had read everything I could find written by her. Her conclusion of an article on the subject of aging was:

> *Old age is not an illness, it is a timeless ascent.*
> *As power diminishes, we grow toward more light.* *

It has taken me about eight years and the writing of this book to begin to understand that philosophic and poetic synthesis of both acceptance and exultancy.

In practical terms, I find I am much less depressed and agitated than I was when I began to write this book. I feel quieter, more tranquil, and at the same time more focused on continuing goals. I think the writing about old age has been my way of dealing with a necessary process—experiencing grief and mourning for my lost youth. Nobody ever

---

* *The New York Times Magazine* (Jan. 30, 1978).

told me I would have to grieve for my life before I could let go. Were any of us prepared for this "developmental task"? How much braver we can be when we know what we must do.

We have mourned the loss of others, but we are unprepared for mourning the loss of the one person we have had with us every minute of our lives—ourselves. Why shouldn't we grieve? No one else is this person; no one else ever will be who we have been and are now. It seems to me that when we allow the mourning to take place—when we truly value our lives, our selves—then perhaps we can go beyond grief to a final and piercing declaration, an exultation, an experience of joyous victory, *because we have lived.*

It is the denial of our pain and fear that interferes with our making courageous choices. One of the most honest responses of the people I questioned was a woman of ninety who said, "Death? I think about it often and I am afraid. Of dying but not death. Will I go gracefully or make everybody miserable? I don't really know what I'm afraid of, but I am. In the meantime, I'm trying to live each day as it comes and make it the best it can be."

Edna St. Vincent Millay wrote one of her most famous and prized poems at the death of her husband. The last verse of "Dirge Without Music" is:

> *Down, down, down into the darkness of the grave*
> *Gently they go, the beautiful, the tender, the kind;*
> *Quietly they go, the intelligent, the witty, the brave.*
> *I know. But I do not approve. And I am not resigned.*

To feel one's feelings deeply—perhaps more than ever before—makes it possible for continuing creativity. To be fully creative until one's last breath requires the hard work of joining all of one's life to some greater design, and what makes that task difficult beyond measure is the denial of the pain and the fear and the anger.

Many who are aging think honest, brave thoughts. Gerry, at seventy-eight, wrote: "As for death, I feel it's a normal process. I only feel disturbed when someone close to me passes away. I wouldn't mind dying as long as there is no pain and suffering involved. I never was afraid of it and feel that life doesn't owe me one thing."

Phyllis, at sixty, said, "My life is rich and full yet I am aware of my mortality in a way that surprises me. Many times I am overwhelmed with a profound sadness about how little I have accomplished. Other times the 'yes' I feel is just the joy of being alive."

I was profoundly moved by the openess with which people shared their deepest feelings. Lester, age eighty-eight, wrote: "The fact is I don't feel ready to die and I am afraid of death. I've been feeling the need to talk to a rabbi about death, but I haven't done so yet." Ruth, eighty-six and in a nursing home, told me, "I throw it out of my mind. I know any day it can happen and I don't like it. When I'm called, I'll go—there is no one to argue with."

Every person I talked to hoped for death with dignity; one woman wrote: "My concern has always been will I die in a dignified way—or will I be a great burden to my children? This weighs on my mind—a quick death is my fantasy." A man told me, "I don't worry, just so I die suddenly!"

We each react differently in terms of our life experiences. Anna, seventy-eight, suffering from a serious heart ailment, told me, "I don't expect anything, good or bad.

Since the age of twenty-three, I have accepted whatever happens. By that age I had lived through World War I in Germany, starved during the revolution, had to escape from Hitler—death is the least of my worries!"

Most of us have had anxieties about death and dying long before becoming old. Paul, sixty-one, wrote me: "Yes, I think about dying. I don't imagine there is a human being alive who doesn't. That consciousness of death is what separates us from the rest of the animal world. I thought about it even as a child and can remember lying in bed in the black of night wondering about the nothingness, and thinking in terror that indeed the world could go on without me."

Those with the strongest religious beliefs had the least conflict. "We know we are going to a higher plane of existence," one said. Another told me, "We have studied this matter with spiritual intensity and are reincarnationists."

Pat Carroll wrote:

Like J. M. Barrie said, through Peter Pan . . . it must be the greatest adventure of all! My god, we can't have lived all these years without KNOWING there's more than meets the eye here, folks. My religious training includes a heavy leaning on the afterlife, but I don't see myself sitting around playing a harp or wafting about from cloud to cloud. It must be a more heightened state of consciousness than we have here, that other plane, wherever it is, whatever it is. We must be able to use our different levels of intelligence in some other form SOMEPLACE . . . I think the "letting go" from the void will be the hardest part, the giving up of what we know to step beyond to what NO ONE knows nor has been able to describe . . . There must be a retraining period, a time to readjust, then upward and onward to whatever. I can't wait for that butterflies-in-the-tummy sensation (if one is aware one is dying) of something NEW, the biggest adventure of all . . . I should hate to leave my darlings here, but you know for sure that they will join you eventually, so what can you lose? You'll even see your enemies on the other side, where it might be decided, since you'll be able to see ALL sides of every question maybe, that they weren't such enemies after all. And perhaps some friends will look less good in the light of truth. Won't it be fascinating? I think we fear death more than the very act itself deserves, unless violence or dire pain are included. The natural act of dying is like being born, it's part of the pattern, it must and will be gone through, so sit back, relax, and enjoy the experience.

There are times when I envy those who can put death in the perspective of a life after death, of a heaven or hell. I've been deeply impressed by the peace and acceptance such belief systems bring to millions of people. It must be great comfort to *know* that someone you love still exists on another plane. Larry keeps telling me that "from a scientific point of view" it is inconceivable to imagine that nothing exists after death, but much as I want to believe him, I find myself unable to believe in an afterlife.

There is a lot of talk these days about "near-death experiences" in which a person who is almost dead comes back to life and describes various sensations and images. Almost always these include moving through some sort of tunnel and coming toward a bright light, and coming upon voices and images of loved ones who have died. And almost always these people describe a sense of peace, a special kind of tranquility and acceptance of what it will be like to die.

My own feeling about these reports is that they are true,

but that they are not necessarily an indication of any future life or of a rejoining with those we love in some version of a heaven. When I think of my own dying, the most comforting thought of all would be that I could be with the people I loved—even go back to being a child, with my mother and grandparents. It seems to me an act of will to think such thoughts, and it does help to prepare us for becoming part of the larger universe, for we are creating guides to help us with this task.

When a friend of ours who had been a very successful talk-show host on local programs died, a minister said, "Now Bob is universally syndicated." It seemed an appropriate comment at the time, and then later I began to think it was too flip. After awhile, I changed my mind again, because I interpreted "universal syndication" as the way in which this man influenced all the lives he had touched. I surely *do* believe that to the degree we live our lives as fully and as intensely as possible is the degree to which we influence the cosmos.

I think quite a lot about immortality, as I get older. I am an agnostic—I have no idea at all what might or might not happen after death. When I was young I was an atheist, but I got over being sure I know everything! I've had some very real experiences that make me feel that nothing in the universe ever disappears completely, and that there may be some "energy" or "life force" which might become part of a universal consciousness. I just don't know.

I guess my attitude about immortality has to do almost entirely with what we do on earth that might live after us. I feel some sense of immortality when I look at my granddaughter. I know the love we feel for our daughter is being passed on to her daughter and that in the years to come, we will pass on feelings and attitudes and memories. I know that in my work I've touched the lives of many people I've never even met, and that my life has made a difference. I love the funny stories the best; I met a woman in a department store and she said, "You kept me from killing my thirteen-year-old when you wrote about yours and promised things would get better!" I've been deeply touched by serious letters, like, "Your book about mourning a dead parent helped me to go through my grief at last." Such statements are my immortality.

I think a lot about the things I've done for which I most want to be remembered. For starting the first interracial council in a southern city; for writing a book called *Roots of Crime* in which I tried so hard to challenge the idiotic, simplistic attitudes of the majority of people about what to do with "criminals." Little things—there is now a YMCA in New Jersey where, because of my discussions with the swim director, no child is ever forced to go into the water. I'm proud of having participated in keeping a dump out of a place near some people's water supply. I'm proud of having done a TV series, *How Do Your Children Grow*. I find peace in thinking of all the good things I've tried to do with my life.

My father, a humanist and agnostic, was looking at a perfect rose from my garden. He said (at eighty-eight), "While I'm looking, I accept age and death." I know what he meant. I also find solace in a sense of wonder at feeling connected to what is beautiful and mysterious in nature. I don't really know if those who firmly believe in an afterlife actually die more peacefully than those who are uncertain or who do not believe at all in such a possibility. As I grow older, I find that my greatest sense of connection to all living things, my awe of nature, what I have learned from Larry about meditation and a sense of oneness with the universe, have helped me to be less afraid.

Some people handle the issue of death with humor. I received one letter which said, "My wife and I bought a cemetery plot on a high hill overlooking the Pacific Ocean. We have both agreed we'd like to be buried in a vertical position instead of horizontally, so we can enjoy the view forever!"

On a different note, Arlene wrote: "I know everyone has to go through it. I think when the time comes I will be able to face it, although at the moment the thought makes me quite sad. The saddest part would be knowing I could no longer watch the children and grandchildren grow and develop. I do *not* want to die in a hospital, but at home, with dignity. I know I will regret having to die, have some fears about it but perhaps whatever illness I'll have may make me so weary and uncomfortable that I shall not mind too much. It is really the thought of not seeing my loved ones that hurts so much."

With all these poignant, complicated feelings, there is one simple truth; the way we prepare for dying and death *matters*. There are terrible deaths and deaths that are the best they can be. And what it seems to come down to, in almost every case, is that we die pretty much the way we have lived. There are styles of living and styles of dying.

In his work for about thirty years on a cancer research project, Larry has met death with many terminally ill patients. What he has found is that the more a person regrets his or her life, the more terrible the death. For those who have fulfilling, loving, creative lives, death is sad but not horrible. One patient, dying in terrible despair, turned to Larry and said, "I never lived, did I?"

Another patient, who was rapidly dying of cancer of the liver, was explaining to his daughter why he was continuing to examine his life, why he had gone on a trip to Europe even though he was very weak and sick at the time, why he was continuing to think about the future. He told her, "I know I'm going to die. Everybody does, but I want to *do it with style.*"

Dying "with style" involves more than anything else a choice to pursue the continuing struggle to find one's own special identity. To some that may seem strange. After all, if you are about to die, what difference does it make? *All the difference in the world.* There is probably no time in all our lives when we need to know who we are more clearly. In a sense one is signing out, and the final signature is really our claim to immortality. We were not the same—not even close—to anyone else who ever lived or is now alive.

There are, of course, the terrible deaths of those who become senile or suffer a lingering illness in the course of which they lose all sense of self. But it has been my experience that with those exceptions the most awful deaths occur when a person has been too frightened to live, to take risks, to search for his or her special identity.

I learned a great deal from the worst death I have ever witnessed. I knew Mona for many years. In all that time she never admitted to having had a single ambivalent emotion during the years in which she was growing up. She actually said, "All my memories are happy ones!" Her mother was perfect; her father was perfect; her sisters were perfect. Her childhood had been blissful. Suspicious creature that I am, I looked for the truth! Mona never talked about her father's death, which occurred when she was thirteen. She never suggested for a moment that perhaps her mother might have been frightened and immature at the time of Mona's birth, when her mother was only sixteen. "We grew up together!" she would declare happily. One sister had died at thirty of colitis; there was never any suggestion that she might have had a stressful or difficult life. Mona married a man who traveled extensively; according to Mona she hadn't minded at all. She had one grown daughter when I met her; the daughter had moved to Alaska as soon as she could leave home and there was almost no contact. Mona never complained, never admitted to a sense of loss. There was never an admission of real anger about anything or anyone.

The flaw in all this perfection was that Mona was the most terrified human being I ever met. She was afraid of restaurant food—it might poison her; she was afraid of ships—she might drown. She was afraid of flying, afraid of the dark—and most of all, terrified of getting sick. She talked endlessly. It was as if silence was her most dangerous enemy, and of course it was; for in silence, feelings might drift up from that closed-in unconscious, where all the "dangers" really lay. She was generous, kind, thoughtful to others, and never allowed herself the luxury of ever showing any real anger, not even displeasure.

When she became terminally ill and had to be medicated because of terrible physical pain, the drugs opened her connection with her unconscious feelings, her early-childhood memories. She became a woman in a towering rage, unable to maintain a facade any longer, losing touch with those she cared about and facing at last, and too late, the emptiness of her charade. She died in terrible bitterness, and after her death a friend tried to account for the fact that there seemed to be nothing left of her to remember. "It's as if she was a bubble, floating in the air, and when it burst there was nothing left." I think this happened because more than any person I had ever known, she had spent her whole life, all of her psychic energy, trying to live on the surface of life, refusing to be touched by a more vulnerable humanity. Having closed herself off so completely from her own inner life, there was nothing for others to find, to remember, afterward.

Sometimes an awful death can be a conspiracy between a husband and wife, or child and parent, or brother and sister. It is an unspoken agreement for denial, for never speaking of the dying. I remember an aunt and an uncle and the awful way they lived through his terminal cancer. Not once in two years did they ever name the disease. They used up all the emotional energy available to them to deny, to pretend. They never said goodbye because they never acknowledged that a goodbye was in order. Later the wife said they were the two loneliest years of her life. His too, I'm sure.

In sharp contrast, when a friend found she had cancer and the chances of survival were not very good, she confided to me, "Jerry and I got into bed and held each other and cried together for most of the night. Even in the midst of my terror and sadness, I knew I would never have to be alone—that my husband had the courage to stay with me, no matter what, and that was a great comfort." Another woman, married and also having an affair, told me, "My husband can't bear to talk about the fact that I may die. My lover encourages me to talk about my feelings. For a long time I felt terribly guilty about having an affair, but now I know which man really loves me."

"Good" deaths are those that seem appropriate because

the alternative is worse. "Inspiring" deaths are those where we are left the gift of someone's life.

My Aunt Renie loved poetry. She had a special collection of works by her favorite poets lined up on her desk. When she died at ninety-two, her daughter called to tell me that her mother had left her a message. Knowing that Hilda would be drawn immediately to the worn books of poetry when she came to dismantle her mother's room, Renie had left bookmarks in place for three or four poems all having to do with being ready for death. Hilda wept and said, "It was her last gift to me—to let me know she felt it was time for her to die."

One day I was standing in line at a bank. Behind me was a woman with a little boy who was getting very restless and hungry. His mother told him that his grandma was going to come and take him for lunch, and when, just then, Grandma came into the bank, arms outstretched, he ran to her and the two embraced in a way that showed so much joy and love, it brought tears to my eyes. As mother and daughter stood talking for a minute, and as grandmother and grandson continued to hold hands, and as he kept jumping up and down with joy and pulled her to take him home, Grandma suddenly, quietly, slipped to the ground. Grandma had died. I heard her daughter say to the doctor, "She's had a heart condition for two years, but we couldn't get her to be careful. Look at that shopping bag. It's full of my son's favorite foods. She knew she shouldn't carry heavy things and she let him jump all over her." I have often worried and wondered how that shock was handled by the little boy—but what a way to go—in the midst of life, with a joyous, loving child pulling at one's skirt!

Hattie, at ninety-three, was in intensive care with heart

failure. Her son said, "We want to keep you with us, but if you and God decide it's time to go, you have a right to that decision." The next morning Hattie said, "I decided God can wait awhile." She recovered and went home.

My Aunt Anne was the funniest woman I ever knew. She loved me and my daughter fiercely and had helped us understand each other. She couldn't stand being sick. She died suddenly of a cerebral hemorrhage in her early seventies standing in the middle of the floor at her hairdresser's, entertaining all the ladies with one of her crazy stories. Everyone was laughing when she suddenly fell to the floor and died. It was terrible for us the living, but even as I mourned, I knew this was the kind of death she would have wished for herself, dying giving pleasure to others, doing what she loved to do.

The kind of dying that most terrified every person with whom I spoke was the kind that is a byproduct of twentieth-century medicine—an age of technology in which medical training has seemed to suggest to physicians that death represents failure, that dying is an unacceptable form of medical practice. Sophie told me, "From the time I was young, I wanted to die before I got old. As you can see, I didn't manage it. My advice to younger people: prepare a potion when you are well, to have it at your disposal when you've had enough of illness and deterioration and crave a dignified exit. I have always tended to be passive and to go with the flow. That can be carried too far. You may not like where the current takes you, but find yourself unable to drown."

In a commentary entitled "Death Is Not the Enemy," Richard L. Landau, M.D., and James M. Gustafson, Ph.D., wrote:

An intense preoccupation with the preservation of physical life
... seems sometimes to be based on an assumption that death is
unnatural, or that its delay, even briefly, through medical and
technical means is always a triumph of human achievement
over the limitations of nature. It is as if death is in every case an
evil, a kind of demonic power to be overcome by the forces of
life, propped up by elaborate technologies . . . The powers of
death are the bad guys, to be vanquished by the good guys
dressed in white coats . . . The emphasis on mortality statistics as
a measure of medical care effectiveness has tended to obscure
the fact that most of the time and effort of practicing physicians
is devoted to improving the life of their patients. The real enemies are disease, discomfort, disability, fear and anxiety. Sen-
sitive, perceptive physicians attempt to guide their patients,
those who are relatively healthy as well as those who are seriously handicapped and ill, to a perspective in which preservation of life is not their God.*

I hope, for all our sakes, that this philosophy will have a
broad renaissance. It is a point of view held by the family
doctors of 100 years ago, who could do no more; it was lost
in the drunken ecstacy of technological and scientific progress during which death itself was to be conquered. What
we aging persons need desperately is the right to the best
care available for as long as life is worthwhile and meaningful, and the right to decide when it is time to die. Marvin Meitus, M.D., a compassionate physician who deals
with the elderly and dying often, says, "At an appropriate
time my concern should be to minimize suffering."

*Richard L. Landau, M.D., and James M. Gustafson, Ph.D., "Death
Is Not the Enemy," *Journal of the American Medical Association* Vol.
252, No. 17 (Nov. 2, 1984) p. 2458.

When Eleanor Roosevelt appeared on Edward R. Murrow's program *This I Believe,* he asked her if she believed in a future life. She answered, "I think I am pretty much of a fatalist. You have to accept whatever comes and the only important thing is that you meet it with courage and with the best that you have to give." Apparently her goal for herself was impossible to carry out; understandably she was so greatly loved and cherished that her last illness was prolonged medically beyond the point where she was able to express her deepest needs and to die with dignity.*

If we greatly fear lingering in a half-life, we need to make plans ahead of time; we need to choose a physician brave enough to allow us to die, as well as being capable of helping us to remain alive and healthy as long as possible.

Until the early 1900s most people died at home surrounded by their families. Today about 70 percent of all deaths occur in hospitals or other institutions. That fact in itself tends to dehumanize the experience of dying. There is an excellent pamphlet available that gives a historical perspective on this and many other issues, *The Right to Die with Dignity* by Elizabeth Ogg.† One of the issues she discusses is the patient's right to refuse treatment when to go on living becomes an inhuman demand on the part of others who prolong life too long after the patient would make the choice to die quickly.

In this connection, the pamphlet describes a Living Will, a document you can sign while you are "of sound mind,"

*Joseph P. Lash, *A World of Love* (New York: Doubleday, 1984).
†Public Affairs Pamphlet #587, 381 Park Avenue South, New York, NY 10016, 50¢.

and which can be attached to your will. Here is a sample of such a document:

If the time comes when I can no longer take part in decisions for my own future, let this statement stand as a testament of my wishes:

If there is no reasonable expectation of my recovery from physical or mental or spiritual disability, I, _____ request that I be allowed to die and not be kept alive by artificial means or heroic measures. Death is as much a reality as birth, growth, maturity and old age—it is the one certainty. I do not fear death as much as I fear the indignity of deterioration, dependence, and helpless pain. I ask that drugs be mercifully administered to me for terminal suffering even if they hasten the moment of death.

This request is made while I am in good health and spirits. Although this document is not legally binding, you who care for me will, I hope, feel morally bound to follow its mandates. I recognize that it places a heavy burden of responsibility upon you, and it is with the intention of sharing that responsibility and mitigating any feeling of guilt that this statement is made.

Witnessed by: _____

_____

Making choices never ends until the moment of death. Dying with dignity means continuing to feel some sense of autonomy about one's life. Dr. Cecily Saunders was a nurse on an oncology service in a London hospital about thirty years ago. She was so horrified by the way terminal cancer patients were being treated by medical personnel as well as by their families that she went back to school, first became a social worker, then eventually a medical doctor and in 1967 founded the first hospice, St. Christopher's, in England. Dr. Saunders tells the patients who come to St. Christopher's, "You matter because you are you. You matter to the last moment of your life, and we will do all we can not only to help you die peacefully, but also to live until you die."

Since then her work has influenced countries throughout the world, and the hospice movement has been growing rapidly. I know of few people who have come closer to the very heart of the matter of staying human through the experience of dying. What Dr. Saunders found she could not tolerate was the loneliness of the dying, the lack of any communication about what was happening, and perhaps most of all, the attempt by the medical profession to deny death by keeping people alive long after it made any decent, human sense to do so.

One example of the kind of ridiculous cruelty that often occurs is when a doctor refuses to give morphine or any other potentially habit-forming drug to a patient who is dying in great pain. The patient may be riddled with cancer in every organ of his body, and when relatives plead for medication to stop the agony, a doctor is too often likely to look at them in horror and say, "But he'll become *addicted!*" Dr. Saunders discovered that heroin and marijuana were helpful in some cases to relieve suffering of terminal patients, and for awhile the American medical establishment treated her as if she were one of the three witches in *Macbeth*. There has been some considerable change in attitudes in the past few years even in the United States. However, the pain reliever made famous by St. Christopher's is called the Brompton cocktail, a mixture of heroin, cocaine, alcohol, and chloroform water dissolved in a cherry syrup, and this is still illegal here. British law permits the dispensing of heroin and cocaine under medical supervision. United States law does not, and morphine and methadone are now being used instead.

Larry visited a hospice near Boston some years ago. When a patient arrived at the hospital, he or she was assigned to a special staff member who would be available as a special friend and counselor. There was an all-night bar and coffee shop where ambulatory patients who could not sleep could go and talk with others. The hospice idea creates more, not less, human contact in the patient's life, since ministers, friends, relatives, specially trained volunteers are encouraged to participate in the patient's life and death.

Fortunately for our generation, the hospice movement has spread all over the country, and its philosophy and services can now be part of our planning. Since what I fear most is being a nuisance to other people, or becoming a whiner, a coward—of not being *me* anymore, but some crazy old crone, gibbering and drooling—I now want to know what hospices exist near where I will be living should I ever want the reassurance that I will be allowed to die.*

For all the validity of remaining close to a dying person, and not prolonging life when a person wishes to die, we need to remember that choice is the real issue. Some people need to do their dying by a process of disengagement. At least for part of the time, they seem to want to start the process of separation and not be surrounded by relatives. Recently I went to visit a friend I hadn't seen for many years. She's in her seventies and her three grown children

*For more information, write to: National Hospice Organization, 1311 Dolley Madison Blvd., McLean, VA 22101.

all live in different cities far away. She finds it increasingly difficult to visit them, and their lives are so busy they rarely get a chance to visit her. She told me, "Somehow, it's all right. I feel less involved. I love them, but I have also let go in some monumental way. I think disengagement is the way we prepare ourselves for the final separation."

A woman dying of cancer refused to see her newborn granddaughter. She said, "I'm leaving—I can't get reattached." I met a nurse a few years ago who told me she was very concerned about a patient she was taking care of in his home. He was very close to death and seemed totally preoccupied with himself and what was happening to him. His wife hovered over him, cried loudly, patted him constantly—even sang to him—and the nurse had the feeling that if her patient had been strong and well he would have told his wife to "buzz off!" but in his weakened condition he just had to endure relating in a way he didn't seem to want at all.

People have as much right *not* to choose to die, as they ought to have to die when they are ready. Aunt Lillie, then in her nineties, had lived alone all her adult life. She wasn't really my aunt, but she was my mother's friend from the time they were little girls, and I always adored her. Very few people in my life ever gave me as much unconditional love as she did; I was always perfect in her eyes. Although she was a secretary and then a real estate agent, and once a children's matron in a movie theater, her real life was dancing. She belonged to a somewhat esoteric school of the dance, and dancing and teaching were the source of her identity. She had a bell-like laugh that was infectious and she told wonderful stories. She taught me how to bark like a dog when I was two, and took me to my first movie at eight. Once, when she had been living in California for many years and she and my mother missed each other a lot, we brought Aunt Lillie to New York, wrapped her in tissue paper with a big red ribbon around her middle, and gave her to my mother for Christmas. Now very ill and weak, unable to get out of bed, it seemed to me she was ready to die. She was so frail, so thin—but one day she looked me straight in the eye and said, "There's always another sunset."

Some sense of autonomy—control over one's destiny—can come when we make plans long before we are dying. One approach that I find comforting is to become clearer about my priorities. Time is really the most precious of all my possessions, and I find myself nurturing it with the greatest of care. Somewhere along about the middle of this book, I knew with absolute certainty that I wanted to retire forever from some of the things I've already been doing for far too many years. I began a process of selection—I'll keep doing this; that is out for good; maybe I'll try this. Every time I reshift the priorities and hold them up to close scrutiny, I feel better.

In recent months Larry and I have been "firming up" our plans for where we would want to be ten years from now, and are in the process of making an application to an adult community that seems to have all the ingredients we feel we might need. We are doing so most of all in order to face the very real possibility that sooner or later one of us will be alone or one of us may become chronically ill and we want to be in a protected environment with all the resources we might need to live without financial panic, with dignity, without one of us feeling guilty about having to be cared for and the other imprisoned by that care. We chose a place one hour away from the Atlantic Ocean, where we can go for refreshment of our souls until we can no longer go anywhere; we chose a place near a university so Larry can have the use of an excellent library and continue doing research as long as he possibly can. We chose a place near a good-sized city with museums and theaters. We chose a place where friends have been, where we have visited often, where the "feeling" of the climate of life seems to us the best one can hope for as aging progresses.

Taking action, planning, allowing the rage and then getting over it, seems to have helped me. I am not resigned about what I must face, but I have come to the realization that I am not helpless, that I can do it my way to a much greater extent than I once thought possible.

Others make plans having to do with the distribution of material things that are important to them. Harriet said, "I've written a letter about minor items and jewelry I want to leave members of my family. I've told my own children the value of the antiques in our home and they should take—or sell—whatever they want. The children are the '*you* take it' type, so I'm not worried about sibling quarrels. Haven't quite decided whether to have a small funeral at home or none."

Another comment was, "I am trying to hang on to such money as I have (and the little I have came just recently, through inheritance) to help my grandchildren go to good colleges and do the traveling I didn't."

And another, "We think it a good idea to have made arrangements for our disposal following death. I'm donating my body to an organ transplant center, and Lori wishes to be cremated. This will relieve undue stress when the time comes. It's a wise idea to get the kids together to see who wants what. If two or more want the same item, let them draw straws, or work out trade-offs. This should all be duly recorded, and copies of the list given to one and all."

Amy told me, "My feelings about death have changed greatly over the years. I used to have a very hard time with the idea that the world would go on without me in it. But aging brings neurological as well as physiological changes that prepare you. I have never been afraid of illness and pain—I've had a lot of pain at different periods in my life—I can handle pain. But death is no longer an active fear. I must be preparing unconsciously. I notice that whenever I leave the house, I look around to see that everything is in order. There is an instinctive sense that I am coming to the end of something. I keep myself and my affairs in better order and perhaps this is connected. I continue to live the way I did, on the whole, since I was old enough to form values and choices. I guess I am me to the core—and to the end."

Because we cannot imagine *not being,* I think it is normal to feel some anxiety about possessions which have special meaning for us. I look around my office in the city, and I see mementos of my whole life—all the souvenirs that led up to my unique and special self. My baby shoe; a china bird that was my grandfather's; pictures of my grandmother and my mother; pictures of a children's television program, where we filmed the opening in Central Park at Columbus Circle, and I'm in a horsedrawn carriage, letting go of hundreds of balloons. Awards of various kinds. What will happen to all this when I die?

If we have been lucky enough to be loved, the things we leave behind which represent our own sense of our identity will be important to those who want to remember us. My daughter knows the stories about how my grandfather would leave the house with money to buy a coat and come back with some art object, and either she or I will probably tell my granddaughter the same stories. Most of our paintings are by close personal friends, and I think Wendy will want some of them. But it is natural to be upset about the loss of identity with loss of life. Ultimately we just have to accept the feelings, and enjoy what is important to us for as long as we can.

For some, any planning is too painful. Dick wrote, "We avoid planning because of the implications of mortality, I guess. Occasionally I think we should update our wills and arrange for death in practical ways but we don't do it."

There is a story about a rabbi who told his congregation, "You should repent and tidy up your life the day before you die." What he meant, of course, is that we can't know that day, and maybe we need to try to "tidy up our lives" every day! Forgive people for things said or done that made us angry; do the things we think need to be done to make us feel proud of our lives.

Some people seem to view "tidiness" in an extreme form, including suicide, as did writer Arthur Koestler and his wife, and many others who design a plan for death either alone or with a spouse. I cannot imagine coming to such a moment myself, but I leave that as an open question. I surely can imagine life becoming unbearable, and wanting a surcease from pain or from a self that is no longer me.

I guess what I ultimately come to is the idea that whenever I die and however I die, the only control I have over that event is how I have lived my life; how I will be remembered. I have control right now, to continue the task of self-discovery as the only real antidote to a preoccupation with death. The never-ending search for one's identity gives meaning to one's life at any age.

Many years ago, after my first book was published, I was a guest on the television program *To Tell the Truth*. A panel of famous people had to figure out which of three people was the real person and not one of two imposters. In a nightmare I had the night before this broadcast, I dreamed that when the host said, "Will the real Eda LeShan stand up," somebody else stood up! It occurred to me recently that the task I now face is to prepare myself for that challenge—to be quite sure who I am. This is a "developmental task" that continues until the moment of dying.

Psychoanalyst Carl Jung told the story of the dying woman who appeared to be talking gibberish as she approached her death. Nobody could understand what she was talking about and assumed that she had become senile. Jung had been her therapist and he was called in to see the woman. It seemed to him she was free-associating, as she had in the course of her analysis. He jotted down the disconnected and often incoherent things she was saying, and then checked these against his notes taken during the therapy. He began to work with her directly, and she lived long enough to finish their work together.

Dr. Robert Butler quotes a Greek lyric poet of the fifth century, B.C., who wrote, "Do not yearn after immortality, but exhaust the limits of the possible."*

What this means to me is discovering new frontiers; not repeating the same things I've done before; letting go of

*Butler, *Why Survive?*

past accomplishments and searching for new risks, new challenges. Whenever I give a lecture on child-raising, I get depressed afterwards. It's because I know that after forty years I could do this blindfolded, and better than almost anybody else. No conquest, no victory. *Enough* already.

"The limits of the possible" seem to me to mean cultivating my own eccentricities, discovering the essence of *me,* with less and less concern for what anybody else thinks.

The continuing search for my own identity is not made any easier by the external world! I never imagined that in my old age *everything* I believed in, everything I worked for, would be in the process of being destroyed by what I view as a frightening change in the politics of this country. It is harder to remember who I am and who I have been in a society that has become ultraconservative, militaristic, cold and unfeeling toward the helpless, willing to weaken if not destroy some of the most precious constitutional rights and freedoms. I know I'm going to have to die a stranger in my land. I despise all the music since Rodgers and Hammerstein! I would close every nuclear plant and destroy every nuclear weapon. I don't think abortion is anybody's business but a doctor's and his patient's. I'm against capital punishment. I'd close every prison and turn them into hospitals. I am for strict gun control. In other words, I now feel like someone from another planet who has gotten lost. I have to fight every day to continue to be this loathsome creature I am—a liberal! Under these circumstances I find myself focusing my attention more on my identity in personal relationships, where the struggle to be most human and most active has at least made a difference among those I love. My sense of terrible sadness about the external world, full of such awful danger, such terror, is

OH, TO BE 50 AGAIN!

somewhat counterbalanced by trying to continue to fulfill myself in personal relationships.

Psychoanalyst Esther Menaker, in a speech given on her seventy-fifth birthday, said, ". . . and what of the future? However long or short it may be, for me it is limitless in the sense that I am involved in exploring the world of ideas and in having young people join me in the enterprise. The world of ideas and creative imagination are infinite and this is where it is good to live as one grows older. If there is any magic secret about how to stay young in feeling, it is to pursue a commitment to the exploration of ideas, for it is such activity that brings about change and inner growth."*

It is that inner experience that must continue as well as contacts with those who still represent creativity, wonder, courage to go on.

Part of becoming more clear about who we are is often going to places that have some symbolic meaning for us. One man took his male nurse and went to Venice where he and his late wife had gone on their honeymoon. A religious Jewish woman wanted to see Israel before she died. Sometimes we go back to a place we've been to rediscover experiences, feelings—to reassess our worth. Larry and I had such an experience a few years ago. We were both going to give speeches in Washington, D.C., at the same time, and we decided to take some time afterward to visit a town in West Virginia, not far from Washington, where we had spent the first two years of our marriage, during World War II. We remembered it as a time of enormous significance, a time when we began to become the adults we have been ever since. I had become the child welfare worker for

*Esther Menaker, *The Psychoanalytic Review,* 71 (1) Spring 1984.

three counties, at the age of twenty-two; I lived there alone for several months when Larry was sent to other places for special training. I worked in rural areas that were so strange to me that I wrote my parents: "Margaret Mead really doesn't have to go all the way to Samoa if she wants to study other cultures!" I was responsible for all the children in foster care, and had some pretty wild adventures. I supervised all the delinquents put in my care by the county judge. What seems so incredible to me is that having had a most protected middle-class life, I was able to meet the challenge. A year after I started, Larry had a leave and went with me through the mountains and orchards of my territory. After a day or two he gave me a choice; either I had to carry a gun or quit! I quit and took the safer job in the section for the mentally ill in the army hospital where Larry was stationed! I've already mentioned his pioneer work with the electroencephalograph, but what we were most proud of was our work in organizing a canteen for teenagers and working with the blacks (in a southern and segregated town) on an interracial council. What we remembered best of all was a fascinating case we collaborated on—a foster child in my care who had very serious problems. Larry helped devise psychological tests that might help me figure out what was bothering her; we had a wonderful relationship with the farm family where she'd been placed, and it was a dramatically successful resolution of a serious disorder. We wondered for thirty-five years what had happened to her and her family.

When we decided to go back, Larry sent a notice to the local newspaper announcing our arrival and where we would be. Some of my foster children turned up—especially one of my delinquents, to tell me he was now a successful farmer. Many of my teenagers—now middle-aged—came to reminisce about the teenagers' canteen. And best of all the little girl, now in her forties, who was the most important triumph of my work, appeared at our motel door and took us out to the farm. We didn't say much about what had gone on between us when she was seven, but she hugged us and let us know she knew that in some way we had changed her life.

The trip was one of the most thrilling—healing—experiences, and came at a time when we were first beginning to think about getting old. It reminded us of what our lives together had been all about—how hard we had worked together to help people with psychological problems individually, and for social change in an entire community. We recalled as well, of course, those first years of trying to learn about each other, and the beginning of the struggle to understand ourselves and each other better. It hadn't all been wonderful; we faltered many times and lived through painful struggles to grow up, to try to make our marriage work.

When we come closer and closer to the time of dying, such trips back into the past can, if physically feasible, add a great deal to that sense of self that is so important. One of the most moving stories in this connection was an article by Audrey Topping, entitled "Family Reunion in China,"* in which she tells of her eighty-nine-year-old father's return to Fancheng, China, the town where he'd been born, and a three-week trip throughout many places in China with his children and friends, who were very apprehensive about his making such a journey since he had had a stroke, but he

* *The New York Times Magazine* (Feb. 12, 1984).

seemed revived and hearty once the trip began. He met people he'd known in China when he'd been with the Canadian Embassy. He spoke fluent Chinese. His parents had been missionaries and he had grown up in China. He visited his mother's grave. There was a ninetieth birthday party with old Chinese associates. They found the church his father had built—it is a touching and beautiful story of a whole family joining an old man in rediscovering an essential part of his identity, his life history.

A woman with a serious heart condition has been on a different kind of adventure into the past. She has been told by her doctors that she could die suddenly, at any moment, but she decided that she wanted to take some control of her dying, and she started to see a psychiatrist who could help her make the journey into herself. She told me, "I'm extremely tired and it's hard to go on, but the thing is, I'm *so curious* to find out about myself, that I am not yet ready to let go!"

Letting go seems to be most possible as that sense of self becomes clearer. One man told me, "I'm totally accepting of my eventual death, which can't be too far away. I want to live as long as possible, but I have no fear of dying because I feel I have lived my life and done the work I wanted to do. I don't have any frustrations."

Another kind of "journey" that seems to bring both comfort and inspiration any time during one's life, and especially toward the end, would be prayer for those who have a specific religious orientation or meditation which can be a part of anyone's life experience. Meditation came into my life through Larry's research into the paranormal. What I have learned is that human beings live on different levels of reality, and that on one level one can experience a sense of oneness with a larger universe; that by training oneself to move into an "alternate reality" one can lose a sense of isolation and become part of the "All."

Older people need meditation as a way of cultivating the special developmental task at hand—to begin to move from a focus on the material world to the larger world of the human spirit. There are hundreds of lectures, seminars, and books* dealing with training methods for meditation. Each person has to find the techniques, the point of view, most suited to him or herself. Unfortunately, the path to enlightenment is obstructed by a number of gurus, teachers, and groups that are making a fast buck out of it. We need to look with a jaundiced eye on anyone who offers us a fancy, expensive package with all kinds of unnecessary gimmicks. Learning to meditate (to focus one's full attention on one thing at a time) is hard work.

Other routes to reinforcing one's connection to the larger universe are available depending on our own interests. For me, looking at an exhibit of Monet's paintings at the Museum of Modern Art was such an experience. Sitting and looking at his paintings of water lilies took me beyond myself, the room, the museum, the city—I was lost in a total sense of beauty, at one with the world and with myself. Others gain such moments from reading or listening to poetry, or praying in a church, or attending a concert. Still others lose themselves in the moment by building a sandcastle with a child or watching a sunset or working with clay.

One day I was waiting for some guests to arrive at my

---

*One of the best, of course, being *How to Meditate* by Lawrence LeShan.

summer home. I was standing in the kitchen cutting the stems off some bright blue hydrangeas, and arranging them in a vase to put in the guest room, to welcome my company. I suddenly felt a great sadness sweep over me. My mother loved this color blue, and with a sharp pain of longing, I remember that she never lived to see the house I was in. I wanted to show her the picnic table and benches I had just painted, because I remember her warning me that if you didn't paint outdoor furniture regularly, it would be ruined. I wanted her to see the goldfinches at the feeder, and talk to the ducks that come to be fed each day. I remember that she took great satisfaction in all the homes I had created before her death—that she loved to watch me feed the seagulls at the Jersey shore one summer, and that when she found flowers in all the rooms of our cottage there, she said, "You are a wonderful nest builder—just like me!" I felt alone, lost, deserted—and then suddenly I felt so connected to her as all my memories flooded to the surface of consciousness.

I started out focusing my attention on putting flowers in a vase—an activity that was part of the "real" world—and I ended up in feeling part of the rhythm of the universe, in which my mother and I are still part of each other, throughout all time. I live in the world of the many, but in my thoughts I am gradually moving to the world of the One.

There is a Tibetan chant for the dying, in which the loved ones say over and over again, "Nothing to hold to, nothing to do." What this symbolizes is the idea of moving from *Doing* to *Being*. It seems to me that this process ought to be part of all living—that one can become accustomed to *Being* long before it becomes a task related to dying, and that we spend too much of our lives doing, achieving, competing, "keeping busy." *Being* is not passive; it is as much an act of choice as those things categorized as doing. It is really focusing all our attention on one thing at a time and not doing anything else. It can be playing a game of tennis, dancing, watching a butterfly light on a flower, singing a lullabye to a baby, or making love. There is no sense of conscious purpose—it's not something that has to be done this minute; it isn't something others demand of us. It's being fully present at one's life, without claims or expectations of results.

Until the moment of dying, life takes precedence. It will, I believe, be helpful to contemplate how we will face our own deaths, but right now, we are alive! The Talmud says that when a wedding procession and a funeral procession meet at a crossroads, the wedding procession has the right of way. While facing the inevitability of our mortality, we still need to focus our energy, our caring, on life.

I hope I don't have to identify my most favorite people, Kukla, Fran, and Ollie, but should there be some poor soul of my generation who missed Burr Tillstrom's television program, which started with TV itself in the late 1940s, Kukla and Ollie and a host of absolutely fascinating and lovable friends are puppets, the creations of Burr Tillstrom's imagination, and Fran Allison is the lovely lady who shared their adventures. I could say that she was the human being on the program, but for me, there was no differentiation—they were all human—more human than most of the people I've met during my lifetime.

One of the peak experiences of my life was meeting and talking with Ollie and Kukla and Fletcher Rabbit and Buelah Witch many years ago, on a television program in Chicago. I was publicizing a book on middle age, and Ollie and I talked about being middle-aged as a dragon—I seem to recall he was several hundred years old at the time. My friendship with Burr Tillstrom has been one of the special joys of my life.* Since Ollie and I had discussed middle age, I wrote to Burr asking if Ollie might have any words of wisdom about old age and dying. Burr assured me this was not possible. Apparently an ancestor of Ollie's had once mentioned his age to a king, who got very upset and told other people about it, and that dragon not only got gray hair but lost his tooth, just from being labeled "old." Burr did tell me that in a conversation with his young cousin, Deloras Dragon, Ollie had told her, "Most of the dragons I know never keep track. Dragons really have no concept of time. They think, rather, of growing. Not growing older, just growing—growing wiser, kinder, braver, and in our case more handsome." (False modesty was never one of Ollie's shortcomings.) Ollie continued, "The point of this kind of growing is that you learn to enjoy living more completely."

I knew I had gone to the right source. I couldn't have said it better myself.

---

*Burr Tillstrom died shortly before publication of this book.

S O U R C E S

~~~~~~~~~~~~~~~~~~~~~~~~~~~~~~~

Books and Pamphlets I Have Found Useful

Ball, Avis Jane. *What Shall I Do with a Hundred Years?* Potentials Development for Health and Aging Services, Inc., 775 Main Street, Buffalo, NY 14203.

Butler, Robert, M.D. *Why Survive? Being Old in America.* New York: Harper & Row, 1975.

Butler, Robert, M.D., and Myrna Lewis. *Love and Sex after Sixty: A Guide for Men and Women in Their Later Years.* New York: Harper & Row, 1977.

Cousins, Norman. *Anatomy of an Illness.* New York: Bantam, 1981.

———. *Healing Heart.* New York: Avon, 1984.

Fisher, M.F.K. *Sister Age.* New York: Vintage Books, 1984.

Hayes, Helen, with Marion Gladney. *Our Best Years.* New York: Doubleday & Co., 1984.

Hunter, Laura, with Polly Memhara. *The Rest of My Life.* Growing Pains Press, 22 Fifth Street, Stamford, CT 06905.

LeShan, Lawrence. *How to Meditate.* New York: Bantam, 1979 (9th printing).

———. *The Mechanic and the Gardener: Making the Most of the Holistic Revolution in Medicine.* New York: Holt, Rinehart and Winston, 1982.

Maynard, Fredelle. *Raisins and Almonds.* Markham, Ontario, Canada: Paperjacks, 1980 (6th printing).

Melamed, Elissa. *Mirror, Mirror: The Terror of Not Being Young.* New York: Linden Press, 1983.

Moffat, Mary Jane, ed. *In the Midst of Winter: Selections from the Literature of Mourning.* New York: Vintage Books, 1982.

Munzer, Martha. *Full Circle: Rounding Out a Life.* New York: Alfred A. Knopf, 1978.

Myers, Albert, and Christopher Anderson. *Success over Sixty.* New York: Summit Books, 1984.

Rollin, Betty. *Last Wish.* New York: Linden Press, 1985.

Sarton, May. *As We Are Now.* New York: W. W. Norton & Co., 1973.

————. *At Seventy.* New York: W. W. Norton & Co., 1984.

————. *The House by the Sea: A Journal.* New York: W. W. Norton & Co., 1977.

————. *Journal of a Solitude.* New York: W. W. Norton & Co., 1973.

Sloan, Bernard. *The Best Friend You'll Ever Have.* New York: Crown, 1980.

Stern, Edith, with Mabel Ross, M.D. *You and Your Aging Parents.* New York: A. A. Wyn, Inc., 1952.

Books Published by AARP (with Scott Foresman):

Write for information to AARP Books, Dept. NBOC, 400 South Edward Street, Mount Prospect, IL 60056.

Fromme, Allan. *Life After Work: Planning It, Living It, Loving It.*

Raper, Ann (editor). *National Continuing Care Directory,* 1984.

Sumichrant, Michael, Ronald Shafer, and Marika Sumichrant. *Planning Your Retirement Housing,* 1984.

Public Affairs Pamphlets

Each is available from Public Affairs Pamphlets, 382 Park Avenue South, New York, NY 10016. Be sure to specify the pamphlet number.

Dickman, Irving. *Ageism—Discrimination against Older People.*
  #575, 50¢.
———. *Nursing Homes: Strategy for Reform.* #566, 50¢.
Lobsenz, Norman. *Sex after Sixty-five.* #519, $1.00.
Milt, Harry. *Family Neglect and Abuse of the Aged: A Growing
  Concern.* #603, 50¢.
Weinstein, Grace. *Planning Your Retirement Income.*
  #634, $1.00.

Other Resources:

Alzheimer's Disease and Related Disorders Association
360 North Michigan Avenue
Chicago, IL 60601

American Association of Retired Persons (AARP)
1909 K Street N.W.
Washington, D.C. 20049

Children of Aging Parents
2761 Trenton Road
Levittown, PA 19056

Elderhostel
100 Boylestown Street
Boston, MA 02116

Friends and Relatives of Institutionalized Aged
425 East 25th Street
New York, NY 10010

Grandparents' Resources:

Equal Rights for Grandparents
7408 Ventnor Avenue
Margate, NJ 08402

Grandparents Anonymous
536 West Huron
Pontiac, MI 48053

Grandparents: A Newsletter for Grandparents
  in Divided Families
Scarsdale Family Counseling Service
403 Harwood Building
Scarsdale, NY 10583

The Foundation for Grandparenting
10 West Hyatt Avenue
Mount Kisco, NY 10549

American Association of Retired Persons (AARP)
1909 K Street N.W.
Washington, D.C. 20049

Gray Panthers
3635 Chestnut Street
Philadelphia, PA 19104

Home Care, National Association for Home Care
519 C Street N.W.
Stanton Park, Washington, D.C. 20002

National Hospice Organization
1311 Dolley Madison Boulevard
McLean, VA 22101

National Institute on Aging
Information Office
Building 31, Room 5C-36
9000 Rockville Pike
Bethesda, MD 20205

National Self-Help Clearinghouse
33 West 42nd Street
New York, NY 10036

National Support Center for Families of the Aging
P.O. Box 245
Swarthmore, PA 19081

Operation Able (coordinates 45 groups)
36 South Wabash Avenue
Suite 1133
Chicago, IL 60603

Self-Help Center
1600 Dodge Avenue
Evanston, IL 60204

The National Council on Aging
1828 L Street N.W.
Washington, D.C. 20036

The Mount Sinai Medical Center
Gerald and May Ellen Ritter
Department of Geriatrics and Adult Development
1 Gustave Levy Place
Annenberg Building, Room 13-30
New York, NY 10029 (publishes a newsletter)

Home Care Resources

All About Home Care: A Consumer's Guide. National HomeCaring Council and the Council of Better Business Bureaus. Send $2.00 with a self-addressed, business-sized envelope and 39¢ in postage to the National HomeCaring Council, 235 Park Avenue South, New York, NY 10003

Home Care. National Association for Home Care. 519 C Street, N.E. Stanton Park, Washington, D.C. 20002. Free.

Information on Home Health Services: A Handbook about Care in the Home. AARP Fulfillment, Box 2400, Long Beach, CA 90801. Free.